A MIND AT HOME
WITH ITSELF

A MIND AT HOME WITH ITSELF

How Asking Four Questions Can Free Your Mind,
Open Your Heart, and Turn Your World Around

BYRON KATIE

WITH STEPHEN MITCHELL

INCLUDING A NEW VERSION OF THE DIAMOND SUTRA
BY STEPHEN MITCHELL

HarperOne
An Imprint of HarperCollinsPublishers

HarperOne

Grateful acknowledgment is made to Alfred A. Knopf, Inc. for permission to reprint an excerpt from "The Snow Man" from *The Collected Poems of Wallace Stevens* by Wallace Stevens, copyright © 1954 by Wallace Stevens and copyright renewed 1982 by Holly Stevens. Reprinted by permission of Alfred A. Knopf, an imprint of the Knopf Doubleday Publishing Group, a division of Penguin Random House LLC. All rights reserved.

HarperCollins books may be purchased for educational, business, or sales promotional use. For information, please e-mail the Special Markets Department at SPsales@harpercollins.com.

FIRST HARPERCOLLINS PAPERBACK EDITION PUBLISHED IN 2018

Designed by Ad Librum

Library of Congress Cataloging-in-Publication Data is available upon request.

ISBN 978-0-06-265159-4

20 21 22 LSC 10 9 8 7 6 5 4

To you

CONTENTS

FOREWORD

1

A Mind at Home with Itself is a book about generosity. How can we be generous not just occasionally but all the time, every day of our lives? It sounds like an unattainable ideal, but what if it's not? What if generosity can become as natural as breathing? This book shows you how. All it takes is an open mind, a mind willing to question any stressful thought that arises within it. When we understand who we really are, behind all our confused thinking, we discover the constant, effortless generosity that is our birthright.

Byron Katie Mitchell (everyone calls her Katie) speaks from the depths of realization. Her method of self-inquiry, which she calls The Work, is a kind of enhanced mindfulness. As we do The Work, not only do we remain alert to our stressful thoughts—the ones that cause all the anger, sadness, and frustration in the world—but we question them, and through that questioning the thoughts lose their power over us.

"Great spiritual texts," Katie says, "describe the *what*—what it means to be free. The Work is the *how*. It tells you exactly how to identify and question any thought that would keep you from that freedom. It gives you a direct entrance into the awakened mind." *A Mind at Home with Itself* will let you see the world through the eyes of someone who has woken up to reality, the radiant moment, the state of grace in which there is no separation and the heart overflows with love.

2

For readers who haven't heard about Byron Katie, here is some background. In the midst of an ordinary American life—two marriages, three children, a successful career—Katie entered a ten-year-long downward spiral into depression, agoraphobia, self-loathing, and suicidal despair. She drank to excess, her husband brought her pints of ice cream and codeine pills that she ate like candy, and she ended up weighing over two hundred pounds. She slept with a .357 Magnum revolver under her bed. Every day she prayed not to wake up the next morning, and it was only because of her concern for her children that she didn't kill herself. For the last two years of this ordeal she could seldom manage to leave her house; she stayed in her bedroom for days at a time, unable even to shower or brush her teeth. ("What's the use?" she thought. "It all adds up to nothing anyway.") Finally, in February 1986, at the age of forty-three, she checked herself into a halfway house for women with eating disorders—the only facility that her insurance company would pay for. The residents were so frightened of her that they put her in an attic bedroom and booby-trapped the staircase at night; they thought she might come down and do something terrible to them.

One morning, after about a week at the halfway house, Katie had a life-changing experience. As she lay on the floor (she didn't feel worthy enough to sleep in a bed), a cockroach crawled across her ankle and down her foot. She opened her eyes, and all her depression and fear, all the thoughts that had been tormenting her, were gone. "While I was lying on the floor," she says, "I understood that when I was asleep, prior to cockroach or foot, prior to any thoughts, prior to any world, there was—there is—nothing. In that instant, the four questions of The Work were born." She felt intoxicated with joy. The joy persisted for hours, then days, then months and years.

When she went home, her children, who had lived in fear of her outbursts, could barely recognize her. Her eyes had changed. "The blue had become so clear, so beautiful," her daughter, Roxann, says. "If you looked in, you could see that she was as innocent as a baby. She was happy all day long, every day, and she seemed to be brimming over with love." She spent most of the time silent, sitting for hours on the window seat or out in the desert. Her younger son, Ross, says, "Before the change, I couldn't look into her eyes; after it, I couldn't *stop* looking into them."

It took Katie years to learn how to speak about her state of being. She had no external context for her awareness; she had never read spiritual books or heard about spiritual practices. She just had her own experience to guide her, and all she needed was the inquiry that was alive in her.

Katie's rebirth was more radical than the kind of conversion experience that William James documents in *The Varieties of Religious Experience*—so radical, in fact, that she had to relearn (or, from her perspective, learn) everything about being human: how to function in time and space, how to break reality apart into nouns and verbs so that she could communicate with people, how to pretend that past and future were real. And its effect was directly opposite from the usual conversion experience in that it didn't result in the acceptance of a religious belief. Her clarity didn't and couldn't permit a single belief. It burned through religious concepts along with all other thoughts. After her awakening, she continued to feel—to *be*—the uninterrupted presence of the love she had awoken as. "I felt that if my joy were told," she says, "it would blow the roof off the halfway house—off the whole planet. I still feel that way."

During that first year, in the midst of her great joy, beliefs and concepts continued to arise in her mind. The way she dealt with them was through inquiry. She would often go out alone into the desert, which began just a few blocks away from her house in Barstow, California, to inquire into these thoughts.

Whenever a belief appeared in my mind—the big one was 'My mother doesn't love me'—it exploded in the body like an atom bomb. I noticed shaking, contraction, and the apparent annihilation of peace. The belief might also be accompanied by tears and a stiffening of the body. It might have appeared to an onlooker that I was affected from the toes to the top of the head with upset and sadness. But in fact I always continued to experience the same clarity, peace, and joy that had arisen when I woke up on the floor in the halfway house, with no "I" left, no world, and laughter just pouring out of my mouth. The belief that had arisen would always fall away and dissolve into the light of truth. What shook the body was the remnant of the belief, which appeared as an uncomfortable feeling. From this discomfort I automatically knew that the story wasn't true. Nothing was true. The awareness of this was experienced as glorious humor—glorious, rapturous joy.

Inquiry continued for a year or so, until all the beliefs and concepts were burned up. The method was tested in the laboratory of her experience, with a more stringent standard of sanity than even the most meticulous scientist of the mind could devise. Any thought or mental event that had the tendency to pull her off balance, anything that caused a reaction in her that was a diminishment of her peace and joy, was subjected to rigorous inquiry, until the thought was met with understanding. "I am someone who only wants what is," Katie says. "To meet as a friend each concept that arose turned out to be my freedom. That's where The Work begins and ends—in me. The Work reveals that you can love it all, exactly as it is. And it shows you exactly how." By the end of this process, during the second year after her awakening, only the clarity remained.

Soon after Katie's return from the halfway house, word spread in Barstow about a "lit lady," and some people found themselves magnetically attracted to her and her freedom. As more and more people came to see her, she became convinced that what they needed, if anything, was not her personal presence, but a way to discover for themselves what she had realized. The Work is an embodiment of the wordless questioning that had woken up in her. She had lived and tested it. Now she formulated it, as if in slow motion, for other people to use. Over the past thirty-one years it has helped millions of people around the world begin to free themselves from stress, frustration, anger, and sadness.

3

A Mind at Home with Itself is structured around the Diamond Sutra, one of the great spiritual texts of the world. The sutra is an extended meditation on selflessness. *Selfless*, in ordinary usage, is a synonym for *generous*; it means "acting for the benefit of another person rather than for yourself." Its literal meaning, though, is "without a self," which means both "not having a self" and "realizing that there is no such thing as a self." You may think that this second meaning is a spiritual concept, since trying to get rid of your self may seem as impossible as walking away from your shadow. But after you have practiced inquiry or meditation for a while, you can see that it is "self" that is actually the concept here, rather than "not having a self." However hard you try, it's impossible to locate anything in reality that corresponds to that noun. To the clear mind there is no self and no other, as the sutra says, and once you understand this truth, selfishness radically subsides. The more your sense of self dissolves in the light of awareness, the more generous you naturally become. In all its variations, that is the central truth that the sutra is trying to wake us up to.

4

One of my jobs as co-writer of this book was to find a balance between what is accurate for Katie and what is intelligible to a large audience. The process had to end in relative failure, though "failure" is a concept foreign to her. "The Diamond Sutra," she emailed me, from the couch three feet away from my armchair, "cries out for an awareness beyond anything that can be articulated. The sutra knows that the simplest way to present the truth is to negate anything that can be said. That is accurate and generous. I speak or write my comments, and you shape them and tidy them and get them as close to my lived experience as you possibly can, and still the words are lies. You have a tough job, dearest. I'm the cat you're trying to herd."

I enjoyed the job of catherd. Where I have failed in these pages, Katie's words may seem to take themselves seriously. Where I have succeeded, the words sound the way Katie does in person: clear, loving, funny, generous, hip, and helpfully alarming.

I have included some Katie stories from the first year or so after her experience of waking up to reality. This has the disadvantage of pointing to what Katie calls "the woman," the person Byron Katie, which is not something she often finds a reason to do; I had to wheedle these stories out of her by the sincerity of my fascination. But including them here has the advantage of making the truths of the Diamond Sutra more vivid and personal. The stories may be unsettling, even frightening, to some readers; they may make it seem as if Katie's experience was some kind of mental breakdown, and therefore dismissible. But as wild as some of them sound, in essence they are about a woman settling, through a process of ecstatic trial and error, into a profound and balanced sanity.

There is very little that has been written from the inside about the experience of deep self-realization. We have just sketches and taglines from the ancient masters: "When he saw the peach blossoms," the old accounts say—or "When the door slammed on his leg and broke it"—"he suddenly awoke." Nothing is said about how the whole world crumbled and changed for the astonished seeker. And there is almost nothing about the aftermath of these experiences. In addition, awakening without any preparation is very rare; there is only one example I know of in the twentieth century that compares with

Katie's in its depth—the Indian sage Ramana Maharshi's. Ramana described the aftermath of his awakening in some detail, but since he was the equivalent of a monk and lived in a culture where this kind of experience was recognized and revered, there was no problem with integration. A few people came to feed and clothe him; otherwise they left him alone, in a state of *samadhi* (deep concentration). He stayed on his mountain. He didn't have to go back to a family or drive a car or shop in a supermarket. ("Neither did I," Katie says.)

The usual awakening that happens through intensive meditation practice is much more jagged: a lightning-flash of insight that gives you immense encouragement and clears up your life to some extent, and afterward a great deal of slogging as that insight settles in and transforms you. "It's not that I'm not joyful," the future Zen master Tung-shan said to his teacher, after his inner eye opened. "But it's as though I have grasped a pearl in a pile of shit." Then later, there may be another insight or insights, and more clarity, and more slogging through your karmic debris. These are extraordinary experiences, and each insight is the pearl of great price, for whose sake you would gladly sell everything you owned. But they are not that uncommon. What happens, though, when there is a total breakthrough? With the Katie stories, we get to see.

One of the benefits of Katie's commentary is that it demystifies the term *enlightenment*. Why does the Diamond Sutra say that there is no such thing as enlightenment? Why did Zen master Huang-po say, "Enlightenment is the realization that enlightenment doesn't exist"? Through Katie's clear words we get to find out. "Enlightenment, at its simplest," she says,

> means a more lighthearted way of experiencing the apparent world. If
> you believe that the world is unkind, for example, and then discover,
> through inquiry, that it's actually kind, you become kinder yourself,
> freer, less depressed, less fearful. I like to use the word *enlightenment* not
> for some exalted state of mind but for the very doable, down-to-earth

experience of understanding a stressful thought. For example, I used to believe the thought "My mother doesn't love me." After I questioned it, realized that it wasn't true, traced the effects of believing it (the effects that belief had on my emotions and actions), saw who I would be without it, turned it around to its opposites, and found living examples of how each of the turnarounds was true, I was enlightened to that thought, and it never troubled me again. . . . This is so important to understand. People think that enlightenment must be some kind of mystical, transcendent experience. But it's not. It's as close to you as your own most troubling thought. When you believe a thought that argues with reality, you're confused. When you question that thought and see that it's not true, you're enlightened to it, you're liberated from it. You're as free as the Buddha in that moment. And then the next stressful thought comes along, and you either believe it or question it. It's your next opportunity to get enlightened. Life is as simple as that.

The stories tell of someone who had no preparation for her experience of waking up to reality. She hadn't longed for it, hadn't practiced toward it, didn't even know what it was. She had no categories for what had happened, nor did anyone else around her. All she knew was that her life had been changed utterly. A paranoid, agoraphobic, suicidal woman had instantaneously become joyful and serene, and had been given a method that could keep her rooted in that state without ever returning to the world of delusion. "I discovered that when I believed my thoughts, I suffered," Katie says, "but that when I didn't believe them, I didn't suffer, and that this is true for every human being. Freedom is as simple as that. I found that suffering is optional. I found a joy within me that has never disappeared, not for a single moment. That joy is in everyone, always."

She had no recollection of her former life, and she stepped into her family's story with a fearlessness one can only be in awe of. Her husband and children suddenly appeared at the halfway house, out of nowhere. "This large stranger is my husband? These three young people, whom I've never seen before, are my children? Okay." The slate had been wiped clean. There was no teacher or tradition to help her or give her a reference for what had happened. She had to figure everything out for herself. She didn't know what our social norms were. So when she saw a stranger on the street and went up to him and stared into his eyes, intoxicated with love, or walked into someone's house because she knew that everything belonged to her, she had no idea that people would see her as crazy. There was never any retrenchment after the initial experience. But there was a gradual process of adjustment. She learned how to modulate her ardor. She learned how to say "I" and "you," "table" and "chair," even though she knew that the words were lies.

These stories also show us how radical the insights of the Diamond Sutra are. When the author of the sutra says that there is no self and no other, he isn't fooling around. He doesn't mean simply that all things are interconnected. He means that there is literally no such entity as a self—that "self" is nothing more than a mental construct, as is the apparent reality of anything outside us (or inside us, for that matter). The Katie stories show what it can look and feel like when someone realizes this truth to the very core of her being. However wild the form of the awareness may seem from the outside, from the inside it moves in perfect harmony. The boat keeps rowing itself gently down the stream, merrily, merrily, merrily, merrily—no dreamer, just the dream. (And not even that.)

Stephen Mitchell

About Inquiry

In the following chapters, when Katie uses the word *inquiry*, she specifically means The Work. The Work consists of four questions and what she calls a turnaround, which is a way of experiencing the opposite of what you believe. The questions are:

1. Is it true?

2. Can you absolutely know that it's true?

3. How do you react, what happens, when you believe that thought?

4. Who would you be without the thought?

When you first encounter them, these questions may seem merely intellectual. The only way to really understand how they function is to use them yourself. But witnessing other people using them may give you a glimpse, even an experience, of their power, and you can find many videos of Katie doing The Work with people at her website, www.thework.com. When the questions are answered honestly, they come alive; they mirror back truths that we can't see when we look outside. (There are instructions on how to do The Work in the Appendix, and more detailed instructions on her website and in her book *Loving What Is*.)

The Work has been called self-help, but it is far more than that:

it is self-realization. As we question a stressful thought, we see for ourselves that it's untrue; we get to look at the cause and effect of it, to observe in sobering detail exactly what modes of pain and confusion result from believing it; then we get a glimpse into the empty mirror, the world beyond our story of the world, and see what our life would be like without the thought; and finally we get to experience the opposite of what we have so firmly believed and to find specific examples of how these opposites are true. Once we deeply question a thought, it loses its power to make us suffer, and eventually it ceases even to arise. "I don't let go of my thoughts," Katie says. "I meet them with understanding. Then *they* let go of *me*."

S. M.

About the Diamond Sutra

> ... the listener, who listens in the snow,
> And, nothing himself, beholds
> Nothing that is not there and the nothing that is.
>
> WALLACE STEVENS, "THE SNOW MAN"

The sutra's title in Sanskrit is *Vajracchedikā Prajñāpāramitā Sūtra*, which means "The Diamond-Cutter Transcendent Wisdom Scripture" ("Diamond-Cutter" because it is a scripture of such highly compressed, adamantine wisdom that it can cut through doubt the way a diamond cuts through glass). Scholars think that it was written sometime around 350 CE, although, according to the usual convention in Mahayana scriptures, it takes the form of a dialogue with the historical Buddha, whose traditional dates are 563–483 BCE. After it was translated into Chinese in 401 CE, it spread throughout East Asia and became popular in many schools of Buddhism, especially Zen. A Chinese wood-block copy of the sutra, published in 868 and now in the British Museum, is the oldest printed book in the world, predating the Gutenberg Bible by 586 years.

Though the sutra is a dialogue, it is not a literary text, and it has none of the charm of Plato's dialogues, for example. It is very repetitious. But when a point is worth making, it's worth repeating. The author's intention is not to impress or entertain us; he isn't trying to be interesting or clever. He wants to awaken us to reality, and in case we didn't understand something the first time around, he will say it a second time, or a third, or a fourth.

The sutra was famous in Zen circles particularly because of a story about Hui-neng, the Sixth Patriarch of Zen, who as a young man was an illiterate woodcutter. One day, standing outside a shop where he had just delivered a pile of firewood, he heard a monk reciting the sutra. At the words "Develop a mind that abides nowhere," Hui-neng's mind opened. After he became a Zen master, he, or a fictional version of him, praised the Diamond Sutra in the highest terms: "The Buddha delivered this discourse especially for very intelligent students. It will enable you to realize the essence of mind. When you realize that wisdom is inherent in your own mind, you won't need to rely on any scriptural authority, since you can make use of your own wisdom by the constant practice of meditation."

It's a radical and subversive text, constantly undermining its own statements, never letting the reader get comfortable in any spiritual concept, even in such a refined one as "non-self." Like inquiry, it keeps pointing us back to the mind that abides nowhere.

There is another famous Zen story about the Diamond Sutra:

Te-shan, a learned scholar of the Diamond Sutra, heard that there was an irreverent doctrine called Zen, which taught that there was "a special transmission outside the sutras." Filled with indignation, he went south to exterminate the heresy. When he reached the road to Li-chou, he stopped to buy a snack from an old woman who sold dumplings at a roadside tea stand. The old woman said, "Your Reverence, what are all those books you're carrying in your cart?" Te-shan said, "My notes and commentaries on the Diamond Sutra." The old woman said, "I hear that the Diamond Sutra says, 'Past mind is ungraspable, future mind is ungraspable, and present mind is ungraspable.' Which mind wants to have the snack?" Te-shan was dumbfounded and couldn't answer.

After a few moments, he asked, "Is there a Zen master nearby?" The old woman said, "Master Lung-t'an lives about half a mile from here."

Te-shan went to Lung-t'an's temple and questioned him far into the night. When it grew late, Lung-t'an said, "You'd better go to bed now." Te-shan made his bows to the master, and lifted the blinds to leave, but it was pitch dark. "It's dark outside," he said. Lung-t'an lit a candle and handed it to him. As Te-shan was about to take it, Lung-t'an blew it out. At this, Te-shan had a sudden awakening.

The next day he brought his notes and commentaries on the Diamond Sutra in front of the Dharma Hall and held up a torch, saying, "Even though you master the profoundest teachings, it's like placing a single hair in the vastness of space. Even though you have learned all the truths in the world, it's like letting a drop of water fall into a deep ravine." Then he set fire to all his writings, bowed to Lung-t'an, and left.

In *A Mind at Home with Itself*, Katie functions as both the old woman who asks the fundamental question and as the Zen master who blows out the candle—the tiny flame that tries to illumine the all-encompassing darkness. If you think you have grasped any truths in this book, you may be delighted later on to find that the breath behind her words has blown them out like the candles on a birthday cake. "Don't believe anything I say," Katie often says. "Test it for yourself. The important thing is to discover what's true for *you*, not for me."

S. M.

About This Version of the Diamond Sutra

I don't read Sanskrit, and the English version in this book is not a translation; it's an interpretive adaptation. In preparing it, I have depended on existing translations into English, especially the ones by Edward Conze, Thich Nhat Hanh, Bill Porter (Red Pine), A. F. Price, and Mu Soeng.

Many contemporary readers have found the Diamond Sutra impenetrable. (One friend of mine, a sincere seeker, tried to read it four separate times, in four different translations, but could never get past the first half-dozen chapters.) For that reason, I thought it would be worthwhile to ground the dialogue in simple, nontechnical language, strip it of its esoteric trappings, and bring it to vivid life, so that everyone can benefit from its wisdom. The original text is even more repetitious, so I have trimmed some of its elaborate phrasing. I have also, wherever possible, shifted the emphasis from the metaphysical to the here and now. My intention has been, above all, to create a text that lets the clear light of the Buddha-mind shine through.

S. M.

A MIND AT HOME
WITH ITSELF

1

THE COSMIC JOKE

Thus have I heard: The Buddha was once staying in Shravasti at Anathapindika's garden in the Jeta Grove with a community of twelve hundred fifty monks. Early in the morning, when the mealtime came, he put on his robe, took his bowl, and walked into the city of Shravasti to beg for his food, going from house to house. When he had finished, he returned to the garden and took his meal. Then he put away his robe and bowl, washed his feet, and sat down.

I come from a little desert town in southern California where people think that the Buddha is the happy fat guy whose statue you see in Chinese restaurants. It wasn't until I met Stephen, my husband, that I learned that the fat guy is Pu-tai, the Chinese god of prosperity. The Buddha is the thin one, he told me, the one with the serene smile on his face. I respect what Stephen says, but for me the guy with the big belly is the Buddha too. He's the one who gets the joke. The joke is that it's all a dream—all of life, everything. Nothing ever *is*; nothing ever can be, since the very instant it seems to be, it's gone. This is truly hilarious. Anyone who gets the joke has the right to laugh that wonderful, whole-body, belly-shaking laugh.

Here's another way of saying it. To me the word *Buddha* means pure generosity: meticulous, joyful generosity, without left or right or up or down or possible or impossible—the generosity that naturally flows out of you when you're awake to what is real. Generosity is what's left of you after you realize that there's no such thing as a self. There's nothing to know, and there's no one to know it. So how do I know this? What fun!

The Diamond Sutra begins with the simple act of begging. I was very touched when I heard that the Buddha begged for his food. Since he understood how the universe works, he knew that he was always taken care of, and he didn't see himself in the position of a lofty transcendent being, or even of a spiritual teacher. He refused to be treated as someone special, someone who should be waited on by his students. In his own eyes, he was a simple monk, and it was his job to go out every morning and beg for food. One meal a day was all that was necessary. He was wise enough to go to any house and stand in front of the door without wondering if the family would feed him. He understood that the universe is always friendly—understood it so well that in silence he could hold out a bowl to any householder and calmly wait for a yes or a no. If the householder said no, the no was received with gratitude, because the Buddha understood that the privilege of feeding him belonged to someone other than that person. Food wasn't the point. He didn't need it. He didn't need to keep himself alive. He was just giving people an opportunity to be generous.

Stephen also told me that the word *monk* means someone who is alone. I love that, because in reality we *are* all alone. Each of us is the only one there is. There's no other! So for me *monk* doesn't describe someone who has entered a monastery. It's an honest description of everyone—of me and also of you. To my mind, a true monk is someone who understands that there is no self to protect or defend. He's someone who knows that he doesn't have a specific home, so he's at home everywhere.

When I woke up to reality in 1986, I realized that all my suffering had come from arguing with what is. I had been deeply depressed for many years, and I had blamed the world for all my problems. Now I saw that my depression had nothing to do with the world around me; it was caused by what I *believed* about the world. I realized that when I believed my thoughts, I suffered, but that when I didn't believe them, I didn't suffer, and that this is true for every human being. Freedom is as simple as that.

Once I opened my eyes that morning, I no longer had a home or a family or a self. None of all that was real. I knew nothing, even though I had Katie's memory bank and could tap into her story as a reference point. People would tell me, "This is a table," "This is a tree," "This is your husband," "These are your children," "This is your house," "This is my house." They also told me, "You don't own all the houses" (which from my position was absurd). At the beginning, someone would have to write Katie's name, address, and phone number on a piece of paper, and I would keep it in her (my) pocket. I noticed landmarks and left them in the mind like breadcrumbs, so that I could find my way back to what people called my house. Everything was so new that it wasn't easy for me to find my way back, even from five blocks away in the small town where I had grown up, so sometimes Paul, the man they said was my husband, or one of the children would walk with me.

I was in continual ecstasy. There was no "mine" or "yours." There was nothing I could attach to, because I had no names for any of it. Often, when I was lost, I would walk up to people and say, "Do you know where she lives?" (In those early days it was impossible for me to say "I." It seemed out of my integrity; it was a lie I couldn't bring myself to tell.) Everyone was unfailingly kind. People recognize innocence. If someone leaves a baby out on the sidewalk, people will pick it up and take care of it and try to find its home. I would walk into any house at all, understanding that it was mine. I would open the door and walk right in. I would always be shocked that they didn't realize that we all own everything. But people were very gentle with me; they smiled and weren't offended. Sometimes they would laugh, as if I had said something funny. Some of them would say, "No, this is *our* house," gently take my hand, and lead me to the door.

Every morning, as soon as I woke up, I would get out of bed, get dressed, and immediately start walking the streets. I was powerfully drawn toward human beings. This was very strange when you consider that only a short time before, "I" had been paranoid and agoraphobic and had hated people as much as I hated myself.

Sometimes I would walk up to a stranger, knowing that he (or she) was myself, just me again, and I would put my arms around him or take his hand. This felt very natural to me. When I saw fear or discomfort in people's eyes, I would step away. If not, I would talk to them. The first few times, I just told people what I saw: "There's only one! There's only one!" But I immediately noticed the imbalance in this. It felt like imposing on people. The words didn't feel natural, and they couldn't be heard. Some people appeared to like what they saw in me and laugh and feel safe in it; they didn't seem to care that what I said didn't make any sense. But some people would look at me as if I were crazy. I also noticed that it didn't feel comfortable not to tell the whole truth. So I would say, "There's nothing! There's nothing!" and I would hold up a zero with my fingers. But when I said this, I had the same feeling as when I told people that there's only one. So I stopped. That turned out to be a kindness.

The truth is that there isn't nothing. Even "There's nothing" is the story of something. Reality is prior to that. I am prior to that, prior to nothing. It's unsayable. Even to speak of it is to move away from it. I quickly realized that none of the things I understood could be put into words. And yet they seemed so simple and obvious to me. They sounded like this: *Time and space don't really exist. Unknowing is everything. There's only love.* But these truths couldn't be heard.

I spent months walking the streets of Barstow, where I lived. I was in a state of continuous rapture, so intoxicated with joy that I felt like a walking light bulb. I would sometimes hear that people called me "the lit lady." I felt that this separated me from other people. Eventually, though the radiance continued (and does to this day), it went inside, and I began to look more ordinary. Until it was ordinary and balanced, it wasn't of much value to people.

Stephen tells me that artists often imagine the Buddha with a halo around his head. But any light that came from him or others like him was an inner glow. It was the radiance that arises from being completely comfortable in the world, because you understand that the world is born out of your own mind. The Buddha has seen through all the thoughts that would override the experience of gratitude. When he goes out to beg, he experiences a receiving that is so deep that it is itself a giving. It's the food beyond food. He comes back to the Jeta Grove and sits with the given and eats his meal, and then he washes the bowl that supports all possibilities, and he washes his feet and sits quietly, in readiness, not knowing whether he will speak or not, whether people will listen or not, serene, grateful, without any evidence of a world before this moment or after it: sitting as the fed one, the supported one, the one who is nourished beyond what any food could supply. And in that quiet sitting, the mind is about to question itself through the apparent other and meet itself with understanding, without past or future, abiding in the self that cannot be named, the self that cannot exist, the radiant non-self.

You say that life is a dream. What motivates you to be kind to other people if they're just characters in your dream?

I love everything I think, so it follows that I love everyone I see. That's only natural. I love the characters in my dream. They are only there as my own self. As the dreamer, it's my job to notice what in the dream hurts me and what doesn't, and lack of kindness always hurts. In this I hear the voice of the Buddha, the antidote and blessing and doorway and unfailing consciousness within.

You say that after you woke up, people had to tell you, "This is your husband," "These are your children," that you had no memory of them. Did the memories come back later?

I found myself married to Paul, out of the blue. The woman who married him in 1979 had died, and something else was living in here. I didn't even recognize him; I literally didn't know who he was. The women at the halfway house brought him in, this large man, and said, "This is your husband." He was a complete stranger to me. I looked at him and said to myself, "This too, God? This is my husband? Okey-dokey." I was completely surrendered to what is, married to it, *was* it. So you could say that whatever had surfaced as Katie in her body that morning had never been married to anyone. And when they told me that my children were coming, I expected babies. I had no idea that "my" children were in their teens and early twenties. I thought that people were going to bring in two- or three-year-old babies. As the children came in, I watched and let the dream unfold. I didn't recognize them as different from anyone else. But I didn't know why I shouldn't accept that they were "mine." I just lived out the story. Love complies. It will meet itself in any form, without condition.

I would always let people define their relationship to me—who they thought they were, who they thought I was. The memory of Paul and the children never came back. It wasn't necessary. They would bring their stories to me, and I would get to see four different women all rolled up into a "me." At the time, there was a kind of echo, a shadow of memory, as they began to define me. If I knew them at all, it was like an essence, like music that was way in the background and couldn't be reached. They filled in the story. They *loved* their stories of me. They would say, "Remember the time when . . . ? Remember when we . . ., and you said this, and I did that?" and it all started filling in, even though it had never really happened. I came to inhabit their stories, and that was fine with me.

For the first seven months or so, people continued to define me. What was left of the one we call Katie was foreign to me, and yet I had her shadow, her memories—some of them, anyway. It was as if I had her fingerprint, and I knew it wasn't mine. It was all her story. I was only the self realizing itself—or, more accurately, the "self" realizing its non-self.

After your experience, you say you had no sense of "mine" or "yours." How is that different from a baby's sense of the world? Isn't becoming an adult a matter of developing proper boundaries and differentiating between "mine" and "yours"?

Without the sense of an identity weighing me down, I would wake up in a bed, and it was okay, since that was the way of it. There was another apparent human being lying next to me, and that was okay. I had legs, it appeared, and they walked me out the door, and that was okay. I learned the customs of this time and place from my sixteen-year-old daughter, Roxann. I would put on a red sock and a blue sock, and Roxann would laugh at me. I would walk out the front door in my pajamas, and she would run after me and pull me back in. *Oh, okay, I would think, no pajamas in public. We don't do that here.* She would take me by the hand (bless her heart) and guide me through it all. She would explain everything to me, again and again. How could she know, through my tears, that I was having a blissful love affair with life? What did I care what the names were? But in a grocery store, for example, she would patiently stop and point and say, "This is a can of soup. This is a bottle of ketchup." She would teach me, as a mother teaches a small child.

So in one sense, yes, I was like a baby. But in another sense I was very practical, very efficient. I could see where people were stuck in their stressful thoughts. I could show them how to question these thoughts and unravel their misery, if that was what they wanted and if their minds were open to inquiry. My communication was a bit wild at the beginning. I have learned to be clearer.

I sometimes say that a boundary is an act of selfishness. You don't need any boundaries when you're clear—about your yeses and noes, for example. In the early days, a couple of men wanted to have sex with me; they were sure that by sleeping with me they would become enlightened. Though I loved these dear, deluded men's honesty and their hunger for freedom, I said, "Thank you for asking, and no. That won't give you what you're looking for."

But isn't "no" a boundary? "No, I won't have sex with you," for example?

Every no I say is a yes to myself. It feels right to me. People don't have to guess what I want or don't want, and I don't need to pretend. When you're honest about your yeses and noes, it's easy to live a kind life. People come and go in my life when I tell the truth, and they would come and go if I didn't tell the truth. I have nothing to gain one way, and everything to gain the other way. I don't leave myself guessing or guilty.

If a man wants to have sex with me, for example, I don't have to decide about my answer. I'm married and monogamous; my "no" pops out with a smile. I'm actually giving the man the greatest gift I can give: my truth. You can see that as a boundary, but if a boundary is a limitation, a contraction, that's not how it feels to me. I see it as integrity. It's not something I establish; it's something that has already been established for me. Saying no isn't an act of selfishness; it's an act of generosity, both to myself and to the apparent other.

You say that you were intoxicated with joy when you first discovered the truth that there is no self and no other. Are you still intoxicated with joy?

Joy balances, yet it remains the same.

How do you relate to the Buddha's begging for food? Can you imagine yourself being penniless and homeless, like a monk, fully dependent on other people for food?

But I *am* fully dependent! If people don't grow vegetables, there are no vegetables in the stores. If people don't pay me or my husband, I can't buy food.

The Buddha asks only for what already belongs to him. He never suffers from hunger, yet he's generous enough to ask for food. He knows when to ask and what to ask for. He knows what to eat, which is precisely what you give him, and no more. I am always free of hunger until the moment food comes; I'm always perfectly fed, perfectly on time, with the right food, gifted out of grace. If you give me food, I thank you not in words but from within your own self. If you don't give me food, I thank you, and maybe, as love would have it, in another time and consciousness, you'll be ready to eat the only food worth eating, the thing we all hunger for, and what I offer truly: to serve what serves.

Generosity is what's left of you after you realize that there's no such thing as a self.

BOWING TO A GRAIN OF SAND

Then the monk Subhuti, who was in the midst of the assembly, stood up, bared his right shoulder, kneeled on his right knee, clasped his hands together in reverence, and addressed the Buddha. "How exquisitely considerate you are, Sir! You are always concerned about the welfare of your students, and you are generous with your teaching. Sir, when sincere men and women seek enlightenment, what should they do, and how should they control their minds?"

The Buddha said, "An excellent question, Subhuti. If sincere men and women seek enlightenment, it is essential for them to control their minds. Listen, and I will explain how."

Subhuti said, "Please do, Sir. We are all listening."

———————

Subhuti stands up and with the most beautiful gestures expresses his reverence for the Buddha. From the Buddha's point of view, everyone is awakened, so *Buddha* ("the Awakened One") is just a word for himself, and it's a word for Subhuti, and it's also a word for each of the monks in the audience. The dialogue that follows is between the Buddha and the Buddha. It's the internal self meeting itself. More accurately, there is no self, and this no-self meets itself. There is no other, and this no-other meets the no-self.

People sometimes approach me with that kind of reverence, and I know that it isn't personal. They come up to me after a public event, when they are very moved because through The Work they have understood something profoundly meaningful to them. They approach me with starry eyes and put their palms together and sometimes even kneel or bow. I know what reverence feels like, and I love that they are experiencing it. Recognition of the Byron Katie woman is only recognition of their own true nature. There can be no "me" in the equation. It's their own recognition; it belongs to them, and as that recognition, I'm thrilled. I am always internally bowing at the feet of everyone and everything, and I understand that anything less than that is a state of separation. When someone bows in front of me, I am what bows and I am what is bowed to. The two positions are equal. There's nothing personal in it.

It would be no different if I bowed in reverence to a grain of sand. It's a falling into, a merging with. That's how I experience reverence. It's the self, intimate with . . . I can't even say "the self intimate with itself"; it's simply the self, intimate. This is true intimacy, the undivided. There's nothing outside it, and nothing inside.

Humility means showing that kind of reverence to the sand, to the dust, to the sound of whatever is heard in this moment. If we were in our right minds, we would show reverence to everything in the world, since everything is the Buddha. That's what realization is. You can't ever grasp what is realizing. The thought that you're realizing anything at all isn't true; it's at least one thought-generation away from the truth. It's a beautiful moment in grace, yet still you're identified as the one who has realized. Once you get past the pain—and eventually the joy—of surrender, you recognize something beyond your ability to identify, and you fall into a state of utter gratitude.

Subhuti says that the Buddha is concerned about the welfare of his students. That's my experience too, though I don't see anyone as a student. To me, there are only friends. And I am concerned only if they are concerned; their concern is all the concern that's left in me. When they ask me a question—"How should I practice inquiry?" "What if a stressful thought still seems true to me after I question it?"—I see them as my confused self. I see them as the Katie I used to believe I was, suffering, with no way out. I would give those people everything I have. The question is needed, just like the begging bowl. It's needed for the enlightened mind; it *is* the enlightened mind, igniting itself. And if they don't question me, I'm never concerned about their welfare, because I know that everyone is perfectly all right, whatever apparent suffering they may be going through.

So Subhuti asks the Buddha a question, and it's a good one. There are men and women who authentically want to go beyond themselves. There are sincere men and women who want to be free of suffering. I was one of those without realizing it. I tested what happened when I didn't respond to the thoughts of "I want," "I need," "I shouldn't," "I should." I witnessed the world beyond those apparent requirements, and I found none of them to be true. None of those thoughts could stand up to inquiry.

You could discover this even if you tested it for just twenty-four hours, with one meal. Someone might give you a small bowl of rice, and that's it for twenty-four hours, and the I-know mind would say, "This isn't enough nourishment; I'm still hungry; I'm too weak; I'll get sick; I'll die." But when you allow each thought to be met with "Is it true?" life will show itself to you. Eventually, you find yourself ending every thought with a question mark, not with a period. You're able to rest in the never-ending enlightenment of the don't-know mind.

When I woke up to reality, I had children in need and property in need and a husband in need and people in need all around me, and none of that turned out to be true. Not even hunger turned out to be true. I tested it. I found that I didn't need food, and that nobody needed me, ever. And with the loss of all this came a further loss of self. It played itself out in the world. Gone was the house, gone the children, gone the husband. There was no "me" to lose them. Everything, without exception, was better taken care of without a Katie; it all fell in to a higher service, a kinder way. Everyone in my family became my teacher, deleting me from the process.

Subhuti's question is a good one, but there's something slightly confused about the way it's phrased, since he asks how to "control" the mind. It's a natural question. In the dream-world, the world of suffering, the mind seems chaotic, and people think that it needs to be controlled. Some people would give anything to know how to control it. But the mind can never be controlled; it can only be questioned, loved, and met with understanding.

The mind is like an unruly child. Thoughts come, one after another, to pester us and demand our attention, like unloved children. Our job is to discern, to know the difference between an internal argument and a state where we're open to listen and receive. Suffering appears when we try to control reality, when we think that we're the source rather than the mirror image or that we're more or less than anything else in the mirror. But everything in the world is equal. It's all a reflection of mind.

We can control the mind only to this extent: as a thought appears, we can simply notice it, without believing it. We can notice it with a questioning mind. The thought that asserts itself and wants to be believed comes from the I-know mind, the supposed teacher. The questioning comes purely from the student. In the questioning mind we experience a flow. There's no interruption, no limitation. "Control" is just a matter of noticing. It doesn't mean imposing an order onto the mind. If you're a true student, the thought will always end with a question mark.

You called this a dialogue between the Buddha and the Buddha. Would you say more?

The Buddha is always generous. There's nothing he would hold back, because for him the giving is the receiving. He is always talking only with himself. This whole sutra is the self (the awareness that is more accurately called the non-self) in discussion with itself. The apparent "other," the person we're speaking to, is a self-image. There's nothing outside our perception; we either perceive it or we imagine that it exists. If I can hear a question, it's inside me; it's coming from inside me, not from an imagined "out there." It's immediate. There's no distance in it, and answering one's own question, as the Buddha answers Subhuti's question here, knowing that it is his own, is what love does, always in service to itself.

The "other" is grateful, naturally, since the other is always a reflection of my own self. I would ask nothing of myself that was beyond me. It's always a refreshment. It's the clear mind, the beloved, always expanding, stretching, soaring as beauty and goodness and creation without limit. Not to answer would be to limit its majesty. When questions appear, the answers are effortless. But the quality of the answer depends on the student.

If I'm sitting with someone who thinks he knows something, he has limited himself, and my answers mirror that limitation. But if the student asks with a mind that is truly open, the answer is free. It comes from the bottomless source. That's why in thirty-one years I have never tired of people asking me the same questions over and over. The questions are always new.

Why would you, as you say, bow in reverence to a grain of sand?

The grain of sand gives itself entirely. Even though I may be totally unaware of it, it waits for the opportunity to show me itself and how it exists through me. It's patient, solid in its purpose, unchanging in its present identity; it doesn't pretend; it doesn't mind if I step on it, praise it, or belittle it; it remains what it is, without disguise or deceit; it is perfectly allowing, doesn't resist the name I give it, lets itself be whatever I call it. Who of right mind wouldn't bow to such a consciousness? I honor it as a teacher, and I meet its nature in everything I witness. If you throw me away, step on me, judge me as useless, overlook me, do I remain with the same constant, generous nature as the grain of sand? This is the Buddha-mind. It's what I woke up to. I also learned from the grain of sand that physical bowing is unnecessary. My bowing is now an unceasing internal experience, like the emptying I underwent in the desert for so many months after I woke up, an emptying that left me with reverence toward everything I met. It left me as the student. Subhuti in the presence of the Buddha. The Buddha in the presence of Subhuti.

What did you learn when you were in the desert?

All I heard in the desert was "I want," "I need," "My mother should love me," "Paul shouldn't watch so much television," "The kids shouldn't leave their dirty clothes on the floor," "They should respect me," "They should be healthy, but only for their own good." It didn't matter how painful each story was, it couldn't withstand inquiry. And to see it for what it was seemed like a gift to the world. "There's a rattlesnake nearby"—can I really know that? I would sit out in the desert with my eyes closed and experience these stories, and I knew I would rather be bitten by a hundred rattlesnakes than open my eyes and not work it out inside me.

What's the difference between humility and humiliation?

Humility looks very ordinary. It's hello and goodbye. Sometimes, at first, it looks like tears; sometimes, like dying. It's total surrender. The thing you were so proud of is seen as selfish; you treasured it, and it falls apart, and there is a change that takes place within you. If there's any hint of humiliation, it means that your ego hasn't yet surrendered; if you feel humbled, it means that your ego is surrendered, and it's the softest, most lovely feeling, and in that experience you see everyone as your teacher. You stand in what's left of you, and you die, and you keep dying. It's like the tree that lets go of its leaves. That beautiful clothing has fallen away, and the tree just stands there in the cold of winter, totally exposed.

You say that to you there are no students; there are only friends. Don't you consider yourself a teacher?

I am always the student. I love to be in that position, bowing, listening, at the feet of all that I see. This doesn't require an open mind: it *is* the open mind. It never has to take responsibility for knowing or for not knowing. It receives everything without defense, without judgment, since judgment would cost it everything it is. The moment you think you're someone or think you have something to teach, the inner world freezes and becomes the realm of illusion. That's what it costs when you identify yourself as the person who knows. It's a concoction of mind. You shrink down into the teacher: limited, separate, stuck.

But aren't there spiritual teachers with open minds?

Yes, of course. But the teacher who thinks of himself as a teacher, the want-to-be teacher, the one who's invested in it—he's trying to teach the student what he himself needs to learn. If I identify myself as a teacher and see my students as any less than teachers, I'm reinforcing what I think I know. The teacher who is always a student, who lives with an open mind, is free to continue expanding his consciousness. For the true teacher (that is, the true student), teacher and student are always equal.

You say that the mind can never be controlled. But sometimes you say that mind is everything. Is the first mind the ego mind and the second mind awareness?

Yes. "Awareness" is a way of saying that the ego is perfectly understood. Awareness is never tricked by what the ego thinks. It always knows the difference between what is and what isn't.

If someone asked you Subhuti's question—"How should people control their minds?"—what would you say?

First, I would invite them to be aware of their stressful feelings. A feeling is like the mate to a thought appearing. They're like the left and the right. If you have a thought, there's a simultaneous feeling. And an uncomfortable feeling is like an alarm clock that says, "You're caught in the dream." It's time to inquire, that's all. But if we don't honor the alarm clock, then we try to alter and manipulate the feeling by reaching into an apparent external world. We're usually aware of the feeling first. That's why I say it's an alarm clock that lets you know you're stuck in a thought you may want to investigate. If it's causing you any kind of discomfort, you might want to inquire and do The Work.

Then I would invite people to question the stressful thoughts that appear in their minds. That's what The Work is, and it shows you exactly how to question these thoughts.

Here's an example I like to give. Many years ago, during one of my public events in New York, a distinguished-looking elderly businessman got up and said that he wanted to do The Work with me on his business partner. "I'm angry with my partner," this man began, "for calling me a troublemaker in front of our employees. He had no right to do that. He damaged my reputation. My partner should apologize." I asked him, "Is it true?" He answered, "Yes, it's true. He insulted me. Of course he should apologize." He was sure of it.

But he was an intelligent man, and he really wanted to be free of his emotional pain. So when I asked him the second question of The Work ("Can you absolutely know that it's true that your partner should apologize?"), he went inside himself and really looked at his statement. After a silence, he said, "No."

"How did you find your no?" I asked.

"Well, I can't really know where he's coming from. I can't know another person's mind. He probably believes he's right. So I can't absolutely know that he should apologize." This answer seemed to loosen something inside him. A statement that he had thought was true didn't appear so obviously true to him now.

Then I asked him the third question, "How do you react, what happens, when you believe that your partner should apologize to you?"

"I get angry," he said. "When he comes up with a good idea, I shoot it down. I criticize him behind his back. When I see him, I avoid him. When I go home, I take the resentment with me, and I complain to my wife." So he began to see the cause and effect of it, the stress that results from believing a thought that might not even have anything to do with reality.

I said, "What would you call someone who shoots down his partner's good ideas and criticizes him behind his back?"

He said, with a look of amazement, "Oh my God. I *am* a troublemaker. He was right!"

Next, I asked the fourth question, "Who would you be without that thought? Who would you be, working with your partner, if you didn't believe that he should apologize?"

The man said, very softly, "I would be his friend. I'd be working with him again, and our company would benefit from that. And I'd set a better example for everyone, and be a lot happier at home."

After these questions, I asked him to turn the thought around—to experience the thought's opposites and see whether they might not be at least as true as his original statement.

"*I* should apologize to *him*," the man said. "Yes, I can see that. He may have insulted me in public—though I'm not even sure of that now—but I can see that I've been mean to him in private." Another turnaround was "I should apologize to myself." "I should apologize to myself," the man said, "because by believing my thought and becoming so angry, I cost myself money, and I cost myself a friend. So I owe myself an apology." A third turnaround he found was "My partner should *not* apologize to me." "Even if my partner *was* inappropriate or out of line in saying what he did, it seems arrogant now to believe that he should apologize. Maybe he didn't intend to insult me. Maybe he was just being honest. Maybe he was really trying to be a good friend by pointing out a problem that was damaging the company."

All this happened during a dialogue that went on for forty minutes or so. By the end of it, this man seemed hugely relieved. He had moved from the position of great anger and upset to a position of more understanding for his partner, a little more humility, and a lot more skepticism about being in the right. When we change our perception, we change the world that we perceive.

If you think that someone else is the cause of your problem, you're insane. You do The Work on your own thinking, clean up your own mess, and the problem disappears. Life always becomes simpler and kinder when we question our stressful thoughts. These thoughts aren't personal; everyone has them at one point or another. They're ancient: in every language in the world there are no new stressful thoughts; they're all recycled, over and over. But when we question them, mind begins to radically shift. Finally, the thoughts have been met with understanding. And then the next time they arise, the exact same thoughts that used to depress us may bring laughter. Like the man in the example: "He should apologize to me." A lot of laughter came from the same thought that used to cause anger, resentment, and depression, because he realized what was really true for him.

The mind can never
be controlled; it can
only be questioned,
loved, and met with
understanding.

3

THE RADIANT MOMENT

The Buddha said, "All bodhisattvas who sincerely seek the truth should control their minds by focusing on one thought only: 'When I attain enlightenment, I will liberate all sentient beings in every realm of the universe, and allow them to pass into the eternal peace of Nirvana. And yet, when vast, uncountable, unthinkable myriads of beings have been liberated, in reality no being has been liberated.' Why? Because no one who is a true bodhisattva entertains such concepts as 'self' and 'other.' Thus, in reality there is no self to attain enlightenment and no sentient beings to be liberated."

In this chapter the Buddha talks about the bodhisattva, someone who attains enlightenment for the sake of all beings. According to some traditions, I've been told, the bodhisattva vows not to enter Nirvana until all other beings have entered it first. This is a very kind idea, but it's confused.

If you think you have to postpone freedom, or that you *can* postpone it, you don't know what freedom is. Postponement is nothing that you do out of generosity. It assumes that your own peace of heart isn't the greatest help you can offer to all beings. It assumes that because of your generosity and compassion you need to keep suffering. That doesn't make any sense. How can your suffering ever help anyone? The only thing that can help is for you to *end* your suffering.

This concept also assumes that beings need to suffer until some sort of wiser, higher being comes to save them. That too makes no sense. The reality is that some well-intentioned but confused person imagines all the apparently terrible things that happen in the world and all the apparent beings that are suffering, and if he attaches to any of those images as though they really existed, in his imagination the freedom of all these beings is postponed, and they keep suffering along with him. But once he realizes the truth of it, all these imagined beings are set free, and in that the bodhisattva is enlightened. Sentient beings are here to serve the enlightenment of the bodhisattva, not the other way around. All beings are within the bodhisattva; it just seems as if they're outside him. They are consistently and without interruption here to enlighten him.

The Buddha talks about enlightenment. But he knows that enlightenment is nothing. There's no such thing. When you wake up from a dream, you realize that it was never real. You've just been asleep. You've been asleep because you've been believing stories that were so compelling that they created even the storyteller.

All beings exist inside the mind. They're all thought-forms, and they pass into Nirvana whether they're allowed to or not. They all go back to where they came from: nowhere. And since time isn't real, they have already passed into Nirvana. There is no "later." Their passage isn't even necessary. All beings are liberated through the enlightenment of the one who created them in the first place. And that one is no more and no less than what just appeared to pass into Nirvana. It includes both the Buddha and the being, both the dreamer and the dreamed.

The Buddha suggests that bodhisattvas should focus on one

thought: "When I attain enlightenment, I will liberate all sentient beings." But then he undercuts that thought with the next one; he rightly says that when all is said and done, no being has been liberated. The vow "When I attain enlightenment . . ." is a noble trick of the ego. It's noble because it points to generosity and compassion. But it assumes a future, and any future is a delusion. Nothing will ever happen in the future. Whatever happens can happen only now.

People used to ask me if I was enlightened, and I would say, "I don't know anything about that. I'm just someone who knows the difference between what hurts and what doesn't." Separation hurts. Any identity, no matter how enticing it may be—bodhisattva, Buddha—understates the truth, since it adds a name to what is already complete. All names are lies; they assume that there are separate beings, and thus they point away from reality. And the name *enlightenment* leaves you with something to attain. It's a word filled with effort. It leaves you as the one who is seeking an authentic identification. At the other end of it, "I am the one who has found" is just as limited as "I am the one who is seeking."

You don't need to know anything about enlightenment, and you *can't* know. The only important thing to know is this: if a thought hurts, question it. "Enlightenment" is just a spiritual concept. It's just one more thing to seek in a future that never comes. Even the highest truth is just one more concept. For me, the experience is everything, and that's what inquiry reveals. Everything painful is undone—now . . . now . . . now. If you think you're enlightened, you'll love having your car towed away. That's the proof of the pudding! How do you react when your child is sick? How do you react when your husband asks for a divorce? Are you thrilled that he's giving himself the life he wants? Do you love him with all your heart as you help him pack his bags? And if you don't, what thoughts are standing between you and pure generosity? Whatever these thoughts are, write them down and question them. No stressful thought, no separation, can withstand the power of inquiry. All the enlightenment you'll ever need is waiting for you to tap into right now.

———————————

Why do you say that the bodhisattva vow is confused—the vow not to enter Nirvana until all other beings have entered it first? Isn't it generous to put others before yourself?

The bodhisattva *is* Nirvana. Nirvana is not a place. He or she doesn't have to enter it. All "other" beings are unrealized bodhisattvas. They're already free, but they're not yet aware of that, and sometimes they begin to be aware and call out for help. The bodhisattva has no job, no purpose, without that call of apparent suffering. It's his nature to respond. He has no sense of generosity about putting others before himself, since for him there are no others; it's himself that he's always serving. It's painful to believe that anyone needs to be saved. I do The Work with people because they ask me; *they* think they need it, and that's what I gave to myself, so of course I give it to them. They are my internal life. So their asking is my asking. Responding to them is an act of self-love. It's perfectly greedy.

Here is an example of the bodhisattva in action: Someone says hello to her, and she says, "Hello. Isn't it a beautiful day!"

You say that enlightenment is nothing. But isn't it obvious that most people are unhappy, whereas people who have had strong enlightenment experiences are happy all the time?

"Nothing" is the state of enlightenment. Suffering is the call of the apparent something. Answering that call is what love does. No suffering: no cause. No cause: no effect. In the absence of suffering, happiness is all that's left.

You say that all beings are inside the mind. Do you mean inside your personal mind?

To be more accurate, there's no such thing as an inside. Mind isn't present inside you. It creates you, and because it begins to identify as a "you," chaos and suffering are born into the world. Stephen tells me that the historical Buddha said that life is characterized by unsatisfactoriness or suffering. But that's only because life is imagination misunderstood. There is an awareness beyond life and death. The Buddha-mind, the questioned mind, wakes up to itself, sees that it's nothing, and thus is free to lead its infinite, unstoppable, creative, brilliantly kind, unimaginable life.

The only important thing to know is this: if a thought hurts, question it.

4

GIVING IS RECEIVING

The Buddha said, "Furthermore, Subhuti, when bodhisattvas act generously, they shouldn't attach to the concept that they are acting generously. This is called 'acting generously while not attaching to form' and 'acting generously while not attaching to sight, sound, smell, taste, touch, or concepts.' If bodhisattvas act generously without attaching to concepts of generosity, their merit will be incalculable.

"Let me ask you something, Subhuti. The space to the east is incalculable, isn't it?"

"Yes, Sir. It is indeed."

"Good, Subhuti. And isn't it the same in any direction of the universe? Isn't space in any direction incalculable?"

"Sir, that is correct."

The Buddha said, "Subhuti, equally incalculable is the merit attained by bodhisattvas who act generously without attaching to the concept that they are acting generously. If bodhisattvas focus on this teaching with one-pointed concentration, they will understand what is essential."

In this chapter the Buddha talks about generosity, and his words go to the essence of it. True generosity happens without any awareness of being generous. You just give. That's it. Nothing sticks to the action. It's an act of receiving as much as of giving. The giving *is* the receiving. And it's not that bodhisattvas *shouldn't* attach to the concept that they are acting generously; it's that they *don't*. It's nothing they have to monitor or strive for. When you're being generous and giving something with your whole heart, you're simply not aware of any generosity. You're not self-conscious. In fact, you would laugh if someone called you generous; it would seem ridiculous. When a mother breast-feeds her baby, does she think, "How generous of me!"? That would be the farthest thing from her mind. Giving to her baby is giving to herself.

When I was five years old my most prized possession was a little brass bell in the form of a doll. It had a carved wooden handle with the faded, hand-painted face of a woman, and the bell was the skirt. I loved it so much that I could barely let it out of my sight. I remember taking it with me when I climbed a hill one day, and my father said, "If you get into trouble, just ring the bell, and I'll come find you." Then, at the kindergarten Christmas party, I gave it to my best friend, a little girl named Betty Jo. I saw that she wanted it, so I gave it to her. This is how we are in our natural state, before we're taught otherwise. The little bell was the first thing I ever thought of as mine, but "mine" wasn't yet a fixed concept; it was fluid, and the bell immediately became "hers."

When I came home, my mother asked me where the bell was, and when I told her, she was furious. "Byron Kathleen!" she said. (She usually called me Katie or Kat, but when she got angry I was Byron Kathleen, with an exclamation point.) "You go straight to Betty Jo and tell her to give it back!" So the next day it was mine again. I never understood why my mother was so upset. She knew how much I loved the toy, and maybe she was projecting a sense of loss onto me. Or maybe she was trying to teach me the value of possessions. Whatever her reason was, I felt mortified. I didn't understand. All I knew was that I had done something wrong. I felt great shame that I had done something so foolish in my mother's eyes.

After my experience in 1986, I never again had a sense of owning things. People would often give me presents, just to express their gratitude, and I would give the present away as soon as someone admired it. I even gave away the gold wedding ring Stephen bought me. I gave it to a young friend of ours, but he returned it to me after a couple of minutes. A few years later I gave the ring away again, after one of my events, to a dear man with multiple sclerosis, and he kept it. Stephen was amused, because he understands where this tendency comes from. We were in New York at the time, and he walked me to Tiffany's and bought me another ring. He said that as long as he had any money, he would always manifest another wedding ring, like a genie in the Arabian Nights. He cares about our wedding rings, and his caring is the only remnant of mine.

Realization is of no value to me if I can't give you everything. And I don't give on purpose; that kind of generosity is simply who we all are without a story. The way you can know how much you're attached to any story is how much you hold back. When you hold back, you feel it. It's not comfortable.

For thirty-one years I have lived my life in service. I have devoted myself to the end of suffering in this apparent world. But I don't do it because I believe that anyone is actually suffering. I do it because I'm serving myself. That's how I think of compassion: as pure selfishness. I'm in love with everyone and everything I see, because it's all me. I sometimes say that it's total vanity. Stephen tells me that the old meaning of *vanity* is "emptiness." I love that.

It's like the imagined bodhisattva who comes back to save all suffering beings. When someone tells me, "Katie, I'm desperate, I need you," I understand. I know that place. And I give them what I myself was given. There's not a choice. If someone is suffering—in other words, if someone is believing a world of suffering into existence— then that is what's left of me. It's my old self; it's one of my cells, one of the cells of my body, that isn't as free as it deserves to be. And I know that the cell is perfect, except that it's saying it's not. So I stay there in my clarity, immovable. I know it's only myself I'm showing up for. I am the one in terror. I am the one in despair. I am the one I'm serving with the four questions and turnarounds of The Work. I am the bodhisattva carried forward, as your imagination. I'm both sides of the polarity, serving myself at all times. Nothing could be more generous than that.

———————

You said earlier that the memory of Paul and the children never came back to you. Yet in this chapter you describe a vivid memory of your doll with the brass bell. Would you explain the discrepancy?

I have no idea. Images arise in my mind or they don't. I don't ask why they do or don't. What people call memories are, in my experience, images with silent words attached to them. I see them, and once they're noticed they're gone. I only see what can't be seen. So I can honestly say I have no memory.

If you don't believe that anyone is really suffering, how can you experience empathy for them or take their problems seriously?

The suffering that people describe to me necessarily comes from either an imagined past or an imagined future, since an identified mind is always remembering or anticipating what isn't happening in reality. I realize that everyone is always okay; they're always in a state of grace, whether they realize it or not. *Empathy*, the dictionary says, is the ability to understand the feelings of another person. To me this makes sense. I understand that when people are suffering, they are me, trapped in a painful past or anticipating a dangerous future, and I respect this, as I respect a child having a bad dream. To the dreamer it isn't a dream. My job isn't ever to wake the sufferers, but rather to see what I see and never override or disrespect their suffering, since it is very real to them. My job is to understand.

Some people think that empathy means feeling another person's pain. But it's not possible to feel another person's pain. What happens is that people project what someone's pain must feel like and then react to their own projection. This kind of empathy is unnecessary for compassionate action; it actually gets in the way. Empathy, in my experience, has nothing to do with imagining pain. It is a fearless connectedness and an immovable love. It's a way of being fully present.

I take people's problems seriously, but only from their point of view, and I remain closer than close. In my world, it's not possible to have a problem without believing a prior thought. I don't tell people that, because telling them what I see would be unkind. I listen to them, and I wait to be of use. I too have been trapped in the torture chamber of the mind. I hear people's delusions, their sadness or despair, and I'm completely available, without fear, without sadness, living in the grace of reality now. And eventually, as love would have it, if their minds are open to inquiry, their problems begin to disappear. In the presence of someone who doesn't see a problem, the problem falls away—which shows you that there wasn't a problem in the first place.

I have devoted myself to the end of suffering in this apparent world. But I don't do it because I believe that anyone is actually suffering. I do it because I'm serving myself.

The Work in Action

"Dave Didn't Acknowledge Me"

Note: This dialogue and the others that follow took place before audiences of between 150 and 1200 people. Each man or woman sitting opposite Katie on the stage had written out a Judge-Your-Neighbor Worksheet; the instructions were: "Fill in the blanks below, writing about someone you haven't yet forgiven 100 percent. Don't write about yourself. Use short, simple sentences. Please don't censor yourself—allow yourself to be as judgmental and petty as you really feel. Don't try to be 'spiritual' or kind."

A first experience of The Work, as a reader or an onlooker, can be unsettling. Katie's deep compassion, which is totally without pity because she sees everyone as free, can seem harsh to those who are used to pitying others and themselves. "I am your heart," Katie has said. "If you invite me in, I am the depth you haven't listened to. It had to get louder, to appear as me, because your beliefs were blocking it out. I am you on the other side of inquiry. I am the voice so covered up with beliefs that you can't hear it on the inside. So I appear out here, in your face—which is really inside yourself." It helps to remember that all the participants—Katie, the person doing The Work with her, and the audience—are on the same side here; all of them are looking for the truth. If Katie ever seems to be insensitive toward someone, you'll realize, upon closer examination, that she's making fun of the thought that is causing the suffering, never of the person who is suffering.

You'll notice that Katie is very free in her use of terms of endearment. This annoys some people (not all of them New Yorkers); one reader of *Loving What Is* grumbled that if she wanted to hear a woman calling everyone "sweetheart" or "honey," she would go to a truck stop in Oklahoma. To her, these endearments sounded conventional and insincere; for Katie, they are the literal truth. Everyone she meets is the beloved.

JOANNA [*reading from her Worksheet*]: *I'm upset with Dave because he walked away without giving me a hug or acknowledging me.*

KATIE: Okay. So what's the situation? Where are you? Give me a picture of where you and Dave are.

JOANNA: We were in the house, and he walked out the door to go to his car.

KATIE: "He walked away without giving you a hug or acknowledging you"—is it true?

JOANNA: Yes. He turned around and walked out of the house, walked to the car; I chased him to the car, and I was throwing my hands up, and he looked at me, and I said, "What's going on?" And he said, "What?" I said, "Are you just going to leave?" I felt completely unacknowledged.

KATIE: Sweetheart, the answer to the first two questions is one syllable: yes or no. When we do The Work, we meditate on a stressful moment in time. Notice how your mind will want to justify your position and defend it and talk about it. Just notice that. Then come back to meditating on the question "Is it true?" until you're shown a solid yes or a solid no. Okay? "He walked away without giving you a hug or acknowledging you"—can you

absolutely know that it's true? You don't have to guess. Images
will show you the answer. It takes stillness. Be a detective. If you
believe it's true, be a detective. Try to prove yourself wrong, but be
authentic. You can't fool yourself. Let the images show you. It takes
courage to look. So can you absolutely know that it's true?

JOANNA [*after a few moments*]: No.

KATIE: Just feel that answer. Give it time to sink in. If you find a no,
good; if you find a yes, that's good too. Then give your answer
some room to be absorbed. Sometimes it's difficult when no is the
answer. We may even feel that it's not fair for him to be right. We
don't want to give him that. [*Pause*] Okay, let's move on now to
the third question. Continue to meditate on that moment in time,
with your eyes closed. Notice how you react, what happens to
you emotionally, when you believe the thought "He didn't hug or
acknowledge me." Does your chest tighten? Does your stomach
flip over? Do you get heated? Do you experience anxiety? Do
you attack him with words or a look? A demand? An insult or
some form of punishment? Notice. How do you react when you
believe the thought "He walked away without giving me a hug or
acknowledging me"?

JOANNA: I get very anxious and needy. Very needy. I doubt myself.
I doubt my worthiness. My self-worth goes down. And then I feel
like I have to beg him for attention. Then I start thinking, "Oh, I'm
too needy." And I question everything. I get a desperate feeling
almost. Reaching, like trying to grasp for something that's not real.

KATIE: Just experience that, and keep your eyes closed. Who or
what would you be in that situation without that thought, as you
witness this man you love as he walks to the car. Who would you
be without the thought "He walked away without giving me a hug
or acknowledging me"?

JOANNA: I would just notice him walk to the car. [*The audience laughs.*]

KATIE: Continue to witness that moment without the thought.

JOANNA: I'd probably notice what a handsome guy he is, too. [*More laughter*] So does that mean in the future when he walks away I should recognize . . .

KATIE: It's only about right here, right now, as you witness that moment, only the one you're contemplating now.

JOANNA: Should I never expect him to give me a hug? Should I just accept that that's what he does?

KATIE: Now we're in a discussion, and discussions will never solve your problem. Let's move back to The Work.

JOANNA: Okay.

KATIE: This Work is about noticing what was really happening, not what you thought onto what was happening. It's not a plan for what to do next. Right now we're just looking at who you would be in that situation without the thought, without this condition that you put on him. It's sometimes hard for us to answer this question. The ego wants to be right, it doesn't want to let him off the hook for not being able to read your mind. We think that if we see who we would be without the thought, then he's right and we're wrong, and it's worth holding on to our anger, because he's wrong and we're right.

JOANNA: I think it's not so much anger. It's just a feeling of rejection. How do you . . .

KATIE: Yes. It hurts.

JOANNA: I don't want to feel that anymore.

KATIE: Do you love him?

JOANNA: Yes.

KATIE: All right. Close your eyes. Drop your story, just for a moment. Look at him going to the car. Look how free he is. He loves you so much he doesn't have to hug you. [*Laughter*] This is one secure guy. If you drop your story, you're open to learning. But as long as you believe your story, you're just open to pain. In fact, you become the cause of your suffering—but only totally. How do I know? It hurts. He's free. He doesn't have to tell you goodbye.

JOANNA: Yes, he's free. He doesn't understand.

KATIE: He's completely innocent. Do you see it?

JOANNA: Yes, I do see it. Very clearly.

KATIE: Good. "He walked away without giving me a hug or acknowledging me." How would you turn that around? What's an opposite?

JOANNA: He . . .

KATIE: "He didn't give me a hug or acknowledge me"—turn it around.

JOANNA: He did give me a hug and acknowledge me.

KATIE: Okay. So, tell me, as you witness that situation, where is it that he did give you a hug and acknowledge you?

JOANNA: Well, when he got to the car, he did acknowledge me when I made it clear he hadn't, or how I felt he hadn't. He looked at me and said, "What do you want me to do?"

KATIE: And did you say, "You are so handsome! I'd like you to give me a hug, sweetheart."

JOANNA: I did say it.

KATIE: You did?

JOANNA: Yes. But I didn't say it like that. [*Loud laughter*]

KATIE: Oh, you're fun to hug. In that moment.

JOANNA: Yeah, I could tell it was not as . . . I said, "Well, are you going to leave without giving me a hug or acknowledging me?" Exactly like that. He was just leaving.

KATIE: So you *didn't* ask for a hug.

JOANNA: You're right. I didn't.

KATIE: You asked a question you already had the answer to.

JOANNA: Okay.

KATIE: And then did he hug you?

JOANNA: He did.

KATIE: And you didn't even ask.

JOANNA: It was . . . a hug. It wasn't exactly what I wanted, but it was a hug.

KATIE: It wasn't the hug you wanted. Did you instruct him?

JOANNA: It felt like he was doing it because I asked him.

KATIE: Because you threatened him. [*Laughter*] You didn't ask him.

JOANNA: Exactly.

KATIE: Is this starting to make sense to you?

JOANNA: Yes, it is.

KATIE: I love this Work. I love that through inquiry you begin to see who he lives with. [*Laughter*]

KATIE: So "he didn't hug or acknowledge me." Turn it around: "I didn't . . ."

JOANNA: I didn't hug or acknowledge him. That's true. I could have run and grabbed him and hugged him.

KATIE: Yes. Other than what you were believing, you're as free as he is. That's a beautiful thing. Okay, let's look at statement 2. In that situation, what did you want from him?

JOANNA: *I want Dave to hold me and look at me before he leaves. Just to look at me.*

KATIE: You want him to hold you and look at you before he leaves?

JOANNA: Right. Sometimes I feel like he looks past me.

KATIE: Okay. Now, witness that situation. Close your eyes. "You want him to hold you and look at you before he leaves"—is it true? You know those things you think you really want? Maybe you don't. You don't even stop to ask yourself. You just go on believing. So in that situation, "You want him to hold you and look at you before he leaves"—is it true?

JOANNA: In that moment, yes.

KATIE: And after what you've seen now? Is it true?

JOANNA: Not as . . . No. Not really.

KATIE: No. Now notice what happens to you and how you react when you believe that thought. And, again, we're not guessing, are we? [*To the audience*] Do you all see the images of the two of them, for yourselves? How many of you have become an instant victim of your thoughts? A martyr? [*To Joanna*] And nothing's happening except that the man's going to the car! [*Laughter*] You're suffering. You're a victim. And it's all his fault! So, who's the cause of the suffering? Is it him? Or you?

JOANNA: It's me.

KATIE: And notice how you treat him when you believe this thought. He's free. He's walking to the car. "I want him to hold me and look at me before he leaves."

JOANNA: I start believing all sorts of stories: that he doesn't really care, that he doesn't love me.

KATIE: So who would you be without the thought, watching him go to the car, without the thought "I want him to hold me and look at me"?

JOANNA: I would just be happy with what happened. I would just be happy and grateful for what he's doing. For exactly who he is, how he is, in that moment. I would just love him.

KATIE: Yes. Now let's turn it around. "I want him to hold me and look at me before he leaves."

JOANNA: I don't want him to hold me and look at me before he leaves.

KATIE: What does that mean to you?

JOANNA: I don't want him to because he doesn't want to. He doesn't want to, necessarily. It doesn't mean anything.

KATIE: He probably doesn't even know you're there. I mean, only you can know as you look at the situation. What else does it mean to you? "I don't want him to hold me and look at me before he leaves." I have one. Would you like to hear it?

JOANNA: Please. Yes, definitely.

KATIE: Did you ask him, "Would you please hold me and look at me before you leave?"

JOANNA: No, I didn't ask. I just assumed.

KATIE: Is he psychic? [*Laughter*]

JOANNA: No. I guess I just wanted him to want to.

KATIE: You wanted him . . .

JOANNA: To just be natural. That it would just be natural that he would want to.

KATIE: He *is* being natural. He's going to the car. Naturally. That's his natural. [*Laughter*] There are two men: there's the man in your head, and then there's him. [*Laughter*] And when he is not the man of your imagination, you punish him. You become cold, or whatever it was you did. Like saying, "Were you going to leave without hugging me?" In that tone of voice. Okay? You become the one he didn't fall in love with.

JOANNA: Right. That's so true.

KATIE: "I want him to hold me and look at me before he leaves"—is it true? I know it's not true because you didn't ask. [*To the audience*] If you ask and he doesn't do it, you again get to meet the man you're with. [*To Joanna*] So let's play that out. Okay? You be the man who doesn't want to. That's where you're going, right? Okay. I'll be you, and you be Dave. "Would you hold me and look at me before you leave?"

JOANNA: "I can't. I'm too mad at you. I can't do it."

KATIE: "Because you're too mad at me? Oh, I understand that completely. And would you hold me and look at me even though you're mad? Could you possibly do that? It's really important to me. I really don't care about how you feel right now." [*Laughter*]

JOANNA: "Well, that's too bad, because I don't care about how you feel either, so have a good day."

KATIE: "Wow! That's really good advice: 'Have a good day.' Thank you, sweetheart. I'm going to work on that one."

JOANNA: So your point is to not take things personally and that nobody . . .

KATIE: No, my point is that I can't change him. Do you want to hug and look into someone's eyes when you don't want to?

JOANNA: No, of course not. But don't we want that from the love of our life?

KATIE: Well, when I want that, I ask Stephen. "Sweetheart, would you look into my eyes and hold me?" If he's busy, I've got an entire population to ask. [*Laughter*] I can just step out the door and ask the first person I see. [*Laughter*] Stephen is never too busy, in my experience. But if he were, and I really wanted to be held, why would that stop me? I'm serious. Do you understand that?

JOANNA: But I want it from one person and nobody else.

KATIE: Well, this is just all about me. I'm the one who wants to be held. I'm the one who wants someone to look into my eyes. What does it have to do with him? He's just handy. [*Laughter*]

JOANNA: Okay, so . . .

KATIE: You want him to fix you. Isn't that all that's happening? "You give me what I need to feel secure, or we've got a problem here. I mean, this is all about me." It would be more honest if you said, "I'm not really doing well, and I know that you don't want to hug me now, and I know you're really mad, but I need you to help me because I don't know another way. Please help me. Help me. Help me. Help me."

JOANNA: And this person is most likely incapable.

KATIE: He says no.

JOANNA: And probably because he's incapable of it, no matter what.

KATIE: Well, he just says no. Okay? So, I'm the one left with me, since it's all about me anyway. I'm left to take care of myself. Can you find another turnaround? Put yourself on all of it. "I want me . . ."

JOANNA: Oh. I want me to hold me and look at me before I leave.

KATIE: Yes, before I completely leave reality. I am a mess. I need to be held. So, as you watch him leave, you might sit there, hold yourself sweetly, and rock, because you've got a big problem and it's not because of him. So put your arms around yourself, hold yourself, get still. If I have a problem, I don't look to my husband to solve it; that's not his job. I look to myself. That's quite a shortcut. It's for people in a hurry. And as a result, I'm close to my husband—closer than close. That closeness is mine. It's intimate. I'm connected. So let's keep traveling. You're doing really well. "I want me to hold me . . ."

JOANNA: I want me to hold me and look at me . . .

KATIE: Yes. If that doesn't hold your interest, why would it hold his? [*Laughter*]

JOANNA: Right.

KATIE: And you can really hold yourself. There are many ways of doing it. And you can go to the mirror and look into your eyes. If you drop your story and really look, you'll meet the love of your life. We can't receive that from another human being until we find it in ourselves, until finally we discover that it's not possible to be rejected. Let's look at statement 3 on your Worksheet.

JOANNA [*giggling*]: *Dave should show me more affection, should initiate physical intimacy more, and should match his actions with his words.*

KATIE: Okay. Now notice how you're laughing at what was very serious for you earlier.

JOANNA: He shouldn't do any of that.

KATIE: "He should show more affection."

JOANNA: He fixes things. He likes to do it. He does say "I love you" a lot, and he likes to fix everything. He's always fixing things around the house, always wanting to fix things.

KATIE: So what is it he should do?

JOANNA: Oh. He's always wanting to fix things, but there's not enough physical intimacy and affection. That's what I was saying. He should show me . . .

KATIE: Yes, sweetheart. And you can have the most amazing time when you go home just showing him how you want to be intimate.

JOANNA: Okay.

KATIE: He may really like that. [*Laughter*]

JOANNA: Okay.

KATIE: "He should show me more affection." Let's turn the whole thing around: "I should . . ."

JOANNA: I should show him more affection, should initiate physical intimacy more, and should match my actions with my words. Yes.

KATIE: So you can see that the turnaround is advice to yourself. This is how to live happily with yourself and with him. Okay? Now let's look at statement 4.

JOANNA: *I need Dave to give me more of his time and to be more present to me.*

KATIE: Okay. Is that true? Is that what you need in order to be happy? Are you noticing how dependent you are?

JOANNA: No, I don't *need* it. I *want* it.

KATIE: The question is, would his giving you more time and being more present with you in that situation really make you happy rather than upset or angry?

JOANNA: No.

KATIE: And notice how you react when you believe that thought. Notice how you treat Dave when you believe that thought, and what that feels like.

JOANNA: I constantly question him. And he gets upset, because he says I'm doubting how he feels and he doesn't understand why. And he always says, "I don't understand why you're saying this."

KATIE: Because you're living a private life. A completely secret life, where you have a whole drama going on that you're not sharing with him. You're assuming that he can read your mind. He's just walking to the car, and all of a sudden he's an enemy, who doesn't love you anymore. And all he's done is walk to the car. [*Laughter*] Probably off to buy a tool to fix something for you.

JOANNA: Yes! He is! He was! [*Laughter*]

KATIE: [*To the audience*] Okay, ladies. Would you rather have affection or your plumbing fixed? [*Laughter*] A little of this, a little of that. Balance. [*To Joanna*] Okay, so close your eyes, sweetheart. Look at him without believing the thought "I need him to give me more of his time and to be more present with me." Drop your story. Look at Dave. What do you see?

JOANNA [*crying*]: A beautiful gift in my life of just . . . A beautiful man who is just a sheer gift. A good man.

KATIE: Yes.

JOANNA: Very loving and generous.

KATIE: Now look at yourself without your story. Look at yourself watching him go to the car. Other than what you're thinking and believing, are you okay?

JOANNA: Other than what I'm thinking and believing, it's heaven. It feels fantastic.

KATIE: Yes. Look at yourself! There you are, healthy, happy, whole, loved. Now look at yourself believing the story. Look at the radical difference.

JOANNA: Believing the story, it's lack and need and abandonment and aloneness. No one's ever there. It's a nightmare. It's a total nightmare.

KATIE: That's with the story. Now look at the situation without the story.

JOANNA: Without the story, there's peace and gratitude.

KATIE: And health and beauty and love. It's all there. "I need Dave to give me more of his time and to be more present with me"—turn it around. "I need me to give me . . ."

JOANNA: I need me to give me more of my time?

KATIE: More of your time to do inquiry on your unquestioned thoughts about yourself and about him.

JOANNA: And to be more present with myself.

KATIE: In that moment.

JOANNA: That's what I need to work on. Just being present and . . .

KATIE: "I need me to give myself more of my time, in that moment, and to be more present with myself, because I am crazed."

JOANNA: It's true, I was like a crazy person. I really do feel crazy at those times. It's irrational. I feel irrational.

KATIE: Yes. So you need to give yourself a little more of your time before you go after Dave. [*Laughter*]

JOANNA: Right. Who's just walking to the car.

KATIE: And to be more present with yourself, for both of your sakes.

JOANNA: Oh, God. So true. Yeah. So when you're present with yourself in that moment, when you've had that moment and it's feeling painful, do you just sit in it and just . . .

KATIE: Well, you just know that you're crazed in that moment, and you know that Dave can't give you what you need. It's time for a Judge-Your-Neighbor Worksheet; you fill it in with what you're believing and then you question it. In other words, exactly what you've done here, only take more time with it. The Work is meditation. It's about getting quiet enough to experience the answers that rise to meet the questions.

JOANNA: Okay.

KATIE: This Work is 100 percent free at thework.com. The Worksheets, the instructions—it's all there on the website, and it's all over YouTube. And we've developed a phone app for $1.99, which allows you to do The Work wherever you go. And we have one for tablets, where you can fill in a Judge-Your-Neighbor Worksheet, and then there's an app where you can question just one belief at a time. So you can fill in a Worksheet while you're waiting for your children at school, or in line at the supermarket, or wherever you are, anytime you're confused, hurt, or stressed out. As Dave drives away, sit down, identify your thoughts, write them down, and do your Work. And then when he drives away, you're honestly able to say, "I love you." It doesn't matter if he hears you or not. When you love someone, what does it feel like? Whom does that belong to? Him or you? Her or you? It's yours. When I say, "Stephen, I love you," he knows that what I mean is "I love," and he's happy for me. Why would I give him the credit? [*Laughter*] And it's so beautiful. Of course I'd want to share it. "Stephen, I love you." I mean, he's me anyway. What do I mean by that? Dave, for example, will only and always be who you believe him to be— no more, no less. Do you understand? You believed him in, and you believe him out. He'll always be who you believe him to be. You can never know him. To know yourself is what's important. To know yourself is truly to know all of us. Okay. Let's look at statement 5.

JOANNA: *Dave is unaware, distant, and doesn't really love me.* Oh, gosh.

KATIE: Okay. "In that moment, I am . . ."

JOANNA: I am unaware, distant, and don't really love myself.

KATIE: At all.

JOANNA: No.

KATIE: You were thinking all kinds of terrible things about yourself. And there's another turnaround. "I am unaware, distant, and I don't really love Dave."

JOANNA: I don't really love Dave?

KATIE: The man you walked up to and put demands on. He wasn't the Dave you imagined him to be, the cold-hearted Dave. He was just the Dave who walked to the car. So you're attacking him for being someone he's not.

JOANNA: Ah. Okay.

KATIE: There's Dave as he is, Dave the person, and then there's the Dave you imagine him to be. One is Dave. One is not. It could be you've never met Dave. I'm serious. I often say, "No two people have ever met."

JOANNA: That's true, because there are times where that same person does everything the way you want, and there can't be two different people; he didn't change all of a sudden. It happened in your mind.

KATIE: Just know that he's always perfect. He's always lovable, except for what you're thinking and believing about him. [*Laughter*]

JOANNA: Okay.

KATIE: And when you're up against that, it's time for a Worksheet.

JOANNA: Okay.

KATIE: Good. Now statement 6.

JOANNA: *I don't ever want Dave to leave me wondering and doubting how he feels about me.*

KATIE: Okay. "I'm willing . . ."

JOANNA: I'm willing for Dave to leave me wondering and doubting how he feels about me.

KATIE: "I look forward to . . ."

JOANNA: I look forward to Dave leaving me wondering and doubting how he feels about me.

KATIE: It's another Worksheet.

JOANNA: Oh, jeez. So, I suppose . . . Is there going to be a day when he leaves and I'm okay with everything and at peace, if I do enough of these?

KATIE: It's called a happy life.

JOANNA: That's what I want.

KATIE: Yes. If Stephen drives away, doesn't say goodbye, never contacts me again, I just assume he's having a wonderful life. And when you love someone, isn't that what you want for him? So if he stays, good; if he goes, good. I love him. That's it. That's solid.

JOANNA: Thank you. Thank you so much, Katie.

KATIE: You're very welcome.

5

EVERYDAY BUDDHAS

The Buddha said, "Let me ask you something, Subhuti. Can anyone recognize the Buddha by some distinguishing physical characteristic?"*

Subhuti said, "No, Sir. The Buddha can't be recognized by any distinguishing physical characteristic, because, as the Buddha has said, physical characteristics of the Buddha aren't actually physical characteristics."

The Buddha said, "Everything that has a physical form is an illusion. As soon as you see the illusory nature of all things, then you recognize the Buddha."

People used to believe that because the Buddha had discovered something extraordinary about the mind, he must have had an extraordinary body, marked by miraculous characteristics like golden skin, a bump on his head, and wheel marks on the soles of his feet. This kind of reverence, though it comes from a genuine place, is limiting; it creates separation. If you believe that someone has to have a

---

* In Indian mythology, the thirty-two physical characteristics of a great man include such traits as a thousand-spoked wheel sign on the soles of his feet, finely webbed toes and fingers, a well-retracted penis, a golden-hued body, a ten-foot aura, deep blue eyes, and a fleshy protuberance on the crown of his head.

bump on his head to be a buddha, how can you see that anyone who has woken up to reality is a buddha, whatever he or she looks like, and that anyone who hasn't yet woken up is a buddha too? Thinking that the Buddha is his body, or that he even *has* a body, makes things difficult. It keeps you limited. The truth is that the Buddha doesn't have a body. Nobody does.

This body is totally imagined. As I sit here on the couch, with my eyes closed, I see images of the body, I feel sensations associated with it, and it all happens within my perception; there's nothing external in it. I open my eyes, I look at my hands and feet, and these so-called parts of my so-called body are still images and sensations within my perception. I can separate them from the rest of my visual world and call them my body, but that separation is still an act of mind, and the images are always of a past, even if the past happened a nanosecond ago. They're part of a movie of reality; they're not reality itself. Why would I believe that a movie on the mind's screen is real? Every time I try to focus on what is real about this body, it's gone, and the "I" who focuses is gone too. There's nothing solid. Not only the dream but even the dreamer is forever gone. And the dreamed body—I sit it, I stand it, I walk it, I feed it, I brush its teeth, I dress it in clothes, I put it to bed at night and lift it from bed in the morning, and none of that is real. It's all a projection of mind. To imagine that there is anything outside the mind is pure delusion.

Even physical pain is imagined. When you're asleep, does your body hurt? When you're hurting, and the phone rings, and it's the call you've been longing for and you're mentally focused on the conversation, there's no pain. If your thinking changes, the pain changes.

I once stuck my hand too far into the mouth of a Champion juicer. I heard the sound of crunching, and when I pulled my hand out it was streaming with blood. The blood was bright red; I had never seen anything so beautiful. Roxann, who was standing beside me, was horrified. She had to be horrified, because her mind was focused on past and future, on images of my hand in the juicer and the sound that was already gone and the pain she projected onto me and a future where she had a mother who was missing some fingers. But in reality the whole experience was beautiful. The blood on the fingertips was healthy and lovely and free. I didn't project a past or a future, so I couldn't feel any pain. There was nothing to obscure the radiant moment. The mangled fingers were the Buddha; the blood was the Buddha; the beloved, horrified daughter was the Buddha too. I waited for pain to happen, and I was open to the illusion that would create pain, but as love would have it, there was none. A couple of fingernails were gone, and one fingertip was a bit chewed up. We got the peroxide and gauze and wrapped the fingers, but there was no need to take care of me, because there was nothing to take care of. The fingers, the blood, the juicer, the daughter, the observer—they were all characteristics of the Buddha.

Another time, in the early '90s, when Paul and I were driving on a busy freeway, the car in front of us stopped short and Paul rear-ended it. This happened up and down the line, and there was a huge pileup. I flew forward, and my head cracked the windshield. What I was aware of was a smile within me that came from the joy of flying through the air. Then I felt the joy of the impact. It was more like a union than an "I" hitting an object. I ended up on the floorboard with the smile on my face. When the policeman got to the car, he said I was in shock and they'd have to take me to the hospital in an ambulance. I said, "You know, sweetheart, I'm okay. If that changes, then we'll do something about it. I'm perfectly willing to, but right now I'm okay." Where could I be hurt? What could ever hurt me? That's not what I told him, of course, because by then I knew that those words couldn't be heard.

These experiences were unusual. It's not as though I don't ever feel pain. After my neuropathy kicked in eight years ago—it appeared out of the blue, as I was walking across the kitchen floor, a violent stabbing sensation on the soles of my feet—the pain was sometimes so intense that I wasn't able to walk. I did public events and one whole School for The Work in a wheelchair or on a Segway, rolling along to each session. But that doesn't change the fact that pain is a projection of mind. If you observe it closely, you'll see that it never arrives; it's always on its way out. And it's always happening on the surface of perception, while underneath it is the vast ocean of joy.

Anything that is perceived by the awakened mind is beautiful. It's the mirror image of mind, as seen by the mind. And to understand this is to lose the concept of mind. What beauty wouldn't want to look at itself in the mirror? If you don't love what you see in the mirror, your vision has to be distorted. This includes suffering, poverty, madness, cruelty, anger, despair: any human experience. All things exist, if they exist at all, within the Buddha-mind, which sees everything as beautiful. To it, there is nothing ugly, nothing unacceptable. This is not to say that the Buddha is passive or that he condones unkindness. He is the essence of kindness, and he does everything he can to end the apparent suffering in the world. But his kindness arises out of the deepest sense of peace with whatever he perceives. If you see anything in the world as unacceptable, you can be certain that your mind is confused. If you think that anything is outside your own mind, that's delusion. And ultimately neither the inside nor the outside is real. One is joy, one is suffering; one is asleepness, one awakeness; and they're all equal in the end.

When you look for the Buddha, don't look for anyone extraordinary. Look for something closer to home, closer *than* home. As you understand your own mind, you'll begin to meet someone who is wise beyond your expectations. Someone has to be a buddha in the space you occupy; someone has to do the dishes or not do the dishes. Watch how this buddha lives. You can't do anything wrong, even though your mind may imagine that you can. Who would you be without your story? Who would you be without comparing yourself to your image of an enlightened being? Most buddhas live secretly; it's rare that the news gets out. When you use your concept of a buddha to make yourself small by comparison, you're creating stress. Without concepts, it's easy to be enlightened. You take the kids to school, you walk the dog, you sweep the floor, effortlessly, and no concepts stick to the actions. That's what a buddha does. You can be the living example, right now, and no one needs to know.

I used to tell my children, "Make friends with mediocrity." You can find perfect enlightenment in just doing the dishes. There's nothing more spiritual than that. Someone can spend three years meditating in a cave, and your practice of just doing the dishes every day is equal to that. Can you love the balance, the harmony, of sweeping the floor? That harmony is the ultimate success, whether you're a pauper or a king. You can achieve it from wherever you are. There are no trumpets blaring; there's only peace.

Peace dwells in the ordinary. It's no further away than that.

You say, "This body is totally imagined." Why did you imagine a body that went blind, had two cornea implants, and developed neuropathy? Why not imagine a body that is forever youthful and never dies?

I would gladly imagine a younger, healthier body if I needed one, but this body is the one for me. Why would I want anything different? I love it with all my heart. It's always youthful, since at every moment it's new. It never dies, since it was purely imagined in the first place.

How can you say that pain is imagined? What does that mean?

I understand where pain comes from, and I understand exactly where it ends. Once you understand where it ends, it has ended. It's already over. This is something you can experience if you pay close attention to what's happening in the mind. When you realize the cause of pain, you understand that all pain is in the past. It's impossible to feel pain in the present, because there never is a present. Freedom is understanding that even "now" is an illusion. It's just one more concept.

How can we maintain our awareness in states of extreme physical pain?

When you're in more pain than you can handle, you shift into an alternate reality. Usually when you think that pain is unbearable, it's a lie. The pain is bearable: you're bearing it. What's so painful is that you're projecting a future. You're believing thoughts like "This will go on forever," "This will only get worse," or "I'm going to die." The story of the future is the only way you can be afraid. As you're projecting what will happen, you miss what's actually happening.

We can track this more closely. When pain is truly beyond what you can bear, the mind shifts into another reality, because it has no control. It can't imagine a future that it hasn't experienced from its past. And because you've never been there before, you don't know how to project what's coming next. The mind has no reference for it, so it shifts out of its body-identification. That's why some people say that while they were being raped or tortured they left their bodies; they were up on the ceiling, looking down. The mind shifts identities, because it can't project what's going to happen to the body next. It shifts out of what it has no reference for.

You say that there's nothing unacceptable. What about genocide and terrorism and rape and cruelty to children and animals? Are these acceptable to you?

All genocide, terrorism, rape, and cruelty to children and animals are in the past. They don't exist in this moment, and that is pure grace. I accept that grace with a sense of deep gratitude.

When you believe that such apparent horrors shouldn't happen, even though they *do* happen, you suffer. So you're adding one more person's suffering to the world's suffering, and for what purpose? Does your suffering help anyone who is being harmed? No. Does it motivate you to act for the common good? If you pay close attention, you'll see that this too isn't so. By questioning the belief that these things shouldn't happen, you can end your own suffering about the suffering of others. And once you do, you'll be able to notice that this makes you a kinder human being, someone who is motivated by love rather than outrage or sadness. The end of suffering in the world begins with the end of suffering in you.

If you see anything in the world as unacceptable, you can be certain that your mind is confused.

6

MIND IS EVERYTHING, MIND IS GOOD

Subhuti said, "Sir, will there always be mature people who, upon hearing these words, gain a clear insight into the truth?"

The Buddha said, "Of course there will, Subhuti! Even thousands of years from now, there will be many people who penetrate into the truth just by hearing these words and contemplating them. People like this, though they may not be aware of it, haven't cultivated mental clarity as students of only one buddha; they have cultivated mental clarity as students of hundreds of thousands of buddhas. When they hear these words and contemplate them, they will see reality in a single moment, clearly, just as it is. The Buddha fully knows and appreciates these people as they wake up to their true nature.

"How do they do this? Once they see reality clearly, these people never again attach to the concepts 'self' and 'other.' Nor do they attach to the concepts 'truth' and 'non-truth.' If their minds attach to concepts of separate things, they will attach to the concepts 'self' and 'other.' If they deny the existence of things, they will still be attaching to the concepts 'self' and 'other.'

So you should not attach to concepts of separate things, and you should not attach to the denial of separate things.

"That is why I tell people, 'My teaching is like a raft.' A raft is meant to carry you across the river; once you have crossed the river, you leave the raft behind on the shore. If even correct teachings must be left behind, how much more so incorrect teachings!"

The Buddha says that mature people will "see reality in a single moment, clearly, just as it is." When they see reality just as it is, they immediately realize that there is no such thing as a past or a future. So all the hundreds of thousands of buddhas they have studied with exist in the present moment; these buddhas are the hundreds of thousands of unquestioned thoughts they have noticed and are noticing in their own minds. Each thought is itself; each thought is the Buddha, showing you where not to go. Love meets these illusions, these figments of the imagination, and sings the song of "Not this, not that." That's why a mature student bows in reverence to every thought as it returns to the nothingness it came from.

When I first realized that the past and future don't exist, I was in a state of continual amazement. I was seeing everything with new eyes; my mind was a clean slate. One day the director of the halfway house asked me to drive to another town to get some books she wanted. I said, "It can't. It doesn't know its way anywhere." The director said, "I know you can do it. I'll give you directions." I said, "It needs someone to go with it." And she said, "No, you're doing this alone." And through her words I could hear the possibility. So she handed me the keys to the van, and she gave me directions. It was very weird.

I didn't have a future, so there was no sense of "going to get" some-thing. There *were* no books; there was nothing except what I could see—if that. It was like being told to drive off a cliff. I couldn't project that I would be hurt, but I knew I was moving straight into the abyss.

And here's what the experience was like: You don't know where the van is, you don't know *what* a van is, you don't know how to get out of the building, or if there is even an outside. But you stand up and walk and just keep walking and somehow the van is there. And then you get in and the thought arises: *Key!*, and you take the key out of your pocket and find a place to put it in, and the steering wheel is new, the windshield is new, the rearview mirror is new, everything's new and strange. You look down, and you don't know which is the accel-erator pedal and which the brake, you don't know which side of the road to drive on, you don't know what green and red lights mean, but somehow everything happens effortlessly. *It* knows what to do and where to go. It's all an effortless flow, and you feel an intense amaze-ment—an intense excitement and awe—that everything is happening by itself, without your involvement, without your having to make any decision at all. And when you get out of the van and walk, you feel that with every step you might fall through the slats of the universe forever, as if you were falling through the empty space between the atoms in the sidewalk. And all this time, I kept seeing that "I" was not the doer. I didn't have the language for that then, but that's what I saw: that something is doing this beyond me—that it's not me, yet it is. So step by step you're going to the edge of the universe and look-ing over and seeing that there's nothing there. And still the next step comes, and the next, and it's all happening by itself. But you're not even looking over the edge, you're *falling* over the edge with every step. Yet you don't ever fall, and you continue to learn that falling is not possible. And that's amazing. So the not-knowing and the amaze-ment are totally intertwined.

That's what the first few weeks of this were like: the amazement of falling off the edge of the universe, the awe of seeing everything being done without a doer, the heart overflowing with the beauty of everything I saw, and the Buddha-ness, the is-ness of it all. And the peace that lives behind everything. I was always consciously coming from that position. There was a constant falling and loss in the foreground, against a background of total peace. The thing always falling apart was nonexistent anyway. The world was always falling away, and nothing remained but the peace. That peace has never changed.

The Buddha's communication in this sutra is impeccable. It is so accurate and fine tuned that any other words are unnecessary. As I listen to Stephen reading the chapter to me, I find myself sitting at the Buddha's feet. I also sit at the feet of anyone who comes to me, and I sit at the feet of a blade of grass, an ant, a speck of dust. When you realize that you are the Buddha sitting at the feet of the Buddha, you find freedom from it all. This clear mind is exquisite. There's nothing to add or subtract.

It's true that there is no self and no other. It's true that there is no truth and no non-truth. There are no separate things, and there are no non-separate things. There is no world outside you, and also no world inside you, because until you believe there's a "you," you haven't created a world. If you believe there's a world, you have two: you and the world; and if you believe there's no world outside yourself, you still have two. But there aren't two. Two is a creation of the confused mind. There's only one, and not even that. No world, no self, no substance— only awareness without a name.

There aren't any truths. There's just the thing that is true for you in the moment, and if you investigated that, you would lose it too. But honoring the thing that's true for you in the moment is simply a matter of keeping to your own integrity.

So-called universal truths fall away too. There aren't any of those either. The last truth—I call it the last story—is "God is everything;

God is good." (I use the word *God* as a synonym for *reality*, because reality rules.) You could also say, "Mind is everything; mind is good." Keep that one if you like, and have a happy life. Anything that opposes it, hurts. It's like a compass that always points toward true north.

The Buddha compares his teaching to a raft that takes people from the shore of suffering to the shore of freedom. He says that that's its only purpose. When you reach the other shore, you leave the raft behind. It would be ridiculous to strap it onto your back and carry it around as you walk. It's the same with spiritual teachings, he says, even the clearest of them, even the Diamond Sutra. I love how the Buddha undercuts his own words and leaves us with no ground to stand on.

The Work too is like a raft. The four questions and the turnarounds help you move from confusion to clarity. Eventually, through practice, you no longer impose your thinking onto reality, and you can experience everything as it really is: as pure grace. At that point the questions themselves become unnecessary. They are replaced by a wordless questioning that undoes every stressful thought immediately, as it arises. It's the mind's way of meeting itself with understanding. The raft has been left behind. You have become the questions. They've become as natural as breathing, so they're no longer needed.

When we reach the "other" shore, we realize that we have never left the shore we started from. There's only one shore, and we are already there, though some of us haven't realized it yet. We think that we need to get from here to there, but *there* turns out to be *here*. It was here all along.

When you sit in the state of contemplation, seeing what actually exists, excluding everything remembered or anticipated, the Buddhamind becomes apparent, and you wake up as the unborn. If you really want peace, if you understand that self-inquiry goes beyond life and death, your practice will leave you on the other shore, which turns out not to be the other but the *only* shore. Thoughts of a different shore were imagination, and when you realize this, you realize that you have always been on the shore that the Buddha points to. No raft necessary.

If you don't have a sense of past or future, how can you get anything accomplished?

A past or future isn't necessary to get things accomplished. I just do what's in front of me, whatever appears in the moment. I watch and witness; I remain as awareness; I continue to expand without past or future, going nowhere, beyond the limits of speed. But if I ever needed a past and future, I wouldn't hesitate to get one.

The Buddha says that people who deny the existence of things are still attaching to the concepts "self" and "other." When you say that life is a dream, aren't you denying the existence of separate things?

"Nothing exists" may feel like a truth, since it's a pointer to something more accurate than a solid self looking out at a solid world. But the nonexistence of things has to be deeply realized before it is anything other than a concept. If you believe that nothing exists, you're still identified as a "you" who believes that nothing exists. If you understand that the world lives only as imagination, you're free; there's no you; it's over. You can't identify as anything. It's the end of belief, and even the most profound thought loses meaning. "Nothing" is the something left to deal with by the I-know mind.

"Mind is everything; mind is good," you say. Are you talking about awareness? Why do you use the word mind *here? Why don't you ever use words like* soul *or* spirit?

What is there to be aware of other than mind? So mind aware of itself is awareness. And when mind is aware of itself, it realizes that not only is it not personal, it doesn't even exist; it's an illusion. Prior to "I," there was nothing. The "I" comes second, out of the nameless first. The apparent mind that questions itself begins to understand where it comes from, which is pure love, for lack of a better word. So if it's not the song of love, it's a distortion of the nature it was born out of.

As for words like *soul* or *spirit*, I don't use them because I don't know what they mean.

You say that when people do The Work as a practice, eventually the words are replaced by a wordless questioning. Would you describe what that's like?

The practice of inquiry requires a careful listening, a witnessing of what meets the questions. Eventually the mind automatically questions every judgment that arises in it and thus finds freedom from its own thoughts. People come to realize that they aren't doing anything, they're being done; they aren't even thinking anything, they're being thought. When The Work is alive inside you, any potentially stressful thought that rises to the surface of the mind is immediately met by the wordless questioning that gives birth to "Is it true?" When a thought is met in that way, it loses its power to cause negative feelings. It unravels instantly, it deconstructs, it evaporates, and you are left with your original nature. The goodness of all things becomes evident with every realized moment. It's all an illusion, but a kind one, not the fearful one I was born into from a mother's womb.

So at a certain point in the practice, inquiry becomes unnecessary?

I have often said that when you realize that the nature of everything is good and that good is everything, you don't need inquiry. It has been clear to me from the moment of that first insight thirty-one years ago. Stephen told me a story that was floating around on the Internet—that according to Einstein there is only one important question: "Is the universe friendly?" (When he later checked the quote, it turned out to be bogus; it didn't come from Einstein after all. But that doesn't matter.) "Is the universe friendly?" In 1986 I woke up to a resounding "Yes," and I wasn't even aware that there was a question. I just immediately understood. I came to see that the whole universe, and everything that happens in it, is kind. The Work's four questions and turnarounds are the internal path to this understanding.

Eventually, through practice, you no longer impose your thinking onto reality, and you can experience everything as it really is: as pure grace.

7

AT HOME IN THE ORDINARY

The Buddha said, "Let me ask you something, Subhuti. Has the Buddha attained enlightenment? And does he have a teaching to offer?"

Subhuti said, "As I understand it, Sir, there is no such thing as enlightenment. Nor is there any teaching that is offered by the Buddha. And here is the reason: the Buddha has nothing to teach. The truth is ungraspable and inexpressible. It neither is nor is not. Every mature person knows that there is nothing to be known."

———————

If you understand that the world isn't separated into self and other, you'll see very clearly that there is no such thing as enlightenment. There can't be. After all, who is there to be enlightened? You would have to *be* someone before you could experience enlightenment. There would have to be an ego to get free. But egos don't get free.

It's true that when you wake up from the trance, you're free of all suffering. But saying it that way still points to a someone, a being who is supposedly "awake." It's only when you see the Buddha as a separate self that you can form the concept that he's enlightened. All these spiritual concepts are just creations of mind. What do "I" know of this imagined form you call "me"?

Many of the monks who were listening to the Buddha must have realized who he was: no one. But some of them may have wanted to treat him like a guru, to put him in a different category, to think that he was superior to them, a more evolved or exalted being. They may have looked at him with starry-eyed adoration. The Buddha's response was to love them and keep helping them to question their thinking, so that they could find their own freedom. How could he play into their projections? He kept saying that he didn't have anything *they* didn't have. He constantly returned them to themselves, to the only way possible. The beauty of inquiry is that this kind of worship doesn't last long, even though, for the person worshipping, it can be very sweet. Inquiry levels everything and leaves us all as equals. The story of having an enlightened master, as sweet as it may feel, is the story of separation.

People think that self-realization is something special. But we're not at home until we're at home in the ordinary. That's where it feels comfortable. Someone will say, "How are you?" and I might say, "Fine." It has joined; it has penetrated. So I'm unrecognizable. I'm standing with everyone else on the corner of the street, eating the hot dog, watching the band go by. I'm neither more nor less than you. If we're even one breath more or one breath less than anyone else, we're not at home.

Subhuti asks the Buddha a question, or the Buddha asks Subhuti a question. In either case, it's the Buddha asking and the Buddha answering. It's the question that gives rise to the truth. Before I can answer, I have to realize for myself what is true, since I wouldn't want to create untruths in my world. "I have a teaching to offer"—is it true? Can I absolutely know that it's true? Of course not. That *is* the teaching. The teaching is always for myself; I don't have a teaching for anyone else. As you ask the questions and I answer, it's only myself that I enlighten, and it's your wisdom—the wisdom asking the questions— that enlightens me. It's the source of my enlightenment. That's how it works. Someone asks me, "Where are you going?" and the question wakes me up. The apparent I, I, I—all inauthentic, all authentic as the perceiver would have it. Believe it or not; enlightened or not.

Ask yourself, "Who is thinking?" There's no answer to that. The question short-circuits the mind. You can never have an answer. You could wait for a million years, and there would still be silence. And really, there's no answer for anything. We can't explain *anything* essential in our lives. But why would you want to explain? Does that make you any happier? I often say, "Would you rather be right or free?" I have no explanations, and I haven't had a problem for thirty-one years.

My job is to take the mystery out of everything. It's really simple, because there isn't anything. There's only the story appearing now: the story of buddhas and non-buddhas, the story that some people are enlightened and some aren't, the story that you need more than you already have, the story that you need to attain some high spiritual state before you can be whole. You can just watch these stories arise and pass away, and be aware that in this moment only the story exists.

Each one of us is a mirror image of the source. That's all I am: woman sitting on couch, woman listening to man read the Diamond Sutra. And when I investigate that statement, is it true? No. I can see that I'm prior to the mirror image. I am the awareness prior to that. I am no one and someone, I am everything and nothing, I am the beginning (mind unreflected) and I am the end (mind unreflected). And I am so vain that I want to see myself in the mirror. Woman listening to man. Woman answering questions.

Subhuti realizes that not only is there no enlightenment, there is also no teaching. There can't be any teaching offered by the Buddha, because all teachings are dissolved, just like the construct that is happening in your mind right now as you read. It's all imagined; there's nothing to teach. Where does the wind go on a still day? And the breath you just took—doesn't it exist now only as pure imagination?

You noticed the breath flowing into your nostrils, and when you don't have any thought of a past, this is the first breath that has ever been breathed, and now it's gone. How can you know that it ever happened at all?

The truth is so simple. Every word said, every teaching given, no matter how valuable, leaves a construct where in reality none exists. It assumes someone listening, someone speaking, something to be known. In trying to tell the truth, it creates something extra. It adds something unnecessary to what is, and thus it becomes a lie.

The Buddha-mind is already complete. It doesn't need enlightenment. It doesn't need to teach. It doesn't need to realize a thing. It's everything it ever thought it wanted—right now. Everything is done for it, effortlessly. It moves without resistance, like a beautiful song. Everything it would ever have or do, it has and does. It just flows as awareness. The story of a problem, when it's investigated, becomes laughable. And even that story is the Buddha-mind.

Is striving for enlightenment a waste of effort?

If the definition of enlightenment is "freedom from suffering," then no. How could the quest to end the illusion of suffering be a waste of effort? Ego too is about the end of suffering, though in a totally self-deluded way: "If only I had more money (or success, or sex), then I'd be happy." So to question the thoughts that are causing your unhappiness makes total sense, and when "out there" is recognized as a projection of mind, it makes even more sense.

If words always add something unnecessary to what is, and thus become a lie, why did the Buddha bother with teaching? Why did you write this book?

Even a text as profound as the Diamond Sutra ultimately doesn't matter. The world without it is equal to the world with it, since neither world really exists. Whoever wrote the sutra wrote it because that's what love does. When someone asks, love answers. That's why I wrote this book. People kept asking for a new Katie book, and Stephen wanted me to talk about the Diamond Sutra, and of course I said yes. I was happy to give him the raw material he needed, and happy to have my words stephened. If you find the book helpful, I'm happy. If you think it's a waste of time, I'm just as happy. "I" project this happiness onto everyone. As I see it, people do their best to believe what they think, yet deep down they can't, and don't, really believe it. I have tested this. As the mind opens to the answers from the clarity within, people find that no matter how hard they try, they don't believe the stressful thoughts they believe they believe.

The Buddha understood that there's no way for him or anyone to bring into the world what can never be brought in. But there's no harm in consciousness appearing to exist. No one really believes, and that's what inquiry makes obvious: the Buddha-mind, no mind, nothing at all.

If we're even one breath
more or one breath less
than anyone else,
we're not at home.

8

THE ULTIMATE GENEROSITY

The Buddha said, "Let me ask you something, Subhuti. If someone amassed inconceivable wealth and then gave it all away in support of charitable causes, wouldn't the merit gained by this person be great?"

Subhuti said, "Extremely great, Sir. But though this merit is great, there is no substance to it. It is only *called* 'great.'"

The Buddha said, "Yes, Subhuti. Nevertheless, if an open-minded person, upon hearing this sutra, could truly realize what it is teaching and then embody it and live it, this person's merit would be even greater. All the buddhas, and all their teachings about enlightenment, spring forth from what this sutra teaches. And yet, Subhuti, there is no teaching."

The Buddha's point here is that when you realize there is no self and no other, you give an incomparable gift. It's the ultimate generosity, both to others and to yourself (neither of whom exist). All Buddha awareness—that is, any mind that sees reality as it truly is—arises from this realization.

There is no distance away from mind. It's all an imagined trip.

Mind never moves as the source. It doesn't "come back" to itself, because it never leaves. Heaven and earth were born when I was, and the only thing that was born is the "I." The whole world arises out of that unquestioned "I." And with it arises the world of naming, and the sleights of mind that match those names. Out of that story come a thousand—ten thousand—forms of suffering. "I am this." "I am that." "I am a human." "I am a woman." "I am a woman with three children, whose mother doesn't love her."

You are who you believe you are. Other people are, for you, who you believe they are; they can be nothing more than that. If you realized that the mind is one, that everyone and everything is your own projection (including you), you would understand that it's only yourself you're ever dealing with. You would end up loving yourself, loving every thought you think. When you love every thought, you love everything thoughts create, you love the whole world you have created. At first, the love that overflows in you seems to be about connecting with other people, and it's wonderful to feel intimately connected to every human being you meet. But then it becomes about mind connected to itself, and only that. The ultimate love is the mind's love of itself. Mind joins with mind—all of mind, without division or separation, all of it loved. Ultimately I am all I can know, and what I come to know is that there is no such thing as "I."

So you discover that even mind is imagined. Inquiry wakes you up to that. When people question the apparent past, they lose their future. The present moment—that's when we're born. We're the unborn. We're born now . . . now . . . now . . . There is no story that can survive inquiry. "I" is imagined by "me," and as you get a glimpse of that, you stop taking yourself so seriously. You learn to love yourself, as no one. Mind's love affair with itself is the great dance, the only dance.

When you realize that there's no self, you also realize that there's no death. Death is just the death of identity, and that's a beautiful thing, since every identity the mind would construct vanishes upon inquiry, and you're left with no identity, and therefore unborn. The "I" of past and future are both nonexistent now, and what remains is imagined. When mind stops, there's no mind to know that there's no mind. Perfect! Death has a terrible reputation, but it's only a rumor.

The truth is that nothing and something are equal. They're just different aspects of reality. *Something* is a word for what is. *Nothing* is a word for what is. Awareness has no preference for one over the other. Awareness wouldn't deny any of it. It wouldn't deny a needle on a pine tree. It wouldn't deny a breath. I am all of that. It's total self-love, and it would have it all. It bows at the feet of it all. It bows at the feet of the sinner, the saint, the dog, the cat, the ant, the drop of water, the grain of sand.

The Buddha says that the merit of someone who realizes this central teaching of the Diamond Sutra is greater than the merit of even the most generous philanthropist. This realization is the greatest possible gift. But ultimately there's no merit. No one is keeping score, after all. How can you acquire merit if you don't even exist as a separate being? "Merit" is just a way of saying that you can do nothing more valuable than realize who you are.

The Buddha-mind holds nothing back. Everything in it is freely given, as it was freely received. It has no storage place; what flows into it flows out of it, without any thought of having or giving. There's nothing to have that isn't immediately given, and its value is in the giving. The Buddha-mind doesn't need it. It's a receptacle; it exists in a constant flow. Whatever wisdom the Buddha may have is something he can't claim. It belongs to everyone. It's simply realized from within and given away in exactly the same measure. The more valuable it is, the more freely it's given.

I can't give you anything you don't already have. Self-inquiry allows you access to the wisdom that already exists within you. It gives you the opportunity to realize the truth for yourself. Truth doesn't come or go; it's always here, always available to the open mind. If I can teach you anything, it is to identify the stressful thoughts that you're believing and to question them, to get still enough so that you can hear your own answers. Stress is the gift that alerts you to your asleepness. Feelings like anger or sadness exist only to alert you to the fact that you're believing your own stories. The Work gives you a portal into wisdom, a way to tap into the answers that wake you up to your true nature, until you realize how all suffering is caused and how it can be ended. It returns you to before the beginning of things. Who would you be without your identity?

We're born as a story. The story stays out there and lives its life, forever. For me, "forever" lasted for forty-three years, and it was every lifetime that has ever been lived—all of time and space. I thought I was stuck there, in hopeless agony, with no way out. Then the four questions brought me back to the storyteller. Once I realized that no one was telling the story, I had to laugh. It turned out that I had been free all along, since the beginning of time.

In this sutra, the Buddha talks about generosity, but he doesn't talk about love. Why do you think that is?

Love is usually thought of as an emotion, but it's much vaster than that. Egos can't love, because an ego isn't real, and it can't create something real. The Buddha is beyond any identity, and that's what I see as pure love.

When I refer to love, I'm merely pointing to the unidentified, awakened mind. When you're identified as a this or a that, a him or a her, any kind of physical self, body, or personality, you remain in the limited realm of the ego. If your thoughts are opposed to love, you'll feel stress, and that stress will let you know that you've drifted away from what you fundamentally are. If you feel balance and joy, that tells you that your thinking is more in keeping with your true identity, which is beyond identity. That's what I call "love."

What's the relationship between love and projection?

When I judge someone, I'm seeing a distortion of my own mind superimposed onto an apparent other. I can't love the one I'm with until I see him (or her) clearly, and I can't see him clearly until I have no desire to change him. When confusion takes over the mind, when it argues with reality, I see only my own confusion. "Love thy neighbor as thyself" isn't a command coming from the outside; it's an observation. When you love your neighbor, you're loving yourself; when you love yourself, you can't help but love your neighbor. That's because your neighbor *is* yourself. He's not the "other" that he seemed to be. He's a pure projection of mind.

I understand how painful the unquestioned mind is. I also understand that love is the power. Mind originates in love and ultimately returns to its source. Love is mind's homing device, and until mind returns, it has no rest.

You say that there is no death. But bodies die, don't they? Is the mind independent of the brain? How can you know that when the brain dies there is any mind at all?

Nothing is born but a thought believed, and nothing dies but that thought once realized, and eventually you come to understand that the thought was never born in the first place. I don't see anyone as alive, since all beings are within me and are only as "I" see them to be.

If you think that bodies die, they die—in your world. In my world, bodies can't be born anywhere but in the mind. How can what was never born die? That's not possible, except in the imagination of the hypnotized, innocent believer.

*You say, "Nothing and something are equal." Doesn't that mean that
nothing matters? And if nothing matters, isn't that depressing?*

All somethings are nothing, since they're all imagined, and "nothing"
is equal to "something." Does anything matter? Yes, to the ego. But the
fact that the ego believes it doesn't make it real.

Once you realize that you're no one, you're *thrilled* that nothing
matters. There's so much freedom in that! The whole slate is wiped
clean at every moment. It means that every new moment is a new
beginning, where anything is possible. You also realize that the turnaround for that statement is equally true: everything matters. That's
just as thrilling as its opposite.

*It's only yourself
you're ever dealing with.*

9

LOVE COMES BACK
FOR ITSELF

The Buddha said, "Tell me something, Subhuti. Do meditators who have attained the level of stream-enterers* think, 'I have attained the level of stream-enterers'?"

Subhuti said, "No, Sir, and here is why. These people realize that there is no one to enter form, sound, smell, taste, touch, or any thought that arises in the mind. That is why they are called 'stream-enterers.'"

"Tell me, Subhuti. Do meditators who have attained the level of once-returners† think, 'I have attained the level of once-returners'?"

"No, Sir, and here is why. Although the name *once-returner* means 'someone who goes and comes back one more time,' they realize that in fact there is no going or coming. That is why they are called 'once-returners.'"

"And in the same way, Subhuti: Do meditators who

---

* People who have begun to practice the Buddha's Noble Eightfold Path.
† People who are partially enlightened and will be reborn into the human world just one more time.

have attained the level of non-returners* say, 'I have attained the level of non-returners'?"

"No, Sir, and here is why. Although the name *non-returner* means 'someone who never returns to the world of suffering,' they realize that in fact there is no such thing as returning. That is why they are called 'non-returners.'"

"One more thing, Subhuti. Do meditators who have attained the level of arhats[†] think, 'I have attained the level of arhats'?"

"No, Sir, and here is why. There is, in fact, no such thing as an arhat. If an arhat should give rise to the thought, 'I have attained the level of arhats,' that would mean that he is attached to the concepts 'self' and 'other.'

"Sir, you have said that of all your students I am the most proficient in meditation, that I dwell in peace, and that I am the arhat who is freest from desire. And yet I never think of myself as an arhat, or as someone who is free from desire. If I were to believe the thought that I have attained the level of arhats, then you wouldn't have said of me that I dwell in peace, since in reality there is nowhere to dwell. That is why you say that I dwell in peace."

---

* People who are reborn in one of the heavenly worlds and from there attain Nirvana.
† People who have attained Nirvana and will never be reborn.

In this chapter the Buddha mentions various categories of attainment, with fancy names: "stream-enterers" for people who practice awareness, "once-returners" for people who will be reborn just one more time, and so on. But without a concept of "self," these categories fall apart. More enlightened, less enlightened; many rebirths, no rebirth; coming, going: they're all just concepts. If you're trying to monitor your progress on the spiritual path—if you think you have any idea how far along you are—you might want to save yourself the trouble. There's no attainment, because you already are what you want to become. Everything separate vanishes in the light of awareness.

When you realize the truth, you also realize that it's no accomplishment. You haven't done anything; the accomplishment is just the joy of being received by the very thing that you already are. It's the mind being met by the mind, without opposition. It isn't personal. The truth sets us free from any attachment to the concepts "self" and "other." There are no humans; there is no mind; it's all a dream. The practice of inquiry deletes everything, as long as mind believes that it exists even as mind. The projected world unravels first, and then mind, and any trace that even mind ever existed. That's my world. When it's over, it's over.

The only thing you need to know about enlightenment is whether believing a particular thought is stressful or not. Does the thought hurt or doesn't it? If it doesn't, good: enjoy it. If it does hurt—if it causes any sadness, anger, or uneasiness of any kind—question it, and enlighten yourself to that thought. Suffering is optional. It doesn't have to last for years. It can get down to months, weeks, days, minutes, seconds. Eventually, when the same thoughts arise, the ones that used to make you suffer, you're at ease with them. In fact, you're lit; you walk down the street shining like a thousand-watt light bulb. When you think, "I need my mother to love me," you just laugh, because you're enlightened to that thought, and the next one, and the next.

Inquiry puts you back into a position of clarity. It lets you realize that you're prior to any thought of "I." What fun to come back to reality! There's nothing I would do to stop that. It's a privilege to open my eyes and see myself in the mirror. But there is no permanent state of clarity, since clarity has no future. We don't wake up forever. We wake up only now. Can you question your thoughts and be happy in this moment? People have these wonderful experiences of spiritual opening, and that's not it. As soon as they think, "I want this to last forever," they've moved into a future and lost the reality. *This* is it, right now. It's that simple. Only this exists.

How do you react when you believe the thought "I want to get enlightened"? You feel stress. You stay stuck in your imagined unenlightenment. Inquiry shows this beyond a doubt. And who would you be without the thought? Free of all that. I'm someone who was graced with not knowing that there even *was* such a thing as enlightenment. (And there isn't.)

But the longing for freedom, the longing that can give rise to these thoughts of attainment—that is genuine. When I was so confused, I used to lie in bed and wail, "I want to go home!" I thought it was physical death that I wanted. I didn't believe in a heaven or a hell; I just wanted to be free of what I considered unbearable suffering, and in my innocence I had it right. I did have to die first. But it wasn't a physical death.

Everyone longs for the authentic. It's always here. It's the true teacher. There's nothing you can do to obliterate it. It's the listener, the one without a story. I call it love, and we can tell all the stories we want about how it doesn't exist, but it does. When you oppose it, you create the only suffering you can experience. It's always cleansing and purifying itself. It spares nothing, and anyone who has had a taste of it would gladly walk into the fire and be burned to a crisp in order to keep that purity. There's not a choice. When the ax falls, just before it chops off your head, the last thought is grace. "Ahh, thank you for this too!"

For forty-three years I had no experience of pure awareness. Then there was one instant of it, and that was enough, because after that instant I had inquiry inside me. It was born. It's *what* was born in that moment. The questioning was awake inside me. There was a perfect circle: the going out and the coming back to peace, rather than the constant going out, with no way back, no possibility of completing the trip that had never happened.

You have to lose everything. Everything that seems to be external dies—everything. You can't have anything. You can't have anything that you love. You can't have a husband—it's not a material husband. You can't have children—they're not material children. You can't have one concept. People think that non-attachment has to do with detaching from the people or things that you love, but it's much more than that. When people talk about detaching from things, I don't have a reference point, because to me everything is internal. But I've learned to understand their language. That's how love joins.

An imagined self is all that exists. You can question it away if you really want to take the trip. Questioning is safe, I assure you. When you question what you think you are, it leaves no self. It leaves you as something more valuable: the unchanging nature of what the dream flows out of, what the dream mirrors. As long as life is a dream, let's deal with the nightmare. Question what you believe, and notice what's left. Until you genuinely realize that you're not the "you" you believe yourself to be, you aren't free to be more. That's why the limited mind is so painful. Mind is always attempting to burst out of its own prison, the identity as a body. When you realize the nature of mind, you realize that it's everything, it's the nature of everything, and that any apparent lack is just a figment of your imagination.

What's it like to live without a self? Nothing happens, not even life. Everything you see, hear, touch, smell, taste, and think is already over before the action begins. My foot just moved, and as I watched it, I was only watching the past. It appeared to be happening now, but the now was gone even as I watched it. This is the power and the goodness of mind realized. I can't even swallow my tea; it's gone before it happens, and there's nothing I can do about it. I look at the poster on the wall, of my beloved Stephen beside the gold mask on the jacket of his *Gilgamesh*, and my eyes remain on the poster, the gaze is held, it seems to exist, and yet as much as I love it, it's an illusion. When there's no thought, there's no world. When no thought is believed, there's no time, no space, no reality. My life is over, and I understand that it never began.

I am my only world. I'm the only one here. The world is my projection, my imagination lived: sight, sound, smell, feeling, humans, dogs, cats, trees, sky. I love the world, both when it appears to live and when it appears to die. The questioned mind loves the infinite way of it. There's a law in this world: when you think life is so good that it can't get any better, it has to. And you're willing to experience whatever life brings; you look forward to experiencing it. Beautiful, beautiful, misunderstood, benevolent life. Anyone who doesn't love the dream-world hasn't understood that life is mind, and that there's nothing outside it. It's lost as long as it believes what it thinks. That is its job, to believe what it thinks, until finally, one day, it sets itself free.

You speak of the longing for freedom. Is it useful for people to hope that they will eventually be free?

I always prefer what is; it works much faster than hope. As you come to love your thoughts, reality eventually replaces hope, and as a result you love the world you appear to live in. Because I understand my thoughts, what I see as a world doesn't require any form of hope. Hope becomes unnecessary, obsolete. "I'm going to get better as I do The Work"—if you have that as a motive, you can afford that hope, since it's true that as you do The Work you do get better, until you catch up to your dear, wonderful self and discover that, except for what you've been believing, you and the world have always been perfect, and you were innocent without being aware of it.

Hope is the story of a future. There's no place for it in my life. I don't need hope, though I wouldn't hesitate to hope if I did need to, because that's what people with a future have to do, until they don't. The mature mind is a peaceful mind, a mind in love with reality. Reality is so beautiful that it doesn't need a plan.

But for people who haven't yet learned to inquire into their stressful thoughts, the concept of hope can be useful. It keeps them going, they think. It's better than the only alternative they see, which is despair. And then, eventually, if they learn to question their thoughts, they begin to see that there *is* no future and that hope is as senseless as fear. That's when the fun begins.

What does non-attachment mean?

It means not believing anything you think. Attachment means believing an unquestioned thought. When we don't inquire, we assume that a thought is true, though we can't ever know that. The purpose of attachment is to keep us from the realization that we're already complete. We don't attach to things; we attach to our *stories* about things.

You assure people that questioning is safe. But you also say that it's necessary to lose everything. Isn't that intimidating for most people?

I can see how it might be intimidating. But are you really safe identifying as a body? As a body, isn't it certain that all the people you love will eventually leave you or die, and that you'll age, get sick, hurt in all kinds of ways, and at last die yourself? Is that "you" safe? So to lose your false identity is to gain everything. In the world of no self and no other, there is no suffering, no decay, no death, no falseness. It's a world of pure beauty. It's yours already, and it only waits to be realized.

If the mind is so invested in believing what it thinks, how can it ever set itself free?

That's easy. You identify any thought that's causing you stress, you write it down, you question it, and you wait for your answers to arise in the silence. The Buddha-mind will enlighten you.

There's a law in this world: when you think life is so good that it can't get any better, it has to.

10

LIVING IN INQUIRY

The Buddha said, "Tell me something, Subhuti. When I studied under the Buddha Dipankara,* eons ago, was there any truth I attained?"

Subhuti said, "Sir, when you studied under the Buddha Dipankara, there was nothing you attained."

"Let me ask you another thing. Does the Buddha create a beautiful world?"

"No, Sir, he doesn't. And here is why. A world that is beautiful isn't beautiful. It is only *called* 'beautiful.'"

"True, Subhuti. Here is what is essential: All bodhisattvas should develop a pure, lucid mind that doesn't depend upon sight, sound, touch, taste, smell, or any thought that arises in it. A bodhisattva should develop a mind that abides nowhere."

This is one of the most profound chapters in the Diamond Sutra. It says what is essential, and it says it in impeccably clear language. Stephen told me the story of Hui-neng, whose mind opened when he

---

* A legendary Buddha who was supposed to have lived a hundred thousand years ago.

heard the last sentence of this chapter; he immediately realized the essence of it all. I wasn't surprised. If you're looking for the clearest, simplest advice about how to stay in peace, this sentence would do very well: "Develop a mind that abides nowhere."

The Buddha talks about studying under an ancient buddha in a former lifetime. At that time in the very distant past, he says, when he attained enlightenment, there was nothing that he attained. He could have made the same point by talking about his present lifetime: "When I was sitting under the Bodhi tree and attained enlightenment, there was nothing that I attained." I don't know if the writer of this sutra actually believed in past lives. I don't think he even believed in past *moments*. He may have been using the language of past lives to illustrate the point that thirty-one years ago, a billion years ago, and a single moment ago are equal, and equally unreal, because the past is just a thought in the present. (So is the present.)

The Buddha's point here is that even someone who is totally dedicated to the practice of enlightenment, someone who has been wholeheartedly devoting himself to awareness for millions of lifetimes, has never attained a single thing. There's nothing to attain that you don't already have. There's nothing that even the most enlightened being in the universe has that you don't have yourself, right now. Isn't that amazing?!

The wisdom of billions of eons ago doesn't change. Because the Buddha is living in inquiry, nothing can stick to him; there's no thought he can attach to. He's always self-testing, self-realizing. People say that there are Tibetan lamas who remember their previous incarnations. But how does a story like that help to end human suffering? Isn't it just another identity—a whole string of identities, in fact? How can it help me to know that once upon a time I was Cleopatra or Marie Antoinette or a beggar in the slums of Calcutta? It's just food for the ego. You can go back to the story of yesterday, you can go back to the story of who you were before you were born; it doesn't matter where you inquire from, it's all a story, and no story is more profound than any other. Suppose you're psychic and you have a vision of a box that's buried beside a tree in a country you've never visited. And they find the tree and dig, and lo and behold, there the box is! Now you can be famous and tell us all about it on *The Tonight Show*. But what does that prove? After it's all over, do you still get upset when you find a parking ticket on your windshield?

Let's stay right here and now, and investigate how the mind works. The world you see is a reflection of how you see it. If your world is ugly or unfair, it's because you haven't questioned the thoughts that are making it appear that way. As your mind becomes clearer and kinder, your world becomes clearer and kinder. As your mind becomes beautiful, your world becomes beautiful. It's not that you consciously create a beautiful world. Everything you see can't help but be beautiful, because you're just seeing yourself in the mirror. You've learned to question your judgments, and you don't attach to the categories of "beautiful" and "ugly," because you're not comparing one thing to another. Your mind has stopped playing those tricks on itself.

Until you question everything you think you know, you can't ever know your true face. There's nothing more beautiful than that; it is beauty itself, beyond description. Sometimes I walk past a mirror and happen to see "my" face in it, and the thought arises, "How gorgeous that woman is!" And then I realize that it's me—what people call "me"—and I smile. But it's that way with everyone. I never meet anyone who doesn't seem beautiful to me. It doesn't matter whether their faces or bodies are what people call attractive. Stephen will sometimes point out what, to him, is a particularly beautiful woman or a handsome man, and I don't have a reference for that. Sometimes I'll sit down on the sidewalk with a homeless person, and it might be a woman who is obese and filthy and muttering to herself, and to me she is as beautiful as a little child. I'll stroke her head and hold her, if she'll let me.

My experience is that everything is good, everything is beautiful in its own way. And here's how I know that everything is beautiful: if I were to see something as less than that, it wouldn't feel right inside me. It's the truth that sets us free, and when I questioned the thought that something was less than beautiful, the whole world looked as beautiful as the sky. I came to see that there was nothing unacceptable. This is very difficult for some of us to take in at first, because in order to understand it we have to lose our entire world. We're afraid of losing the world of opposites that we depend on to maintain our precious identity as the one who is justified in suffering. Some of us would rather be right than free.

The Buddha says that anyone who wants to be free of suffering should develop a pure, lucid mind that doesn't depend upon sight, sound, touch, taste, smell, or any thought that arises in it. This is entirely accurate, in my experience, and it couldn't be said more clearly. Anything that you see, hear, touch, taste, smell, feel, or think isn't it.

The mind is prior to whatever it perceives. It is pure and lucid and completely open to everything: the apparently ugly just as much as the apparently beautiful, rejection as much as acceptance, disaster as much as success. It knows it is always safe. It experiences life as an uninterrupted flow. It doesn't land anywhere, because it doesn't need to; besides, it sees that landing somewhere would be a limitation. It notices each thought it thinks, but it doesn't believe any of them. It realizes that there is never any solid ground to stand on. What flows out of its realization is freedom. "No place to stand" is where it stands; that's where its delight is. When inquiry is alive inside you, every thought you think ends with a question mark, not a period. And that is the end of suffering.

How can we develop "a mind that abides nowhere"?

Mind has to exist before it can abide. To realize that mind doesn't exist is to realize that there's nowhere it can abide. For me, staying inside the questioning was enough.

Does your mind abide anywhere?

It would if it could.

Why do people think that becoming enlightened means attaining something?

I don't know. It actually means losing everything.

What does it mean to develop a pure, lucid mind that doesn't depend upon sight, sound, touch, taste, smell, or any thought that arises in it?

Sight, sound, etc. all come from the mind. Mind creates them, but that doesn't make them real. If you understand that they're all dreamed, you understand that the dreamer is dreamed as well.

When inquiry is alive inside you, every thought you think ends with a question mark, not a period. And that is the end of suffering.

11

THE GIFT OF CRITICISM

The Buddha said, "Subhuti, if each of the grains of sand in the Ganges River were its own Ganges River, wouldn't the number of grains of sand in all those Ganges Rivers be uncountable?"

Subhuti said, "Yes, Sir. If the number of Ganges Rivers were themselves uncountable, how much more so their grains of sand!"

"Now tell me this: If a good man or woman filled worlds as many as the grains of sand in all those Ganges Rivers with treasure and gave it all away to support charitable causes, wouldn't the merit gained by this person be great?"

"It would be immeasurably great, Sir."

The Buddha said, "I assure you, Subhuti: if an open-minded person, upon hearing this sutra, could truly realize what it is teaching and then embody it and live it, this person's merit would be far greater."

———————

When you realize that there's no such thing as a self or an other, you also realize the value of criticism. Since everyone is yourself, criticism is always coming from inside you; it's you talking to you. Criticism is the greatest gift you can receive, if self-realization is what you're interested in. It shows you what you haven't been able to see yet. What could anyone say to me that I wouldn't be able to acknowledge? If someone were to say, "You're unkind," I would become still, I would go inside, and in about three seconds I'd be able to find it—if not in the present situation, then at some time in the apparent past. If someone were to say, "You're a liar," I'd think, "Duh," because I can easily join them there. Or I might say, "Where do you think I lied? I really want to know." This is about self-realization, not about being right or wrong. Whatever someone might call me, I can go inside and find it. My job is to stay connected. The only thing that could cause me pain would be my defense or denial. "Oh, no, you can't be talking about *me*—I'm not *that*!" Well, yes I am. I am that too. I am everything you can think of. Keep coming at me. Show me what I haven't realized yet.

When the mind begins inquiry as a practice, it learns as a student of itself that everything is *for* it. Everything adds to it, enlightens it, nourishes it, reveals it. Nothing is or ever was against it. This is a mind that has grown beyond opposites. It's no longer split. It keeps opening, because it's living out of a fearless, undefended state, and it's eager for knowledge. It realizes that it's everything, so it learns to exclude nothing, to welcome it all. There's nothing gentler than open-mindedness. Because I don't oppose, it's not possible that someone will oppose me; people can't oppose anything but their own thinking. When there's no opposition, the chaotic mind hears itself. It notices that the only opposition is its own.

There's nothing anyone could say about me that wouldn't be true in some sense. Though I appear as this body—the perfect height, the perfect weight, the perfect age—some people may have a different idea. A few years ago, a producer proposed a television series called the *Byron Katie Show*, on which I would be doing The Work with a different person every week. I was delighted. I knew this would mean I'd have to spend a lot of time in a studio in L.A., but I thought it would be a wonderful way of getting self-inquiry out into the world. So he shot a few video samples and took them to the chairman of the network. A week later, he came back to me with a disappointed look on his face. His boss said I was too old and too fat for TV. I was delighted. I thought, "He could be right. The man's a pro. What a blessing!"

Even if someone called me a murderer, I could see how that would be true. I can remember a time in my life when I was so confused that I would have wished for someone to drop dead. I have killed mice and wiped out hundreds of ants when they invaded my house. I could go on and on. If they locked me up for killing someone I didn't kill, I could go to jail, even to death, knowing that I finally got caught; it was the wrong body but the right crime. Not that I wouldn't hire the best defense attorney I could afford. But if I were convicted, I would be at peace with that. As I sat in prison for a crime I didn't commit, I would get to see where I was still arguing with reality, if anywhere. If there was something other than gratitude in my mind, I would have the opportunity to question the thoughts that were causing me discomfort. The worst thing that can happen always turns out to be the best thing that can happen.

What's the connection between happiness and realizing that there is no self and no other? Why is this a joyous experience?

It's a joy to see that everything that isn't, isn't. It's a joy to see that everything is unreal, without exception. This leaves you with a mind awake to its true nature, a mind at home with itself, at home *in* itself. Amazing grace!

Would you say more about happiness?

I use the word to mean a natural state of peace and clarity. It's a state that is free of sadness, anger, fear, and any other stressful emotion. It's what remains when we meet our minds with understanding. That's what The Work gives us.

The only place we can be happy is right here, right now—not tomorrow, not in ten minutes. Happiness can't be *achieved*. We can't get it from money or sex or fame or approval or anything on the outside. We can only find happiness within us: unchanging, immovable, ever present, ever waiting. If we pursue it, it runs away. If we stop pursuing it and question our minds instead, the source of all stress disappears. Happiness is who we already are, once our minds are clear. When the mind is perfectly clear, what is is what we want. We're happy with whatever life brings us. That's enough, and more than enough.

Here's the bottom line: suffering is optional. If you prefer to suffer, go on believing your stressful thoughts. But if you'd rather be happy, question them.

How can we not take criticism personally, especially when it comes from the people closest to us?

Just consider the suffering you create when you believe their thoughts about you, and yours about them in return. It's huge, and it goes on and on. As for the how, it's simple. Question the thoughts you had while your mother or father or husband or wife or apparent enemy was criticizing you. Hurt feelings or discomfort of any kind cannot be caused by another person. No one outside you can hurt you. That's not possible. Only when you believe a story about them can you be hurt. So you're the one who's hurting yourself. This is very good news, because it means that you don't have to get someone else to stop hurting you or to change in any way. You're the one who can stop hurting you. You're the only one.

Criticism is the greatest gift you can receive if self-realization is what you're interested in.

12

TEACHING A CAT TO BARK

The Buddha said, "Furthermore, Subhuti, if an open-minded person, upon hearing this sutra, could truly realize what it is teaching and then embody it and live it, that person would become a buddha, worthy of the deepest respect from all beings in the universe. Even one glimpse of the truth is worthy of respect. How much worthier is a life fully transformed by insight and lived in perfect clarity! Wherever this sutra is embodied and lived, the Buddha is also present."

The Work deals only with reality. Everything in the world is doing its job. The ceiling sits on the walls, the walls sit on the floor, the curtains are hanging in front of the windows; they're all doing their jobs. But when you tell yourself a story about how reality is *supposed* to look, you end up arguing with the ceiling or the wall, and it's hopeless. It's like trying to teach a cat to bark. The cat won't ever cooperate. "No, no," you may tell it, "you don't understand. You should bark. It would be so much better for you if you barked. Besides, I really *need* you to bark. As a matter of fact, I'm going to devote the rest of my life to teaching you how to bark." And many years later, after all your sacrifice and devotion, the cat looks up at you and says, "Meow."

Trying to change people leaves you in a hopeless state of mind, because you just can't do it. That's what I love about reality: it is what it is. It won't accommodate itself to you, however you try to will it or force it or trick it or positive-think it into changing. As I often say, if you argue with reality, you lose—but only 100 percent of the time. People change or they don't. It's not your business; your business is to understand your own mind. When you understand your mind, you feel gratitude when they change and gratitude when they don't. You can argue with reality all you want, or you can stop arguing long enough to understand it and be free. You come to know for yourself what's true, and that's where your freedom is; it has nothing to do with anyone else in your life. People will just keep pressing your buttons until you understand. Isn't that wonderful? It's a setup for total enlightenment, as long as you're willing to question your thoughts. I call it "checkmate."

The Buddha says that even one glimpse of the truth is worthy of our deepest respect. The basic realization that other people can't possibly be your problem, that it's your *thoughts* about them that are the problem—this realization is huge. This one insight will shake your whole world, from top to bottom. And then, when you question your specific thoughts about mother, father, sister, brother, husband, wife, boss, colleague, child, you watch your identity unravel. Losing the "you" that you thought you were isn't a scary thing. It's thrilling. It's fascinating. Who are you really, behind all the façades?

The Buddha talks about a life fully transformed by insight and lived in perfect clarity. This might sound exaggerated or idealistic, but it's the simple truth. It really is possible to live a life of perfect clarity, without a single problem. All it takes is the willingness to question whatever stressful thoughts arise in the mind: "I want," "I need," "He should," "She shouldn't"—the unexamined thoughts that argue with reality and cause all the suffering in our lives. Once the nature of the mind is understood, suffering can't exist. Emotions such as sadness, anger, and resentment are the effects of believing our stressful thoughts. When we learn how to question these thoughts, they lose their power over us. Eventually, if a stressful thought arises, the questioning arises at the same instant and the thought unravels before it can have any effect. This leaves us with nothing but peace. Peace, and a lot of silent laughter.

It's not possible for someone with a questioned mind to feel sorrow. Sorrow is a kind of suffering, and suffering can only come from a confused mind that projects an unkind world and believes that its projections are real. But it's the mind's unquestioned story that causes the sorrow. The questioned mind is in love with reality. It loves everything it thinks and therefore everything it sees. It can't project a confused world. Since it sees only reality, sorrow is no longer possible.

When you attach to any identity, you suffer. Only the unidentified mind is free. If the Buddha thinks he's a buddha, he's not. The very thing that makes him a buddha is that he has no concept of buddhas and non-buddhas. For him, there's no separation. All beings are enlightened, though they may not be aware of that yet. The Buddha-mind is free of identity. It is love's expansion, the mind awake to itself, questioning itself, responding to itself out of its own pure intelligence, dancing with itself, traveling through its own unlimited continuum, with no trace of existence, no evidence that it has ever traveled at all. It flows freely, effortlessly, without interruption, without opposites, and there's no identity that is enticing enough to interrupt its flow. And even if the flow is momentarily interrupted, awareness immediately realizes the identification and dissipates it, leaving only the whisper of a thank-you as it goes on in its continual, joyous creation.

The whole world is a reflection of mind. The mind must eventually come back to itself, because everything that flows out of it is less potent than original cause. Just as the streams flow back to the sea, the mind flows back to its conceptless source. No matter how brilliant the mind is, no matter how large the ego that clings to its identity, when it realizes that it knows nothing, it returns to the beginning, in all humility, and meets itself as original cause, prior to any existence.

You can't control people or dictate to them or silence them.

You can only listen and put yourself in their position—not only in their position, but in the lowest position you find. And as you realize for yourself what is true, everything apparently above you flows down toward you, the way streams flow down to the sea, since you have become an example of what is true and humble and wise. The Buddha, the self that is realized, the self that sees no self or other, is master of nothing and no one, not even mind; it is simply a master of understanding. When the mind understands itself, it's no longer seen as an enemy and is no longer at war with itself. It finds its peace in the humblest position. Everything creative is born out of that.

———————

"Emotions such as sadness, anger, and resentment are the effects of believing our stressful thoughts." Are you saying that it's wrong to feel sad or angry? Aren't these natural human emotions?

No, I'm not saying that it's wrong to feel sad or angry. And yes, these emotions are natural for the unquestioned mind. But they, and all other forms of suffering, are always effects of believing untrue thoughts. They go against your nature. The thoughts are the cause; the emotions are the effects. In the third question of The Work—"How do you react, what happens, when you believe that thought?"—I encourage people to identify and experience these effects in great detail. They're an important way to recognize when, and exactly how, you're out of your right mind.

Are you sure that emotions are the effects of thoughts? I've read that newborn babies and animals show evidence of having emotions such as sadness and anger.

We can't know whether babies and animals have what we would call thoughts. Babies and animals do what they do, and we superimpose onto them whatever we believe about their movements and the sounds they make. We write down our observations and take our measurements with the same identified mind that our own stories are created out of.

When my baby is crying, if I believe she is sad or angry, that's just me believing suffering onto her. Who would I be without these beliefs? I'd just be holding her, changing the diapers or feeding her, doing all that I know to do, in the name of love. I'd also be grateful that I have believed her into my life, and grateful that I have believed myself into it as the mother, love itself, shining without sadness, anger, or worry.

You say that it's not possible for someone with a questioned mind to feel anger or sorrow. Do you ever feel anger or sorrow?

No, not for a long time. But I had an interesting experience when my mother died of pancreatic cancer. She died in her apartment in Big Bear, California, on Christmas Day, 2003. I had been living with her for a month. Usually I was with her twenty-three hours a day. (Stephen came by at least once a day, in the morning, to take me out for a walk and a cup of coffee.) I cared for her, bathed and dressed her, helped the hospice nurses, administered her pain medications, slept with her in the same bed, loved her with all my heart, and never for a moment felt any sorrow. She was heavily drugged, but when she wasn't sleeping, we would talk, or I would do her nails or shower her; our time together was very lighthearted and intimate. Whenever my sister or one of her children came into the room, the whole experience changed. They saw her as a victim, and there was a lot of pity going around: "poor Mom," "poor Grandma." My mother would segue right into that and become a victim in her own mind, and she too would get weepy, and the room would become a sickroom. But as soon as they left, she would shift back into my world and begin smiling again.

It was snowing on the day she died. When she stopped breathing, someone called the mortuary. I bathed her, put her favorite earrings on her ears, and arranged her hair. There was no war with reality in me, just love, gratitude, and connection. It was wonderful. Then the mortuary people arrived, put the body on a gurney, and covered it with a fuzzy chenille blanket that was colored an intense royal blue. Somewhere in the background one of her grandchildren had the radio on, and as the people were wheeling her out of the room, I could hear Elvis Presley singing "I'll Have a Blue Christmas Without You." My mother wasn't sad, she was just blue. She was a Willie Nelson fan; she didn't particularly like Elvis, but she would have loved to go out that way. Life, when you understand it—what a trip! What an amazing trip! It doesn't matter how heartrending something may seem; if you're of right mind, you can see the humor in it.

Then we all gathered in her living room. People were reminiscing and crying; there were a lot of tears. All I felt was love and connection. My heart was full to bursting. At one point, my son Ross approached my chair, and I found myself standing up and moving into his arms. And as I stood there, a wail arose inside me. I had a quick thought that it might upset the children, but I wasn't going to shut it down. So the wail came out of me, and it was very loud. It didn't feel like sorrow; it was more elemental than that, and it was so "not-I" that I could have stood there and filed my nails as it was wailing. It lasted for maybe thirty seconds, but if it had gone on forever, I would have allowed it to. I love reality, however it shows up. I wasn't going to con myself out of that sound. Every emotion that arises has a right to life.

Once the nature of the mind is understood, suffering can't exist.

The Work in Action

"My Mother Attacks Me"

ARTHUR [*reading from his Worksheet*]: *I am furious with my mother because she attacks me, judges me, and thinks I'm not good enough.*

KATIE: Okay, there are three things we can question there. One: "She attacks me." Two: "She judges me." Three: "She thinks I'm not good enough." These are three separate inquiries. Or we can do them all at once. When you're filling in statement 1 on the Judge-Your-Neighbor Worksheet, I invite you to see if you can identify which one of your statements has the most charge for you and to begin there. And what you've written is okay. You could take yourself through inquiry using all three at once. But I'm more curious than that. I've got to know the effects of each concept on my life. I don't want to wait to be free. I'm going to answer all four questions for each concept and then turn it around. And then I'm going to do a whole new inquiry on each of the other two. I'll give you pointers here, and at the same time, just know that you can't do it wrong. I'm just going to show you from experience, from a lot of experience, how to cut to the chase to get what you came for, in the most powerful way possible. So read it again.

ARTHUR: *I am furious with Mom because she attacks me, judges me, and thinks I'm not good enough.*

KATIE: I'm not going to have you question the part where you say, "I'm furious with Mom." I'm going to have you question what's causing your furiousness. So read those three things again.

ARTHUR: *She attacks me, judges me, and thinks I'm not good enough.*

KATIE: Okay. So "she attacks you." That's the first one. Let's go there. "In that situation, your mom attacked you"—is it true? [*To the audience*] How many of you just saw this man, in your mind, being attacked by his mother? [*Many people raise their hands.*] [*To Arthur*] And we've never even met your mother.

ARTHUR: Lucky you. [*The audience laughs.*]

KATIE: So "your mother attacked you"—is it true? Now, how are you going to answer the question? Are you going to guess? Or are you going to meditate on that moment in time and let *it* show you the answer? The Work is meditation. Get very still, and look closely at the situation, at the image of you and your mother. The images may be really vague, but just sit in them until you see that she did or she didn't. [*To the audience*] As a facilitator, I don't know if he's talking about a physical attack or a verbal attack or if she just gave him "the look." So I'm just going to hold this space and witness what I can through him. [*To Arthur*] Now, the answer to the first two questions has one syllable only: it's either yes or no. So watch how your mind is going to say, "Well, not really, but, well, yeah, she really did." That's not it. You need to get still until a clear answer of yes or no appears. "Your mother attacked you"—is it true?

ARTHUR: No.

KATIE [*to the audience*]: Now, because he answered no, we skip the second question and move to the third. And I'm going to keep reminding him of that one-liner. "Your mother attacked

you"—how do you react, what happens, when you believe that
thought? One reason I do that is so that I can remember the
concept we're working with. And I don't have to know what I'm
doing. I don't have to remember the one-liner: I can just write it
down. [*To Arthur*] Now, go into that situation where you believed
she was attacking you. In that silence, witness how you reacted.
Did you attack her in return? Did you pout? Did you give her the
cold treatment? Notice your emotions. Just witness and report.
Report how you reacted in that situation as you witness it. We go
through life mother-realized. We know what she did. But we're
not self-realized. We're so busy judging other people that our
self-realization is hidden under our judgments. So be still. Witness
how you react in that situation when you believe the thought "She
attacked me."

ARTHUR: I lash out. I shout at her. I feel trapped. I feel angry. I feel
like there's nothing I can do. I'm powerless.

KATIE [*to the audience, after a pause*]: Now we'll go to the fourth
question, because I feel like he is empty and ready to move on.
He's said everything he needs to say in answering question three.
I've given him enough space. [*To Arthur*] So in that situation, who
would you be without the thought "My mother attacked me"?

ARTHUR: Umm . . . I'd be . . . I'd be peaceful. I'd be . . .

KATIE: Just witness that situation without your story that she attacked
you. Drop your judgments and witness you and her without all
these thoughts on top of her. Who or what would you be without
the thought "She attacked you"?

ARTHUR: I'd just be someone standing in a kitchen, talking on the
phone.

KATIE: So, go into the image. "I am . . ."

ARTHUR: I am standing in a kitchen listening to my mother, open to what she's saying, there for her, there for myself, I suppose.

KATIE: Okay. And I want you to get closer than "I suppose."

ARTHUR: Yeah.

KATIE: Closer, closer. And sometimes "I suppose" is as close as you can get, and that's okay too. But we're going for the real deal here. No one can give that to you. It's already in you. You can see it. It was already there, and now you're dropping your story long enough to see something else. What is she saying to you? Listen.

ARTHUR: She was . . . She was saying to me . . . She was asking if she was welcome to come and visit me. She'd asked the question many times before, and I'd always said yes.

KATIE: In other words, she said, "Can I come see you?" And you put a story onto it.

ARTHUR: Yes.

KATIE: So who would you be without the thought "She attacked me"? Who would you be just answering her question?

ARTHUR: Well, yeah. I answered, you know, yes, and then I freaked out. But I could have just answered yes.

KATIE: Or no.

ARTHUR: Or no? [*Looking astonished*] Wow! I could have answered no! That would have actually been more honest. "I'd prefer you didn't." [*The audience laughs.*] Wow! It never occurred to me that I could have done that. Okay. I could have answered no. Okay. Yeah! [*Laughter*] "Actually Mom, no." Oh, wow! Okay. Wow!

KATIE: We're meditating on a moment in time, and allowing that moment to enlighten you. So "your mother attacked you"—turn it around.

ARTHUR: I attacked my mother.

KATIE: Give me an example, in that situation, on that phone call, of where you attacked your mother.

ARTHUR: Well, yeah, I very liberally attacked her, actually. I shouted at her. I told her she was impossible. I told her . . .

KATIE: Slow it down. Close your eyes. And tell me, as it's shown to you.

ARTHUR: I said a lot of really hurtful things to her, actually. I said that no matter how hard I tried I was never good enough for her. That she was impossible. I was screaming at her.

KATIE [*to the audience*]: So now he's witnessing the situation in his mind's eye and seeing how, in fact, he attacked her. He's asking himself how that turnaround is true, what it means to him. It's not necessary to make turnarounds difficult. In other words, don't claim something that you don't actually remember, that you don't actually see. In the stillness, allow yourself to be shown, and experience the emotions that come with that. [*To Arthur*] Can you find another turnaround for "My mother attacked me"? What's another opposite?

ARTHUR: I attacked me.

KATIE: Yes. In that situation, as you look back, where did you attack yourself?

ARTHUR: I attacked . . . [*Crying*] I attacked me because . . . I . . . I was . . . The reason I, um, felt the way I did about my Mom was because she, and I could question this, but I perceived that she didn't—doesn't—accept that I'm gay. I wasn't there for me in terms of supporting myself and knowing that it's okay to be who I am. And if Mom believes otherwise, that's not my problem, it's hers. But I felt that that was true. And so I did attack me because I didn't think I was good enough.

KATIE: Yes. Your own fear. Your own homophobia.

ARTHUR: Yes.

KATIE: Because you were homophobic, you projected that onto your mother, and all she said was "Can I come see you?" She doesn't sound very homophobic to me. [*Laughter*]

ARTHUR: No, not in that instance. But yeah.

KATIE: Who knows? After this Worksheet, you might call her and say, "Mom, you know, during that phone call (and spell it out for her), did you know I was gay?"

ARTHUR: Yeah.

KATIE: We believe our thoughts about people, and we punish and attack them for what we're believing. We believe our thoughts so strongly that people don't have a chance with us. And some of us hold on to those thoughts to our deathbed. So, this is like a coming-out party. Okay. "I attacked my mother." I saw another example. Would you like to hear it?

ARTHUR: Yes, please.

KATIE: You lied to your mother. In that situation.

ARTHUR: That's true, yeah. I did.

KATIE: You said yes when your honest answer was no. That's how you attacked yourself.

ARTHUR: Yeah. I wasn't honest about what I felt comfortable with.

KATIE: So do you see the pattern?

ARTHUR: It never occurred to me that I could have said no. Maybe that would have been more loving.

KATIE: I'd drop the "maybe." You attacked her!

ARTHUR: Yeah. I did. Yeah, yeah. It's true. I did.

KATIE: You're trying to spare her on the one hand, and you're attacking her on the other.

ARTHUR: Yeah.

KATIE: Okay, sweetheart. Do you see another turnaround? We've done "I attacked my mother" and "I attacked myself." "My mother attacked me"—what's another turnaround?

ARTHUR: My mother didn't attack me. She was . . . She was actually . . . She actually felt really rejected by me, I think. And I realize that she wasn't attacking me. She was asking me a question, and also she was trying to reach out to me. She was actually trying to have a connection with me, where she didn't feel that anymore.

KATIE: "My mother didn't attack me." Can you find another turnaround? What's the opposite of *attack*?

ARTHUR: My mother reached out to me. Yeah. Yeah. It was her way of reaching out.

KATIE: So specifically, how did your mother reach out to you? She called. She asked if she could come stay with you.

ARTHUR: Come see me, yeah. "Are we welcome?" Yeah. And I could have said no. But she was actually trying to reach out to me.

KATIE: "My mother reached out to me." Can you find another example on that phone call?

ARTHUR: That she reached out to me?

KATIE: Uh-huh.

ARTHUR: Yes. She . . . She actually wanted me to come home more often.

KATIE: I have one. Would you like to hear it?

ARTHUR: Sure. Absolutely.

KATIE: When you were attacking her, she didn't hang up on you.

ARTHUR: No.

KATIE: She continued to reach out.

ARTHUR: She did keep listening to what I said, yeah.

KATIE: Okay. So, statement 2. "I want . . ." In that situation, with your mother on the phone . . . Just read what you wrote.

ARTHUR: *I want Mom to stop attacking me. I want her to accept me, love me, and embrace me as good enough for her.*

KATIE: So, "you want your mother to stop attacking you"—is that true? Now, look at all the information we have, because we've questioned statement 1. Did you find one place where she attacked you?

ARTHUR: No.

KATIE: So do you see how that changes your answer?

ARTHUR: I haven't spoken to my mother in twelve years, and that was the last full conversation I ever had with her. It's a story I've believed for so long.

KATIE: It cost you your mother.

ARTHUR: Yeah.

KATIE: You became motherless because you've been believing these thoughts.

ARTHUR: Yes. Well, yeah.

KATIE: You haven't talked to her in twelve years.

ARTHUR: Well, I perceive that *she* doesn't want to talk to *me*. But then it doesn't matter.

KATIE: So let's look at it. "You want your mother to stop attacking you"—is it true? Be open-minded. When you're doing this Work, it requires a very open mind. How can she stop attacking you if she never started? So is that what you want?

ARTHUR: No.

KATIE: And how do you react, on the phone, when you believe the thought "I want my mother to stop attacking me"?

ARTHUR: I get really angry and defensive and insulting.

KATIE: Do you see yourself on the phone, in your mind's eye?

ARTHUR: Yeah, and it's not good.

KATIE: It's how you react when you want someone to give what she can't give or stop doing what she isn't doing. Now let's look at who you would be without the thought. In that situation, who would you be without the thought "I want her to stop attacking me"?

ARTHUR: I'd be sane. I'd be listening to her. I'd be peaceful. I'd be . . . I'd be clear about her questions, and I'd be clear about my answers. The crazy, crazy thing is that I have replayed this in my head for a decade or more, and it never occurred to me that when she said, "Are we welcome?" I could have said, "No." I could have said, "I'm gay, and I don't want you to be uncomfortable." That never occurred to me.

KATIE: "You want your mother to stop attacking you"—turn it around.

ARTHUR: I want me to stop attacking me. Yeah. That's really true.

KATIE: Can you find another turnaround?

ARTHUR: I want to stop attacking my mother. I do. In my mind, in my life.

KATIE: And you haven't found a single attack on her part.

ARTHUR: Yeah, it's true. She was just asking a question.

KATIE: Unless you can find one place during that phone call where she attacked you.

ARTHUR: I can't find a place where she wasn't reaching out.

KATIE: Now, do you see another turnaround? "I want my mother to stop attacking me." Turned around: "I want my mother to keep attacking me."

ARTHUR: Hmm.

KATIE: Just to see what's valid and what's not. And also, from the point of view of pure ego, "I want my mother to keep attacking me." How else can you be right? She's a monster, and you're completely innocent and justified in your attack.

ARTHUR: Bam!

KATIE: It's been a very important thing in your life that you continue to believe that she attacked you when she didn't.

ARTHUR: It just . . . for a really long time I had this belief. I mean, other things happened afterwards, blah, blah, blah, but I created a really strong identity for myself as the person who was disowned by his parents for being gay. And the image of my mother as this monster was so important to me. I realize that if I didn't have that, then I would think that it wasn't okay for me to be gay. But the two things aren't related. She doesn't have to be a monster for me to think I'm okay. Wow! [*Crying*] I didn't realize that. I thought as long as I thought she was wrong, I'd be okay. But me being okay doesn't have anything to do with how she feels. It's been so long that I've been angry with her in my mind, and I didn't realize that I could have just been, like, no, I'm fine. What she feels doesn't change how I feel about me or my life. I didn't even think I loved her anymore. And now I just . . . All I feel is all this love for her, because it must be so sad for her to feel that way. I just didn't realize that I'm fine. I had this belief that if she were different, then I'd be fine. And it's just not true.

KATIE: You understand that she didn't attack you in any way during that phone call. She was just trying to reach out, to see her son and invite him to come home more often. All the rest was yours.

ARTHUR: Yeah. And it was . . . She could have said anything to me and it wouldn't have mattered, if I had been right with myself. It was me believing that my being the way I am was wrong.

KATIE: And projecting it onto her.

ARTHUR: Yeah.

KATIE: And you still don't know.

ARTHUR: Not in this moment, no, I don't. I have no way of knowing.

KATIE: No way of knowing whether she knows you're gay or . . .

ARTHUR: Yeah, I know she knows.

KATIE: Well, there's no way for you to know whether she's okay with it or not.

ARTHUR: Not in this moment, no.

KATIE: Nothing that I've heard so far. She didn't attack you.

ARTHUR: Well, I mean, later on she flooded my email with stuff about how homosexuality is an illness that can be cured. But . . .

KATIE: Well, that's her world. She saw her son as ill and was only trying to heal him.

ARTHUR: Yeah.

KATIE: So say that to me, the way she said it to you.

ARTHUR: That she emailed me? The email was: "My dearest Arthur." Well, first she rang me when she found out I had a partner she didn't know about. And she said, "Do you want to hear your father crying? This is what you wanted, isn't it? You're having a gay relationship."

KATIE: Okay. It was a question. *Did* you want to hear your father cry? [*Laughter*] She was reaching out.

ARTHUR: Did I want to hear my father crying? Not particularly, no.

KATIE: Well, think about it.

ARTHUR: Did I want to hear my father crying? No.

KATIE: Have you ever really listened to your father crying?

ARTHUR: No. No, I haven't.

KATIE: Well, then there's your answer. And if you want to hear him cry, then the answer is yes.

ARTHUR: Yes. Maybe I might.

KATIE: It's good to be there for people when they cry.

ARTHUR: Yeah, that's true.

KATIE: It's kind, it's loving, but only a man who is right in himself could do that from the heart.

ARTHUR: Yeah. And then she emailed me saying, "My dear Arthur," and then in capital letters "YOU'RE NOT GAY. Read these articles about cures. And, you know, we love you as you really are." But that's only a problem to me if I agree. Because otherwise . . .

KATIE: It's just a mother reaching out with a couple of little antidotes just in case you're not sure. She's a mother worried for her son.

ARTHUR: Yeah. And rightfully so, I suppose, because last time I spoke to her I sounded like a crazy person. [*Laughter*] And then I blocked her emails. I did that. But that's the thing. Because . . . I thought, if I accept her trying to reach out to me, then that means it's not okay for me to be gay. But the two things are completely unrelated. They have nothing to do with each other. I could say, "Well, thank you, Mom. And, no, I won't be reading those things."

KATIE: Exactly so. Or "Thank you, Mom. And if I ever have a problem with this, I'll take a look. I appreciate you for being so concerned."

ARTHUR: Yeah. "But so far I'm doing really well." [*Laughter*]

KATIE: Yes, you are. [*Laughter*]

ARTHUR: Wow! Okay.

KATIE: People don't have to get along with me. Do I get along with them?—that's the important question. People don't have to understand me. Do I understand myself? Do I understand them? And if I understand myself, I understand everyone. As long as I remain a mystery to myself, people remain a mystery. If I don't like me, I don't like you.

ARTHUR: Yeah.

KATIE: Now, turn all those "want" statements around. "In that situation with my mom, I want me . . ."

ARTHUR: I want me to stop attacking me. I want me to accept me, love me, and embrace me as good enough.

KATIE: Okay. So that is how to live. That's what you want. When you turn around the wants, needs, and shoulds—statements 2, 3, and 4 on the Judge-Your-Neighbor Worksheet—that's your advice to yourself. It shows you what will give you a happy life. The world's not telling you what you want. No one else is telling you. There it is. You wrote that. I call it your prescription for happiness. It comes from within you. Now turn the statement around to your mother.

ARTHUR: I want me to stop attacking my mother. I want me to accept her, love her, and embrace her as good enough for me.

KATIE: Yes, sweetheart. That's your prescription for happiness. That's what you want in that situation. And it's what you didn't have available to you.

ARTHUR: Yeah.

KATIE: But you do now, and there it is.

ARTHUR: I want me to accept her. Wow! Wow! The thing is, I actually do want that.

KATIE: Well, it comes from what you wrote. It automatically flows out of inquiry. I love that.

ARTHUR: I've never wanted that before, and I do now. I do want that. I do want to accept her and love her and embrace her, and it doesn't mean anything about how I live.

KATIE: Yes. Now read the statement again, turned around to its opposite. "In that situation, I don't want her . . ."

ARTHUR: I don't want her to stop attacking me. I don't want her to accept me, love me, and embrace me as good enough. Well, yeah. Why should she?

KATIE: And when you consider how you behaved on that phone call, how *could* she?

ARTHUR: Oh, gross. Yeah, I agree.

KATIE: Stay in the situation; otherwise you'll generalize and turn this onto yourself and start to feel guilt. In that situation, "I don't want her to do all those things, when I consider my part."

ARTHUR: Why would she? Yeah. That's true.

KATIE: And you didn't give her a lot of room.

ARTHUR: No, I gave her no room.

KATIE: Let's look at statement 3. This is advice to your mother.

ARTHUR: *Mom shouldn't be angry with me. She should love me uncondi-tionally and not make me feel rejected and alone. She should be a loving, respectful mother.*

KATIE: When you consider that situation, "she shouldn't be angry with you"—is it true?

ARTHUR: No.

KATIE: Pretty clear, isn't it?

ARTHUR: Yeah.

KATIE: And how do you react when you believe this thought, that she shouldn't be angry with you? What happens to you in that conversation?

ARTHUR: Well, I get angry with her. I just don't want to listen. I shut her out. I defend.

KATIE: And lie.

ARTHUR: And lie. Oh, yeah. Well, there's a lot of lying. She used to accuse me of . . . well, I say "accuse." She used to say, "You've rejected me."

KATIE: She's a wise woman.

ARTHUR: She was right. She was right on the money. [*Laughter*] I did.

KATIE: She was reading you in that respect, long before you did.

ARTHUR: Yeah.

KATIE: So you got angry and lied to her, because you didn't want her to be angry.

ARTHUR: Yeah.

KATIE: That's why you didn't say, "Mom, I'm gay. I'm comfortable with it." Because you didn't want her to be angry.

ARTHUR: Yes.

KATIE: You didn't even want to hear your father cry, because you kept seeking love, approval, and appreciation.

ARTHUR: Yeah.

KATIE: Who would you be without the thought "She shouldn't be angry with me"?

ARTHUR: I'd be fine, because I'd be, like, "I understand. Go for it. It's all good."

KATIE: Let's turn it around. "She shouldn't be angry."

ARTHUR: She *should* be angry with me.

KATIE: So in that situation, she should be angry with you. Give me examples. What does that mean to you as you look back at that situation?

ARTHUR: She should be angry with me because I am rejecting her. She should be angry with me because she accused me of shutting her out, which was true. She should be angry with me because she accused me of keeping secrets from her, which was true. She should be angry because she felt like I didn't want to be part of their lives, all of which was true. Yeah. She had good reasons.

KATIE: Okay. Now read your whole list.

ARTHUR: *Mom shouldn't be angry with me. She should love me unconditionally and not make me feel rejected and alone. She should be a loving, respectful mother.*

KATIE: So turn it around. "She should . . ."

ARTHUR: Mom should be angry with me. She shouldn't love me unconditionally, and she should make me feel rejected and alone. She shouldn't be a loving, respectful mother.

KATIE: Yes. When you consider your part and what you are discovering, what better way to bring you to The Work? Is there anything more powerful that your mother could have done to bring you to self-realization and freedom from suffering?

ARTHUR: It's true. Yeah.

KATIE: We all have the perfect parents.

ARTHUR: Wow!

KATIE: Now, here's what you need on that phone call to be happy. Look at your list, and turn it all around to the self. This is your advice to yourself. "I shouldn't . . ."

ARTHUR: I shouldn't be angry with me. I should love me unconditionally and not make me feel rejected and alone. I should be a loving, respectful son. Oh, yeah. Okay.

KATIE: That's great advice.

ARTHUR: I shouldn't be angry with me. Oh! Oh, yeah. That's true.

KATIE: That's your prescription for happiness.

ARTHUR: Because I would have been fine. Because I would have been there for myself.

KATIE: And statement 4?

ARTHUR: *I need Mom to tell me that it's okay for me to be gay, to respect my choices, to not attack me or judge me or invade my privacy anymore.*

KATIE: "You need your mother to say it's okay for you to be gay"—is it true? On that phone call?

ARTHUR: No. No, I don't.

KATIE: And notice how you react when you believe that thought.

ARTHUR: And she doesn't say it's okay? To be honest, the bottom falls out of me.

KATIE: And you attack another human being.

ARTHUR: Yeah.

KATIE: And how can we expect countries to stop making war if we can't stop doing it with the people in our own lives?

ARTHUR: That's true.

KATIE: It's like you just nuked her, and in that you nuked yourself.

ARTHUR: That's really true.

KATIE: Yes. But only for twelve years.

ARTHUR: And I nuked myself in my mind so much. Like, I'll never forget, I was in Venice, the most beautiful place, years later, and I was alone, and I was just thinking about that conversation over and over again and making myself miserable.

KATIE: There goes Venice.

ARTHUR: There go the canals. Gone.

KATIE: So again, "I need . . ."

ARTHUR: "I need Mom to tell me that it's okay for me to be gay."

KATIE: Who would you be on that phone call without that thought?

ARTHUR: I'd be fine. Because I could actually just really be present and, yeah, because . . . Well, the word that comes to mind is free.

KATIE: So turn it around. This is how to be happy on that phone call and in that situation and in your life. "I need . . ."

ARTHUR: I need me to tell me that it's okay for me to be gay.

KATIE: Yes. And continue. "I need me . . ."

ARTHUR: I need me to respect my choices.

KATIE: Yes.

ARTHUR: Yeah. Yeah. I need me not to attack me or judge me.

KATIE: Or her.

ARTHUR: Or her. I need me not to attack her. I need me not to judge her or invade her privacy anymore.

KATIE: Yes. Stop invading her privacy.

ARTHUR: Because she has the right to think whatever she thinks.

KATIE: Just like you.

ARTHUR: Yeah. That's true. Yeah.

KATIE: Different worlds. And it's a wonderful thing to share them. If you share your world with me, it doesn't affect my world. Now I have two worlds to appreciate.

ARTHUR: So I . . . Wow! Okay.

KATIE: Different planets. Different solar systems.

ARTHUR: It's just . . . [*Laughing*]

KATIE: In her world, it's not okay to be gay. In your world, it's okay.

ARTHUR: Yeah.

KATIE: And why do we have to fight with these worlds that have different traditions, different ideas, different ways of being?

ARTHUR: That's true. Yeah.

KATIE: And the next statement, statement 5, where you say what you think of her?

ARTHUR: Oh, God. Umm. You asked us to let loose when we filled this out. *Mom is a judgmental bitch who doesn't listen and is cruel when she doesn't get her own way.* Uh-oh, I can see where this is going. [*Laughter*]

KATIE: Now, it's really important that you stay in the situation, because this doesn't define you. It's just how you are in that particular situation, on the phone, and you test it as you go to see how it fits. It's like trying on a new pair of shoes. "In that situation with my mom, I am . . ."

ARTHUR: It's true. I'm a judgmental bitch who doesn't listen and is cruel when I don't get my own way.

KATIE: And this is so good to know about yourself. "When I don't get my way . . ."

ARTHUR: Yeah. I'm a nasty bitch when I don't get my way.

KATIE: You are everything you accused your mother of being.

ARTHUR: I can't disagree with that.

KATIE: Well, you're waking up to reality. Now, denial is an interesting thing. We can't change what we're not aware of. It's not possible. So what The Work does is reveal yourself to yourself. And everything starts to shift, because you're becoming more aware of what was hidden. So this is waking up to reality.

ARTHUR: It's true.

KATIE: Now turn the list around to the opposite. "On that phone call, my mother was . . ."

ARTHUR: She was . . . Do I reverse it to Mom?

KATIE: You just see where there are opposites that apply to each judgment. What's the opposite of "judgmental bitch"?

ARTHUR: She was . . .

KATIE: An understanding mother?

ARTHUR: Understanding mother. Yeah. Yeah. "Who doesn't listen . . ."

KATIE: Who does listen.

ARTHUR: Who does listen. And who is kind when she doesn't get her own way.

KATIE: You just contemplate these. You test them. It doesn't mean that the turnaround is true, but you stay focused on that phone call until you can see how the turnaround is true, even if it doesn't seem true at first. You meditate. You test. You stay focused on it. This is really important, if freedom from suffering is your goal.

ARTHUR: She wasn't cruel. Yeah, well . . . She actually just really, really crazy loved me and just wanted me to be happy, according to her particular definition of that, which is the only definition anybody ever has.

KATIE: Let's move on to your last statement: what you don't want to experience again.

ARTHUR: *I don't want to ever feel judged, unloved, attacked, or rejected by my mother again.*

KATIE: "I'm willing . . ."

ARTHUR: Oh, wow! Okay.

KATIE: "I'm willing . . ."

ARTHUR: I'm willing to feel judged, unloved, attacked, and rejected by my mother again.

KATIE: Do you understand?

ARTHUR: Well, yeah, because, like, that's the litmus test for how not homophobic I am.

KATIE: Yes. And it shows you where you are still at war with yourself and, as a result, with others in your world. It shows you what to question on another Worksheet.

ARTHUR: Because she can say anything, and I'll be like . . .

KATIE: Bring it on.

ARTHUR: Yeah, exactly.

KATIE: Bring it on. And if you feel anything less than connected to your mother, it just means you need another Worksheet. So, "I look forward to . . ."

ARTHUR: I look forward to feeling judged, unloved, attacked, and rejected by my mother again. Which might just happen if I call her.

KATIE: If you call her and you perceive it that way again, it's time for another Worksheet. If you notice that you're attacking her, it's time for a Worksheet. You're going against your happiness. You're going against what you want and what you need to be happy any time you attack anyone, including yourself. And this inquiry made it very clear.

ARTHUR: It really did.

KATIE: So you be your mother on the phone and attack me.

ARTHUR: Um. Oh, God. I can't even . . . "Do you want to hear your father crying? This is what you wanted, isn't it? You're having a homosexual relationship."

KATIE: "I *am* having a homosexual relationship, and no, having Dad cry is not what I wanted. I don't want him to suffer, and I don't want you to suffer either."

ARTHUR: "Well then, why are you doing this?"

KATIE: "I was born like this. I can't be any other way for you or for me."

ARTHUR: "No, you weren't. That's not true. You can change."

KATIE: "I'll take a look at that, Mom. I'm open."

ARTHUR: "Well, you need to not live with the man that you're having a relationship with."

KATIE: "Well, actually, I adore him. Would you like to meet him?"

ARTHUR: "That's disgusting."

KATIE: "Oh. Well, maybe not quite yet. But when you're ready." [*Laughter*] "If you're ever ready to meet him, I would love for you to visit."

ARTHUR: "I don't want to meet your pansy friends."

KATIE: "Well, I understand that."

ARTHUR: Wow! Okay. Oh . . . I don't know. I don't know what she'd say. Umm.

KATIE: What are you afraid she'd say?

ARTHUR: "You've ruined my life."

KATIE: "What can I do to make it right?"

ARTHUR: "You can stop being gay."

KATIE: "Well, Mom, that's the one thing I can't give you."

ARTHUR: "Why not?"

KATIE: "Because I'm gay." [*Laughter*]

ARTHUR: And then she'd probably say, "No, you're not."

KATIE: And I would listen to her world, to her suffering, to her beliefs, and how some we have in common and some we don't.

ARTHUR: Yeah. Yeah.

KATIE: "I know this is hard on you, Mom, and it was really hard on me, too, for a while. I really understand why Dad would cry. And I'm here anytime you want to talk."

ARTHUR: That's really lovely.

KATIE: Well, I learned it from your Worksheet.

ARTHUR: Thank you.

KATIE: Our minds, written down on a Worksheet and questioned, wake us up to reality and show us how to live out of love, not out of our fear and confusion. Good work, honey. Good work. Thank you. It's a privilege to be your facilitator.

ARTHUR: Thank you so much, Katie.

KATIE: And you. [*Applause*] [*To the audience*] And for those of you whose mothers have died—even if she's dead, you can still do The Work on her. It's never too late. She doesn't have to be alive for you to get this done, for you to have a relationship with her as you've never had before. And that goes not only for mothers but for every human being you haven't forgiven yet. Every human being, every cat, dog, tree, thing—to be separate from anyone or anything goes against your heart. The only time those people or things are not okay is when you believe they're not. So I continue to invite you to write down what you believe about them. To question what you believe is an amazing gift to give yourself, and you can have it all the days of your life. The answers are always inside you, just waiting to be heard. The Work isn't a philosophy. It's not anything. It's just four questions and the turnarounds. All it takes is an open mind.

13

THE WORLD BEYOND NAMES

Then Subhuti said, "Sir, what should we call this sutra, and how should we embody it and live it?"

The Buddha said, "This sutra is called 'The Diamond-Cutter Transcendent Wisdom Scripture,' because it can cut through any form of ignorance or delusion. You should embody it and live it with this name in mind. But tell me, Subhuti: Does the Buddha have a teaching to offer?"

"No, Sir. The Buddha has no teaching to offer."

"How many atoms are there in a world system of a billion worlds?"

"An inconceivably great number."

"The Buddha teaches that atoms aren't atoms; they are only *called* 'atoms.' The Buddha teaches that worlds aren't worlds; they are only *called* 'worlds.'

"Subhuti, if a good man or woman dedicated lifetimes as numerous as the sands in the river to charitable acts, and another person, upon hearing this sutra, truly realized what it is teaching and then embodied it and lived it, the merit of the second person would be greater by far."

In the same way that a diamond can cut through any substance, inquiry can cut through any stressful thought, any blindness or delusion of the mind. Inquiry is the unfailing practice of cutting through delusions. Self-realization pours forth from the Buddha into the Buddha. It's already present in you, though unknown until it is received, listened to, and understood in the silence.

The Buddha truly doesn't have a teaching to offer: he lives as the answered question, self-realized, without self. He acts without doing anything. He teaches without saying anything. Anything that has been said can exist only in the world of illusion we call the past. If he taught, the Buddha could teach only what is not, and in doing that, he would be no buddha at all. Whatever he truly teaches happens in silence.

In this chapter, as in previous ones, the Buddha says that names aren't real. That's why "atoms" and "worlds" aren't real. They are simply mind-plays of apparent *not-now*s, and are therefore *not*s: though they are "worlds" and "atoms" in the dream-world, they are *not*s in the world as truly seen. Whatever you call something isn't the thing itself. The name is what creates the thing; it's how the infinite becomes separated, as if there could ever be parts, as if each part were not the whole.

The ultimate desire is the desire not to exist. That desire is the mind's way back to its true self, the self before naming, where there is no self and no other. The mind is afraid that without anything, there would be nothing. And how can that be? *Nothing* is just another word for a something. When the mind believes that it exists, it also believes that it can be annihilated. What silly opposites these are! The don't-know mind doesn't name, doesn't fear, has no wish to control or foresee, steps off the cliff of the moment with absolute trust that the next step will land somewhere, and the next step somewhere else, and the feet will take us wherever we need to go. Without believing in words, there can be nothing to fear. Fear is born only to words believed, and

what believes those words is a concoction of prior words believed.
Who started all this confusion? You did. Who can end it? Only you.

How does inquiry cut through delusion?

Inquiry ends suffering by cutting it off at the root. No stressful
thought can withstand sincere questioning. Even people who are very
attached to a thought, and who answer The Work's second question
("Can you absolutely know that it's true?") with a resounding Yes,
get a chance to look deeper when they meditate on the questions that
follow. When they answer the third question ("How do you react,
what happens, when you believe that thought?"), they can realize, in
detail, precisely how the thought causes suffering. And in answering the fourth question ("Who would you be without the thought?"),
they can see what the world would look like if they didn't believe the
thought, if they didn't even have the capacity for thinking it. Then,
when they find turnarounds for the original thought, they can experience how its opposites are just as true, or maybe even truer. When
a thought is thoroughly questioned in this way, it loses its power to
cause suffering.

*You say that the ultimate desire is the desire not to exist. Does that mean
that spiritual longing is a form of suicide?*

Yes, for the ego, the "you" you believe you are. People usually identify
themselves with a particular body. They look in the mirror and say,
"That's me." But a few people get a glimpse that they aren't physical,
and if they're not frightened by this, they may want to discover who
they truly are. So the desire not to exist as a separate ego is the desire
for freedom from any false identity. It's a longing for the disappear-
ance of the dream-world. Physical suicide, killing the body, doesn't
solve the issue, since the body wasn't you in the first place. You don't

kill your ego just because you stop one particular object from moving. The clear mind sees that even though the body stopped, the mind didn't, and so there is still work to do, until there isn't.

*No stressful thought
can withstand
sincere questioning.*

14

NOTHING BELONGS TO US

When Subhuti heard these words, he was moved to tears. He said to the Buddha, "It is a rare privilege, Sir, that you have offered us this teaching. Since the moment, long ago, when I understood, I have never heard a teaching so profound and so direct. Sir, if someone is able to hear this teaching with an open mind, that person will surely have an insight into reality and see things just as they are, beyond all concepts. Such a person is worthy of the utmost respect. I have understood your teaching and am deeply moved by it. But thousands of years from now, if an open-minded person hears this sutra and truly realizes what it is teaching and then embodies it and lives it, that person will be extraordinary. He or she will be free of the concepts 'self' and 'other,' which aren't real. Those who have freed themselves from all concepts are called 'buddhas.'"

The Buddha said, "Yes, Subhuti, exactly so. If someone hears this sutra and isn't frightened or upset by its teaching, that person is indeed extraordinary.

"Subhuti, what the Buddha calls the highest spiritual qualities aren't in fact the highest spiritual qualities. They are only *called* 'the highest spiritual qualities.' For example, the quality of patience that I teach isn't in fact patience. In a former lifetime, when my body was dismembered by the king of Kalinga, I wasn't attaching to concepts of 'self' and 'other,' so there was no need for me to be patient or forgiving. If, when my body was being dismembered, I had been attaching to the concepts 'self' and 'other,' anger and hatred toward the king would have arisen in me. During five hundred lifetimes as an ascetic practicing patience, I was free from the concepts 'self' and 'other,' so patience was unnecessary.

"The only thing bodhisattvas need to do is to free themselves from all concepts and nurture the aspiration for freedom. They shouldn't allow the mind to dwell on concepts that arise from anything they can perceive— from sight, sound, smell, taste, touch, or any other qualities. The mind should be kept independent of any thoughts that arise within it. If the mind depends upon anything, it has no sure refuge.

"Subhuti, when bodhisattvas want to practice generosity for the benefit of all sentient beings, they should realize that generosity isn't in fact generosity and that sentient beings aren't sentient beings. When

---

* In a legend about a previous incarnation of the Buddha, the king of Kalinga once went hunting with his concubines, who wandered off into the forest. There they found the ascetic Kshanti (who was later to be reborn as the Buddha) sitting in meditation. They were so enchanted by his serenity that they laid flowers at his feet, and he began to teach them about patience. When the king found them there, he was enraged by jealousy, and in order to test Kshanti's patience, he cut off his hands, then his feet, then his ears and nose. During the torture, Kshanti remained unmoved, and not a trace of anger arose in his heart. When the king realized this, he felt remorse and begged Kshanti to forgive him.

bodhisattvas realize this, they will be able to practice generosity for the benefit of all sentient beings.

"You should understand that what I teach is true, it is authentic, and it points to the way things are. There is nothing wishful or inaccurate about this teaching. You should further understand that the truth I have attained is neither true nor false.

"Subhuti, if bodhisattvas practice generosity while attaching to concepts, they are like people walking in total darkness. If bodhisattvas practice generosity and are free of concepts, they are like people walking in the sunlight with their eyes wide open, seeing all things clearly, exactly as they are. If, in future ages, open-minded men and women hear this sutra and truly realize what it is teaching and then embody it and live it, I will be fully aware of these people and will recognize each one of them, and each will be worthy of the deepest respect."

———————————

This chapter contains a variation on the truth that the Buddha stated in chapter 10: "A bodhisattva should develop a mind that abides nowhere." Here he says, "The mind should be kept independent of any thoughts that arise within it. If the mind depends upon anything, it has no sure refuge." To see things just as they are, you would need to think only in what I call "first-generation thoughts": single nouns, with no other words attached to them—for example, "tree," "sky," "table," "chair." But even tree, sky, table, and chair have to be questioned, since any point of reference is pure imagination. So it's not a table, though you call it a table; it's not a tree, though you call it a tree. Calling it something doesn't make it the something you call it.

Nothing is ultimately true; there's nothing that can't be questioned. The last reality is "There is no reality," and I invite you to go beyond even that. You can find no anchor, no identity, no self. And that's the safe place. That's the sure refuge.

If the mind depends upon anything, it becomes the I-know mind, an ego flailing around in apparent space and time, always trying to define itself, always trying to prove that its judgments are real, that its whole world is real. The mind's only way out is in: the mind inside itself, Buddha-mind, responding to the illusion of a self. Once the illusion is questioned, it can no longer exist. It appears as inconsequential, funny, and completely insane.

In the story that the Buddha tells in this chapter, about when he was being tortured, he was awake to the fact that the hands, feet, ears, and nose that were being chopped off weren't his. The body wasn't his body. It was no one's body. He realized that it was all imagined, so no thought could arise that would cause anger or hatred in him.

I haven't been tortured, but a number of times I have been threatened by violent people, and I know that it's possible to stay rooted in the real even when you're in apparent danger. To my mind, this isn't a matter of patience; it's a matter of noticing, witnessing, and staying connected to reality.

For example, sometime early on, in 1986 or '87, I was doing The Work with a woman from Kansas City who had come to stay with me for a few days. She said she suffered from chronic pain. One day, as she was leaving, I put my arms around her. According to her, a shock went through her, and she said, "Oh my God, the pain is gone!" She burst into tears and said I was a great healer. I told her that whatever had happened resulted from her projecting this role onto me so powerfully, but it was all her; *she* was the one who had healed herself. After this, she kept flying back to Barstow and spent as much time as she could hanging out with me, living in my house. This went on for several months.

Then one day her husband appeared at the front door, furious. I invited him in. He stood in the living room and began screaming accusations at me, yelling at the top of his lungs. He said he had forbidden his wife to come to my house again. She was growing more and more obsessed with me, he said. I must be controlling her mind somehow. She no longer listened to him or loved him the way she loved me. Then he started pacing back and forth in the living room. He was a large man, and he looked like a character in an animated cartoon, waving his arms and shouting. At times he put his face within inches of mine and screamed out his accusations, and I could feel his breath on my face. What I saw was a man terrified of losing control over his wife, a man who was driving himself crazy with fear. I said that I understood his fear, but that if she came to see me, I wouldn't turn her away—or anyone else, for that matter.

At this point he threatened to kill me if I didn't stop seeing his wife. I was very still as I listened to him. The identified mind would interpret this ranting as dangerous. But if you take away the meaning, he was like a tree in a strong wind, swaying its branches, strong and limber and beautiful. In reality, nothing was going on but a man sharing his fears with a listener who cared. He said he was a policeman in Kansas City, and he knew how to deal with someone like me. If he didn't kill me now, he would do it later. "I understand," I said. That made him even more furious. He said he would burn my house down, with me and my children in it, and make it look like an accident—that I would never know when it was going to happen, and there was no way I could prevent it. It was obvious how confused he was and how much he was suffering. I could only continue to connect with him at a level that was deeper than deep, since it was my own self I was connecting with, and I felt the love inside me expand as he threatened. There was no "him" outside; it was all me. "I really do understand," I said. When he heard it this time, he looked at me, and his whole face softened, his body began to shake, and he fell into my arms, sobbing. I held him for a while, then I helped both of them out the door. Neither one ever came back.

An onlooker might have said that I was being patient, but in reality I was simply aware that what that man was threatening—this Katie person—couldn't be harmed in any way. The whole time, I was witnessing his unhappiness and confusion, and his anger at facing something that can't be moved. I was listening to just one thing: his mind, which was a part of my own mind, not separate from it. Being impatient with his mind would have been the same as being impatient with my own.

That's why meditation and stillness are so important when it comes to inquiry, especially for beginners. If you can do The Work in slow motion, meditating on a situation when you were upset or angry, taking five, ten minutes or more with every question, it becomes a pattern of mind, a natural state of listening. Inquiry becomes a way of unscrambling anything that isn't your truth, anything other than the clear mind. Awareness isn't a trick or a special kind of thinking. It's simply the ego unscrambled.

———————

Why would someone be frightened or upset by the teaching of the Diamond Sutra?

The ego is always fighting for its life. You might be frightened or upset to hear that you don't exist as a "you," that the whole identity you're so invested in is an illusion. It's the end of the world as you understand it to be, the end of time and identity and the physical body. Of course, the ego will continue to bring you back into its imagined world as long as you value anything more than the truth. But once the ego is understood, it has no way of believing itself back into apparent existence, so you can't possibly be frightened or upset by any truth or untruth.

Not everyone has huge breakthroughs when they're doing The Work. How important is patience?

The Work is a practice. I suggest that people have it for breakfast every morning, and have a good day. Even if you're graced with the deepest experience of enlightenment, you still need to practice awareness, because there are ancient thoughts that will keep arising in you, and if you don't question them, they'll take you over, however enlightened you are. For me, the major thought was "My mother doesn't love me." I worked on this one, and dozens of variations, every day for a whole year. I would write down the thoughts as they came to me, and I would meditate on each one, using the four questions and turnarounds of The Work, for hours, sometimes for days. I knew I wasn't dealing with a person; I was dealing with concepts, and once I investigated the concepts about my mother, I had unraveled all my concepts about everyone and everything.

It does take patience to continue doing The Work as a daily practice, or at least as a regular practice. People who truly want to end their suffering are able to find that patience. Questioning your stressful thoughts can be difficult, but it's a lot more difficult *not* to question them. When people are interested in The Work, they notice that sometimes they do it and sometimes they don't—at first. But if you make a commitment to doing The Work for breakfast every day, it starts waking up in you. You no longer do it; *it* does *you*. It becomes natural, automatic, like breathing.

The Work is a way to step in between *thinking* a thought and *believing* the thought. When you do The Work on any stressful thought, amazingly enough you may see that it's just not true. You've been tying yourself in knots, and often your partner too, over a false belief. And you get to see, in detail, the cause and effect of the thought, exactly how the thought has power over you and causes your suffering. Not only that: Through doing The Work on a thought you get to see, in depth, who you would be—who you *are*—without it. The reversal can be immediate. I keep seeing people turn their lives around, their relationships, health, finances, in five, ten, fifteen minutes, because of the simple realization that what they've been believing for years is untrue. Anyone with an open mind can achieve that. It comes with an incredible feeling of freedom. If it's not immediate—if it takes more inquiry and effort at undoing—that's also the way it *should* be, and it's wonderful.

How do we bring The Work into our everyday lives?

By doing it.

But our lives are filled with many difficult relationships and moments. How do we navigate this life of inquiry?

You do The Work, and your perceptions change naturally. There's no need to navigate. As your mind changes, the world you perceive changes, since the world is your projection. Every time you question your stressful thoughts, you become a clearer, kinder human being. You may not even notice that. But little by little, over the months, over the years, life becomes simpler, and your mind settles into a peace that you weren't even aware of before. Your relationships become easier and happier. You realize that your enemies are really your friends, that the difficult people in your life aren't really difficult: it's your own mind that created the difficulties. And the clearer your mind gets, the more it projects a friendly universe, until one day it occurs to you that you haven't had a problem for a very long time.

For how long did you write Worksheets on your mother? And when was the last time you actually filled in a Worksheet and questioned it?

I don't remember exactly how long I did The Work on my mother. I think it was for about a year. I haven't filled in a Worksheet since then, because I haven't had a problem. I don't remember if any stressful thoughts arose in the years following, but if they did, they dissolved in the light of the wordless questioning that lived inside me. As they arose, they were met with the questioning and were instantly seen for what they were and, in that realization, undone. But if I had a problem today, I wouldn't hesitate to bring it to life on paper, and I would have no trouble meditating on the exquisite illusion of life that it brings to mind. Mind is not a danger. It's only when we attach to mind that the false world of suffering appears.

The mind's only
way out is in.

15

COMING HOME

The Buddha said, "Subhuti, suppose there is a good man or woman who in the morning does as many charitable acts as there are grains of sand in the Ganges, and does that many charitable acts at noon, and again in the evening, and keeps doing this for hundreds of thousands of millions of billions of eons. Now suppose there is someone who hears this sutra with an open mind and lets it penetrate into his or her heart. The merit of the second person would be far greater than the merit of the first. How much greater is the merit of someone who wholeheartedly embodies this sutra and lives it!

"We can summarize it like this: This sutra has inconceivable, inestimable, limitless value, and the Buddha teaches it to those who are mature enough to understand. Those who are able to realize what it is teaching, and then embody it and live it, stand in the same place as the Buddha, and take the Buddha's enlightenment wherever they go. They are worthy of the deepest respect from all beings in the universe."

Every thought leads back to the beginning of thought. It doesn't matter what the thought is; however deluded it may be, the Buddha recognizes it and guides it back to inquiry, as if he were guiding it into a vast funnel, and every thought swirls down through the funnel and reaches the simplest element and dissolves.

In the process, the Buddha repeats himself over and over. It's necessary for him to repeat himself. As long as there is any apparent suffering in the world, he helps people dissolve it by whatever means he can. Suffering is what creates buddhas. Where there's no suffering, there's no buddha, because there's no reason for a buddha to exist. To his own mind, in fact, the Buddha doesn't exist. Buddha-mind is simply the mind that has fallen back into itself. It's the mind that has called itself back to its true nature.

In these passages where the Buddha repeats himself, he's like a mother standing in front of her house and calling her child home to dinner. "Come home! It's time for dinner! Come in, come in!" The child is out on the street, distracted; maybe he has fallen down, scraped his knees, gotten into a fight; maybe he's lost in the dark, he's frightened, and then, in the distance, he hears the mother's voice calling his name, and he knows where to go. The Buddha is like that mother, standing there for her child, calling the child's name over and over. He remembers when he himself was lost in the darkness, and he is unmoving in his understanding of what it is to be lost and what it is to be found. That calling is always there for the one who listens. The Buddha would wait a thousand years for one lost child.

The nature of the questioned mind is kindness, and it has absolutely no quarrel with itself. When something appears that is unlike its nature—a negative concept, any thought of defense or rejection or resistance—mind splits away from its enlightened self. It has become identified as something unlike itself, and it keeps straining to be what it isn't, what it never can be. The moment it's identified as something other than itself, it gets stuck as a thing, a body, an "I." When it understands its true nature, it becomes an unceasing flow of delight. It watches as it appears to create something, but it never becomes identified as that something. It realizes that there is nothing to have or be. Eventually it realizes that it is the beginning and the end, that it was never born and can never die.

Peace comes by invitation only, the invitation from yourself, and if that's your goal, welcome to inquiry. The great spiritual texts describe the *what*—what it means to be free. The Work is the *how*. It gives you a direct entrance into the awakened mind. Some people spend years trying to figure out what's the matter with them. When you come to The Work, you don't have to figure it out. You already know what's the matter with you: you're believing your stressful thoughts. You don't even have to know *which* thoughts. You just pick the first one that occurs, and *that's* what's the matter with you. And when you question your thoughts, the thing that was the matter with you begins to show up as nothing.

———————————

You say that the Buddha "is unmoving in his understanding of what it is to be lost and what it is to be found." For many years you felt lost. Who found you?

"I" did. Then I questioned even that.

You say, "The nature of the questioned mind is kindness." How do you distinguish between kindness to others and kindness to yourself?

When I do a kindness to you, it's a kindness to myself, and when I do a kindness to myself, it's a kindness to you, even if you never realize it.

*The great spiritual texts
describe the what. The Work
is the how. It gives you a
direct entrance into the
awakened mind.*

16

EVERYTHING HAPPENS
FOR YOU, NOT *TO* YOU

The Buddha said, "Furthermore, Subhuti, if good men and women who hear this sutra truly realize what it is teaching and then embody it and live it, nothing in the world will be able to upset them. Enemies may slander them, friends may turn cold and leave them, but on all occasions their minds will remain undisturbed. Because they no longer entertain the concepts 'self' and 'other,' they can't take anything personally. Thus, their minds are free.

"Billions of eons ago, before the time of the Buddha Dipankara, I served eighty-four thousand millions of billions of buddhas, and I served them with wholehearted devotion. But if, thousands of years from now, someone hears this sutra and truly realizes what it is teaching and then embodies it and lives it, that person's merit will be a hundred billion times greater than the merit I gained when I served all those buddhas. In fact, no number could express how much greater his or her merit would be.

"If I were to be accurate about the merit gained by good men and women thousands of years from now who hear this sutra and truly realize what it is teaching and then embody it and live it, no one would believe me. You should know that the value of this sutra is beyond conception and that its rewards are beyond conception."

Reality unfolds perfectly. Whatever happens is good. I see people and things, and when it comes to me to move toward them or away from them, I move without argument, because I have no believable story about why I shouldn't. It's always perfect. A decision would give me less, always less. So "it" makes its own decision, and I follow. And what I love is that it's always kind. If I had to name the experience in a word, I would call it gratitude—living, breathing gratitude. I am a receiver, and there's nothing I can do to stop grace from coming in.

It's personal and it's not personal. It's personal in that the whole world is me, a mirror image that I am and love. Without it, I'm bodiless. And it's not that I need to look; it's just that looking is such a delight. On the other hand, it's not personal, because I see nothing more than a mirror image. Every movement, every sound, every breath, every molecule, every atom is nothing more than a mirror image. So I don't move, I'm being moved; I don't do, I'm being done; I don't breathe, I'm being breathed; I don't think, I'm being thought. There is no me. There's nothing real about it.

When you realize that there's no such thing as a self or an other, you realize that all human relationships are reflections in the mirror. It's not you that people like or dislike; it's their *stories* of you. They aren't attacking you or leaving you; they're attacking or leaving who they believe you are. What does any of that have to do with you? You're their projection, just as they are yours. Realizing this makes it easy not to be affected by praise or blame.

I love it when people blame me. I learn what I can from their criticism, but I can't ever take it personally. I also love it when they praise me, though I know that they're just praising the person they believe I am. But praise is more like our true nature; blame hurts the blamer. So when people praise me, I feel happy for them. They say, "Oh, Katie, you've changed my life. I'm so grateful," and I hear it as a turnaround. *She* has changed her life, or *he* has changed his life. They give me the credit, but the credit is all theirs. To think that any of it has to do with me is confusion. Their gratitude is pointed toward the me they think I am, but eventually, as they grow more mature in inquiry, it gets pointed back to them, and eventually it gets pointed nowhere at all. It becomes pure gratitude, with no direction.

If someone rejects you, he could only do that because you don't match his beliefs about how he wants the world to be. Only an inflated ego could say that you had anything to do with it. Suppose your hand moved for no reason, and he found that unacceptable—wouldn't it be obvious that it was all his show? If he criticizes you, and you take that personally, *you're* the one who hurt you. The story you impose onto his criticism is where the pain begins. You're arguing with reality, and you lose.

My love is my business; your love is yours. You tell the story that I'm this, or I'm that, and you fall in love with your story. What do I have to do with it? I'm here for your projection. I don't have a choice in that. I am your story, no more and no less. You've never met me. No one has ever met anyone.

If you find internal work exciting, you'll look forward to the worst that can happen, because you won't find a problem that can't be solved from the inside. It's the perfect setup for the end of suffering. And it becomes a mystery why you ever thought there was a problem in your life. You begin to realize that there are no mistakes and that whatever you get is what you need. This is paradise found. Everything you need, and even more than you need, is always supplied to you, in abundance.

Even the subtlest upset is a form of suffering. It doesn't feel natural. Meeting people with understanding feels more like you. So when an annoyed or angry thought appears, can you meet that thought with understanding, through inquiry? When you learn to meet your thoughts with understanding, you can meet *us* with understanding. What could anyone say about you that you haven't already thought? There are no new stressful thoughts—they're all recycled. We're not meeting anything but thoughts. The external is the internal projected. Whether it's your thinking or my thinking, it's the same. Only love has the power to heal.

Whatever people say or do, how can you be upset with them when you know that they're projections of your own mind? When the mind realizes this, there's nothing to project itself *as*. Even the mind is its own theory. There's no one to be upset. There's only mind playing in the apparent world of itself. The Buddha-mind can never be stuck in the nonexistent past or future. So it's impossible that it would ever experience anything but the joy that comes out of that understanding.

The fact is that you've never reacted to someone else. You project meaning onto nothing, and you react to the meaning you yourself have projected. Loneliness comes from an honest place—you're the only one here. There are no humans. You're it. When you question your thoughts, you come to realize that. It's the end of the world—the joyful end of a world that never existed in the first place.

You've said, "The litmus test for self-realization is the constant state of gratitude." Did you ever experience gratitude before your experience of waking up?

One day in February 1986, just before I checked in to the halfway house, when I was in so much mental pain that I didn't believe I could bear one more breath, things came to a head. For no particular reason I started screaming, and I couldn't stop. I couldn't stop screaming and thrashing around on the bed. Paul and Bob, my older son, came in and held me down, to keep me from hurting myself. The suffering got more and more intense; it was beyond what I thought was bearable, with no way out, no end to it. I felt it was beyond what anyone could endure.

They were holding me down, and I was very frightened. They were too—they were panicked—and one of them began making calls to try to find a doctor who would talk to me on the phone. He kept calling different hospitals, different doctors. "What can we do? Will you talk to her? Is there someone there who can talk to her?" They were desperate. Finally, somewhere, in some state, in some city, they found one person who said he would talk to me. He was a psychologist on a psych ward.

They put the phone to my ear, and I experienced love coming from his voice. I felt that he genuinely loved me and wanted to listen. My screams became quieter, and I could hear him. I don't remember what he said; it was probably something like "I hear you. I understand. You must be hurting very badly." But whatever he was saying, it made sense to me. What mattered was where his kindness came from. I knew he couldn't want anything from me; he didn't know me, there were no strings attached, so I trusted what he said. He said I needed help, and the agony shifted a bit.

This was the first time in my life that I ever experienced love. I couldn't get it from my parents, or from my first or second husband, or from my children; I just got it from this simple act of kindness. Today I give others what that man gave me, and each time I do, I receive the original gift again.

Often when I tell this story, tears run down my cheeks. It's the experience of gratitude all over again. When anyone is hurting to the extent that I used to hurt, I know how simple it is to step out of it. And I know that you're what's left of me. So when you say, "Help me," I do what that kind man did. He showed me who I was—who we all are.

"It's not you that people like or dislike; it's their stories of you." Can't this insight become an excuse for not taking a look at yourself? "Oh, she called me selfish," someone might think. "Well, that's not me; it's her story of me. So I don't need to take a look or do anything about it."

Anything can become an excuse for asleepness. If people are believing an insight because they read it in a book, or because it sounds true, or for any reason other than what they themselves have actually realized, it's not an insight; it's just one more defense. You can tell when you're being defensive; a lack of connection makes it obvious. If someone says he doesn't like me, I honestly want to know why, since I realize that in certain respects he may see me more clearly than I see myself—in other words, his story about me may be more accurate than my story about myself. His attitude may grow me. I get to know why he doesn't like the Katie he believes I am, and this puts me in a state of intimacy with him. If I'm not connected and grateful, I'm the one who is off.

You say that realizing we are people's projections makes it easy not to be affected by praise or blame. But isn't it human to be affected by praise? Why shouldn't we just enjoy it?

I do enjoy praise, as I enjoy blame. Blame gives me something to consider. Could they be right? I test what I heard them say, as part of my unending vigilance.

As for praise: when I praise something, I'm showing respect, a sense of gratitude that what I'm praising is so visible in the apparent other. It's an experience of connection, and I love sharing my appreciation with the person I praise. So when someone praises me, I appreciate his state of mind, and I love that he's seen something worthy of praise in what he sees as me. But I can't take his praise personally, even though it may match what I witness in myself.

If you find internal work exciting, you'll look forward to the worst that can happen, because you won't find a problem that can't be solved from the inside.

17

LIFE WITHOUT SEPARATION

Then Subhuti said, "I ask you again, Sir: When sincere men and women seek enlightenment, what should they do and how should they control their minds?"

The Buddha said, "Sincere men and women who seek the truth should control their minds by focusing on one thought only: 'When I attain perfect wisdom, I will liberate all sentient beings and allow them to pass into the eternal peace of Nirvana.' And yet, when vast, uncountable, unthinkable myriads of beings have been liberated, in reality no being has been liberated. Why? Because no one who is a true bodhisattva entertains such concepts as 'self' and 'other.'

"Let me ask you something, Subhuti. When the Buddha was with Dipankara Buddha, did he attain enlightenment?"

"No, Sir. As I understand your teaching, when you were with Dipankara Buddha, you did not attain what is called enlightenment."

"That is correct. In reality, there is no such thing as enlightenment. There is no such state of mind that the Buddha has attained. If there were any such thing, Dipankara Buddha would not have predicted, 'In the future you will become a buddha named Shakyamuni.' It is precisely because there is no such thing as enlightenment that Dipankara Buddha made this prediction.

"Subhuti, those who say that the Buddha has attained enlightenment are mistaken. The enlightenment that the Buddha has attained is neither real nor unreal. That is why the Buddha has said that all things are Buddha things. But 'all things' aren't, in fact, all things. They are only *called* 'all things.'

"If a bodhisattva says, 'I will liberate all sentient beings,' then he or she isn't a true bodhisattva. In reality, there is no separate being that can be called a bodhisattva. There is nothing in the universe in which you can find a self. So if a bodhisattva says, 'I will make the world into a beautiful place,' he or she isn't a true bodhisattva. In reality there is no separate world to make into anything. Only when a bodhisattva realizes that there is no self and no other does the Buddha call that person a true bodhisattva."

Here the Buddha repeats what he said in previous chapters. These chapters make important points that are worth repeating: that the bodhisattva's focus is always on selfless service to others, that there are no others, and that there is no such thing as enlightenment. If you understand these three points, you understand everything. If you understand just one of the points, you understand everything. Each is a different aspect of the same truth.

What the Buddha says may seem confusing, but only because he is so clear. How can you use words that are somethings to describe nothing? How can you describe the world of apparent things when you understand that it doesn't really exist? You can't. You can only point away from any concept the mind would be tempted to land on. And every teaching is a misteaching, because there's really nothing to teach. If you point to an apparent truth, you're pointing to what isn't. But when you point away from what isn't, you point toward loving what is, which leads back to nothing.

You might think that it would be depressing to realize that nothing exists. Actually, it's the opposite: it's thrilling. There's no separation left. There's nothing to be separate *from*. There's just gratitude and laughter.

When I first discovered The Work, I wanted to get as close as I possibly could to understanding the thoughts that the mind was ceaselessly producing. This is the only way to control the uncontrollable mind. I got very still with these thoughts. I met them as a mother would meet her confused child. The child is having a nightmare, but the mother sees that the child is really safe; he's just caught in a frightening dream. So I listened intimately to every thought and loved it as I would love my own child. I wrote down everything the child said about the nightmare, and then I questioned it. I questioned the validity of every thought written down, thought by beloved thought. When the thoughts are met with understanding, through inquiry, the child is able to see what the mother sees: that it's just a dream. And when you wake up, you see that there's no dream, and not even a dreamer.

In those early days, whenever a belief appeared in my mind—the big one was "My mother doesn't love me"—it exploded in the body like an atom bomb. I noticed shaking, contraction, and the apparent annihilation of peace. The belief might also be accompanied by tears and a stiffening of the body. It might have appeared to an onlooker that I was affected from the toes to the top of the head with upset and sadness. But in fact I always continued to experience the same clarity, peace, and joy that had arisen when I woke up on the floor in the half-way house, with no "I" left, no world, and laughter just pouring out of my mouth. The belief that had arisen would always fall away and dissolve in the light of truth. What shook the body was the remnant of the belief, which appeared as an uncomfortable feeling. From this discomfort I automatically knew that the belief wasn't true. Nothing was true. The awareness of this was experienced as glorious humor— glorious, rapturous joy.

I had seen that everything was backward, that my thinking opposed everything that was real. I used to suffer from thoughts like "Paul should be kinder to me" or "The children should listen to me." After questioning these thoughts, I saw that the opposite was true. Paul should *not* be kinder to me; the children should *not* listen to me. It was all so simple: the truth was that he was as kind as he could be, given what he was thinking, and that they listened to me as much as they were capable of doing. All of these "shoulds" were just thoughts. They had nothing to do with reality. Everything was perfect, just the way it was.

On the floor of the halfway house, I instantly became a lover of what is. I noticed that this felt more natural, more peaceful. I understood that it was I who should be kinder, I who should listen. This understanding became what I later called the turnaround. It's a way of living that is stress-free. When you understand this, it's the end of suffering. The dream becomes a happy one.

I saw that for the belief "My family should love and understand me" the turnaround is "I should love and understand myself." Why had I ever thought that it was *their* job? That was crazy! Let it begin with *me*. Until I can do it, let me give the world a break. I looked at the belief again and saw another turnaround: "I should love and understand my family." It was a humbling experience to realize this. For all my life, understanding is what I had expected from friends and family, and when I didn't get it I was hurt or resentful or furious or unsettled in some way. I had always tried to get understanding and recognition from the people I knew. I now noticed that this was hopeless and left me feeling disconnected and empty. Now I understood why they didn't love and understand me. Look how I had treated them!

I woke up turned around. I was a walking turnaround. The thought would arise "It's too hot," and I'd go "Pfft! That's not true. It's not too hot. That has to be truer, because in reality it's as hot as it is." I experienced the cause and effect of believing an untrue thought. Because I came from such confusion and loathing, some of the profoundest inquiries that I experienced were from inquiry on thoughts from my old world. And all I experienced now, after questioning them, was their opposites. "The world is a terrible place," for example, became "The world is a beautiful place." The accuracy of these turnarounds was so obvious that I would often burst into laughter. I didn't have to make the world into a beautiful place at all. It was already everything I could ever have wanted. Nothing was required of me but to notice.

This is so important to understand. People think that enlightenment must be some kind of mystical, transcendent experience. But it's not. It's as close to you as your own most troubling thought. When you believe a thought that argues with reality, you're confused. When you question the thought and see that it's not true, you're enlightened to it, you're liberated from it. You're as free as the Buddha in that moment. And then the next stressful thought comes along, and you either believe it or question it. It's your next opportunity to get enlightened. Life is as simple as that.

Why do you say that the realization that nothing exists is thrilling?

It's thrilling to watch the ego dance, no matter where it goes—left, right, up, down, all around—none of it valid, none of it real. You just can't help delighting in its antics, its brilliant attempts to be something that has never been, is not, and never can be.

You say that in the early days, beliefs would explode in your body like atom bombs, but that you continued to experience peace. Were you observing the explosions from inside your body? From outside it? Where was the peace, amid all the uproar?

It was like being visited by a world that had been extinguished billions of years ago and feeling one of its ancient convulsions. I noticed it. I welcomed it. It was something/nothing, real/unreal. I didn't feel it from the inside or outside. There *was* no inside or outside. The peace was at the center of everything. And not even what was observing could exist. I was in a state of fascinated rapture, continually loving what is—in other words, continually loving what isn't.

You invite people to realize that a turnaround may be as true as or truer than the original stressful thought. But elsewhere you say that nothing is true. If a turnaround isn't ultimately true, what good is it to recognize that it's as true as the original thought?

Realizing that a turnaround is at least as true as the thought that is causing your suffering is a liberating experience. It gives consciousness an opportunity to expand, rather than being stuck in one limited reality. The nature of mind is infinite. When mind gets caught in the I-know position, it's as if someone has bound it in chains and thrown away the key. It's stuck in the illusion of time and space and suffering. But when you question a thought that your whole identity is invested in and then realize that its opposite is at least as true as the original thought, you can step outside that thought and look at your life with a new clarity and freedom.

*Enlightenment is as
close to you as your own
most troubling thought.*

18

FREEDOM IS NOT BELIEVING YOUR THOUGHTS

The Buddha said, "If each of the grains of sand in the Ganges River were its own Ganges River and there were a world for each grain of sand in all these Ganges Rivers, would these worlds be many?"

"Very many, Sir."

The Buddha said, "However many beings there are in all these worlds, Subhuti, the Buddha knows how their minds function, and he knows the quality of their thoughts. But mind is not in fact mind; it is only *called* 'mind.' Why is that? Because past mind is ungraspable, future mind is ungraspable, and present mind is ungraspable."

When you imagine any scenario, that is your world in the moment, and there are many worlds within the illusion of time—as many worlds as there are grains of sand in the Ganges or stars in the sky. You think that you know what other people are thinking, but it's just you thinking. Even if they tell you what they're thinking, that doesn't mean it's so. You hear and see only from the perspective of your own world. In all possible worlds, the Buddha knows how people's minds function, because he knows that they don't function at all. That is Buddha consciousness.

When I do The Work with people, I help them clarify their minds by seeing that mind doesn't exist and world doesn't exist. The ultimate clarity is to realize that there are no thoughts and you're not the one thinking them.

It's easy to see how the mind functions: no thought is true. So it's easy for me to guide people to nothing, if they're open to that, because that's where they are in the first place. I just guide them to unravel everything they think. I don't move; they're the ones who move. I ask questions and occasionally point to nothing. I help them notice that the thoughts and images in their minds are pure imagination. However substantial a belief appears to be, there's no substance to it, and I point them to that no-substance. When the mind is tempted to land on any thought, it's because it believes that thought. And to believe a thought is to exist in an imaginary world, however real it may seem. So I guide people out of their imaginary worlds, into Buddha-mind—in other words, into nothing. You can't describe Buddha-mind. You can only point to it with words such as *serene, joyous, whole.*

People sometimes compare thoughts to clouds that come and go in the sky of the mind. But if we want to be really accurate, nothing comes and nothing goes. Something would have to exist before it could come or go. It may seem radical to say that not even thoughts exist, until you begin to notice that every thought is in the past. Even the present moment is the past as soon as you notice it, and that is obvious to anyone who has spent much time in meditation. So how is a thought possible? It's not. Just because you believe that thoughts exist doesn't mean that they do. The imagined past is your only proof that there is even a "you" who thought the thought.

The Buddha ends this chapter with the essence of it all: "Past mind is ungraspable, future mind is ungraspable, and present mind is ungraspable." That's it. Period. The end.

I love the elegance of the Buddha's statement. It's so crisp and clear. It's the complete truth, and the best news there could ever be.

———————

You say that that there are no thoughts. Do you mean that thoughts happen so quickly that by the time we're aware of them they're already in the past?

When I say that thoughts are already in the past, it's with the basic understanding that there is no past. What past? Where's your proof? Only another thought.

Why is the truth that past mind, future mind, and present mind are all ungraspable the best news there could ever be?

Because that is mind realized. The mind delights in itself as the creator of everything, which is nothing. It experiences itself as pure awareness, with nothing outside it and nothing inside, and no "it" that is doing the awareness.

To believe a thought is to exist in an imaginary world, however real it may seem.

The Work in Action

_____

"Sophia Doesn't Listen"

PHILLIPE: Hello, Katie. I have been living for a while believing that I am the creator of my own problems. So it was hard for me to find a person to judge. And I have to say also that it has not been an easy life with that belief. But then I just wrote a Judge-Your-Neighbor Worksheet on my daughter, and I am impressed with how much I'm affected by it. And I was wondering if I can do The Work with you on that.

KATIE: Good, sweetheart. Let's do The Work.

PHILLIPE: Thanks.

KATIE: So, you're in perfect peace, and then your daughter wants something, and you're upset. That's a Worksheet. If you're not experiencing peace, it belongs on a Worksheet. All war belongs on paper. What did you write?

PHILLIPE [*reading from his Worksheet*]: *I'm angry at Sophia—she's my daughter—because she doesn't listen to me and she doesn't do what I tell her to do.*

KATIE: What's the situation?

PHILLIPE: I'm picking her up from day care. I want her to get into her car seat, and she doesn't want to.

KATIE: How old is she?

PHILLIPE: Almost two.

KATIE: "She doesn't listen to you"—is it true? [*To the audience*] Do you all see Sophia in your mind's eye? He's putting her in the car seat. How many of you see that? [*Almost all the people in the audience raise their hands.*] Okay, now we're all in the same dream. So let's do this inquiry as we witness that moment in time. [*To Phillipe*] "Sophia doesn't listen to you"—is it true? Can you absolutely know it's true that she's not listening to you?

PHILLIPE: No, I can't.

KATIE: The answer to the first or second question is one syllable long. We meditate on the first two questions until a one-syllable answer is shown to us. It's either yes or no.

PHILLIPE: No.

KATIE: "No." Do you feel it? If the answer is just one word, without elaboration, you have to experience it on a deeper level. Just sit with the question, meditate on that situation, and your mind will show you the yes or no. It will show you through images. Everything you need in order to find the truth is given to you in that silence.

PHILLIPE: When I said no, I could see that she actually does listen to me. And it felt very liberating, because I really believed that she wasn't listening to me. She doesn't get into the car seat, but she does listen.

KATIE: That's a powerful insight.

PHILLIPE: It *is* powerful. For almost two years I've believed that she hasn't been listening to me.

KATIE: Now question three. Notice how you react when you believe the thought "Sophia doesn't listen to me." How do you treat her, how do you treat yourself, when you believe that thought?

PHILLIPE: It's coming to my mind now that for a while she has been shouting and screaming a lot.

KATIE: She's been listening. But what is she listening to when you believe she isn't listening? How do *you* react? How do you treat her? Close your eyes and describe it. [*To the audience*] And all of you, witness *your* reactions when you believe that someone isn't listening to you.

PHILLIPE: I get really frustrated, and I feel tense in my stomach. I start making up stories of why it's good to go home. So I lie to her. I literally lie to her. And when I get more upset, I force her to get into the car seat. I use physical force to get her into the car seat.

KATIE: Now in that situation, as you force her into the car seat, who would you be without the thought "She doesn't listen to me." And notice that you're still putting her into the car seat, though you're not believing that thought.

PHILLIPE: What I notice is that she just wants to wander around. She wants to take my hand instead of going to the car. To walk around a little bit outside her school. That's all she wants.

KATIE: And who would you be if you didn't believe the thought "She doesn't listen to me"?

PHILLIPE: I'd be gentler. I'd be patient. I'd be speaking to her kindly as I put her into the car seat.

KATIE: "Sophia doesn't listen to me"—turn it around. "I . . ."

PHILLIPE: I don't listen to Sophia.

KATIE: But you're listening now. It's all there in the image. It doesn't cheat or put you into denial. It shows you what you may have missed.

PHILLIPE: Now I can't wait to see her again!

KATIE: Yes. It becomes so exciting to start over, to listen to a different daughter, your real daughter, not the one you imagined her to be. Without your story, without the lie that she doesn't listen to you, you feel connected to her. "She doesn't listen to me." Can you find another turnaround?

PHILLIPE: She does listen to me. Yes, she was listening. She didn't want to get into the car seat. She heard what I wanted, and let me know that that wasn't what she wanted.

KATIE: And another turnaround?

PHILLIPE: I don't listen to myself.

KATIE: You were believing your thought, and you didn't ask yourself, "Is it true?" You were like a two-year-old child, like a baby. You believed your thoughts, and you lost control, like Sophia not wanting to get into her car seat. You started to force things. We teach our children at an early age, and then we wonder why they are so like us.

PHILLIPE: Also, I've been experiencing this for some time now, and I knew I had to do something about it. So I wasn't listening to myself.

KATIE: Good one. Let's move on to the second part of your statement. "She doesn't do what you tell her to do"—is it true? In that situation?

PHILLIPE: Yes. In that situation, yes.

KATIE: "She doesn't do what you tell her to do"—can you absolutely know that it's true?

PHILLIPE: Yes.

KATIE: And how do you react, what happens, when you believe the thought "She doesn't do what you tell her to do"?

PHILLIPE: I feel powerless. It's funny, because when I'm listening, I feel that nobody listens to *me*. In the whole world. So I project that onto her. And I get louder. I shout, just to get her attention.

KATIE: So in that situation, close your eyes and witness. Who would you be without the thought "She doesn't do what I tell her to do"?

PHILLIPE: I'm sorry, I'm still stuck on the last one. I was being a baby myself—a really needy baby. [*Pause*] Okay. I'm ready now.

KATIE: I love how introspective you are. When this Work found me, I used to sit in one question the way you're doing. Sometimes I would sit in it for days. And my daughter would keep showing me how I reacted, prior to The Work, when I believed the thought, and who I was without it.

PHILLIPE: I'm realizing the gifts I haven't been open to receiving from her. When she cries, when she shouts.

KATIE: Yes, they take on our ways of getting what they want, our ways of communicating. So "Sophia doesn't do what I tell her to do"—turn it around.

PHILLIPE: Sophia does do what I tell her to do. [*He closes his eyes and is silent for a minute.*]

KATIE [*to the audience*]: If these turnarounds don't make sense to you, remember this man's example of meditating on the situation and being enlightened to what is and what isn't true, what is suffering and what is peace. Remember how he is going inside himself to receive the answer. We meditate on turnarounds to see what we couldn't see when we were believing what we believed in that situation.

PHILLIPE [*opening his eyes*]: More often than not, I tell her how proud I am of her, because she can understand very complicated orders and perform them. She does most of what I ask her to do. I don't know if this is part of The Work, but it's coming to my mind.

KATIE: Whatever you find, whatever is shown to you in that meditative state, is okay. The Work is simply the questions. Whatever arises you can look at. "Sophia does do what I tell her to do." Give me an example of how this is true.

PHILLIPE: Actually, she does do what I tell her to do, except when it's silly, when it doesn't make sense. Then she doesn't do it. Like getting into her car seat.

KATIE: Sweetheart, you're catching this while she's so young—while you're so young. In that situation, there were two two-year-olds. As you become aware, she becomes aware. So she does do what you tell her to do. How do you get your daughter into a car seat? Eventually you may notice that you do it the way your father did. That's how you get things done. Or there's another way. You can do it forcefully or with awareness. In anger or in peace.

PHILLIPE: I'm having all these thoughts about how The Work is the end of war. And I'm thinking that if, now that I have more tools to put her into her car seat . . .

KATIE: Tools or clarity?

PHILLIPE: Clarity.

KATIE: Wisdom. Your own.

PHILLIPE: If people do The Work, more kids will be able to get into their car seats, and that can save them.

KATIE: We learn the old paradigm from you, or the new paradigm from you. A world with or without war. It's up to you. And Sophia will give you every opportunity to find the way to peace as she grows up. She will grow you up as she grows. That's what Sophia's all about. She's here to enlighten you. "Sophia doesn't do what I tell her to do." Another turnaround? "I don't . . ."

PHILLIPE: I don't do what Sophia tells me to do. I don't take her by the hand and take a little walk with her before we go to the car.

KATIE: In that situation. Close your eyes, sweetheart. Now, without your story, put her into the car seat, even though she doesn't want to go. Get really connected with her. She doesn't want to get in. Stay connected. Walk with her first, if that comes to you. Get her into the car seat. Look into her eyes. That sweet little face. Fall in love. Without the thoughts you're believing, are you okay?

PHILLIPE: Yeah.

KATIE: Without your thoughts, is she okay?

PHILLIPE: We're both okay.

KATIE: Always. Sometimes you'll have time to walk. Sometimes you won't. Either way, you'll be awake. It will be a win-win situation. But you don't have to disconnect with her. And if you do disconnect, you know how to identify and question the thoughts that are the problem. Let's move to statement 2.

PHILLIPE: *I want Sophia to listen to me and be happy about it.*

KATIE: You want her to be happy about being forced into a car seat after she's been in school all day? Now, look at her little face. Look at her. Look at her. She's pushing away from the car seat. You want her to be happy about that. Is it even possible?

PHILLIPE: No. And the car is too hot.

KATIE: And how do you react when you believe the thought "I want her to be happy about all this"?

PHILLIPE: I get angry at her. And in my mind I blame her for being such a crybaby. And in my mind I say, "What's wrong with you?"

KATIE: So now you're teaching her there's something wrong with her. And we wonder why they think there's something wrong with them!

PHILLIPE: I compare her with other kids. That's what I'm teaching her.

KATIE: So when you put her in the car seat, you're comparing her with other kids in your head. Are those real children, or is that imagination?

PHILLIPE: That's only a little information about the few times I saw babies not crying.

KATIE: And is that a real baby in your head, or imagination?

PHILLIPE: It's imagination.

KATIE: So if it's imagined, it's really nothing. I just want you to realize you're comparing your baby with an image in your head—in other words, with nothing. That's the powerful ego dream-world you're up against. So "you want her to be happy about it." Who would you be without the thought "I want her to be happy" about being forced into the car seat in a hot car?

PHILLIPE: Without the thought, I see myself looking forward to her reaction of what she likes and what she doesn't. Her personality. Who she is.

KATIE: You'd just be connected with her. No separation. No confusing her with those images of dreamed-up babies in your head. "I want her to be happy about it"—turn it around.

PHILLIPE: I don't want her to be happy about it. Because I wouldn't like her to get used to something that isn't right for her, like a hot car.

KATIE: "I don't want her to be happy about it." Any other examples of why this is true?

PHILLIPE: Well, in that situation I don't want her to be happy about it because the alternative is to walk with me hand in hand, which I love to do with her.

KATIE: I have another example. Would you like to hear it?

PHILLIPE: Of course.

KATIE: When you're not happy, can you make yourself happy in that moment?

PHILLIPE: No.

KATIE: That's what you're expecting of her.

PHILLIPE: Yeah. Yeah. I'm expecting her to go from crying to being really happy and saying, "Yes, Daddy, I'll do it in a second."

KATIE: "Great idea, Daddy. I'm so happy." Impossible. And how do you react when you believe the thought "I want her to be happy about it"? Again, we teach them that there's something wrong with them when they're not happy. And then they learn to pretend. They learn how to fake happiness. And at some point, we never see our daughters again, even though we live with them. They think, "Here comes Dad. He'll be upset if I'm not happy."

PHILLIPE: It's like it's okay to get into the car seat when you don't want to, but it's not okay to want to walk with your dad. That sounds awful to me.

KATIE: It's no fun to walk with dad if you're not happy. It really flows into our relationships, doesn't it? It runs so deep.

PHILLIPE: I can't believe all this is coming from just one thought about a car seat.

KATIE: And it's so far reaching. Just like when your daughter is unhappy, when your wife is unhappy you believe the thought "She should be happy." It flows from your daughter to your wife to your parents to the world. Eventually, though, if inquiry becomes your practice, you don't expect anyone to be happy, and that leaves you happy. Your happiness isn't dependent on anyone else. And in your presence, we have permission to be authentic, because you're a safe place. Let's move on to statement 3.

PHILLIPE: *Sophia should think about the needs of the family.*

KATIE [*to the audience*]: How many of you have put these thoughts on your toddlers? [*Many people raise their hands.*] It's what the mind does, sometimes. Our reactions are caused not by our children, but by what we're believing about our children, and we think we're justified. That's how powerful the dream-world is, the world of the ego. When we're believing our thoughts, we're angry even at our innocent children. And then we're angry at ourselves for being angry at a toddler. For any of you who get angry, it's as elementary as this. War can't be justified by anything but an ego. The ego depends on that illusion. "She should think about the needs of the family"—how do you react when you believe that thought?

PHILLIPE: I treat her like she's selfish. And I really think that it's never going to change.

KATIE: And how do other parents react when they believe this thought? Some people become child abusers. We hit babies. We lock them in closets. We do horrible things, and then we hate ourselves. So, how do we react when we believe these thoughts? Everything from minor irritation to violence. And it's almost always followed by guilt. Now look at that little pumpkin without believing that she should think about the needs of the family. Who would you be without that thought?

PHILLIPE: I would understand that she's just a baby. She's doing what she's supposed to be doing. Sometimes she's happy and sometimes not.

KATIE: And you don't even know that she's unhappy. You don't even know if she has an identity or not.

PHILLIPE: I know nothing about it.

KATIE: You haven't met her yet. But you're beginning to meet her now.

PHILLIPE: A little bit.

KATIE: So, the next one. Statement 4.

PHILLIPE: *I need Sophia to be more relaxed and to cooperate.*

KATIE: Have you ever had that thought about your wife or about someone you have lived with?

PHILLIPE: Pretty much everybody I've ever met.

KATIE: "You need Sophia to be relaxed and cooperate"—is it true?

PHILLIPE: No.

KATIE [*measuring with her hands*]: She's this big. And you're *that* big. You can get her into that car seat happily. And on your second statement—"I want her to be happy"—we didn't do the turnaround "I want me to be happy." I want *me* to listen to myself and be happy about it, in that situation with Sophia. Right? It's not so easy.

PHILLIPE: It's true, though.

KATIE: You were a believer then, and you have a more questioned mind now. It's how to be happy with every thought you think, every thought that brings war into your life. "I need Sophia to be more relaxed and to cooperate"—turn it around.

PHILLIPE: I need me to be more relaxed and to cooperate. Of course.

KATIE: And there's another turnaround, a turnaround to the exact opposite. Can you find it?

PHILLIPE: I *don't* need her to be more relaxed and cooperate.

KATIE: How *could* she?

PHILLIPE: Yes, I see that. She's learning everything from me.

KATIE: She's a mirror image of the way you see life. Let's move to statement 5.

PHILLIPE: *Sophia is a stupid baby, unreasonable, capricious, and a princess.*

KATIE: Turn it around. "In that moment, I am . . ."

PHILLIPE: In that moment, I am a stupid baby, unreasonable, capricious, and a princess. I see especially the last one. I'm like a princess, who says, "Okay, now you do this, and you do that. Get into your car seat. Be happy. That's my command."

KATIE: A dictator. Can you find a turnaround to the opposite? "Sophia is . . ." What's the opposite of stupid?

PHILLIPE: An awesome baby.

KATIE: The opposite of unreasonable?

PHILLIPE: Smart.

KATIE: What about reasonable?

PHILLIPE: Reasonable.

KATIE: In that situation, she's reasonable.

PHILLIPE: Thanks for that.

KATIE: And statement 6—let's move to that.

PHILLIPE: *I don't ever want to lose my patience or feel a desire to slap her.*

KATIE: "I'm willing . . ."

PHILLIPE: I'm willing to lose my patience and to feel a desire to slap her.

KATIE: Yes, sweetheart. It could happen again. There are thoughts in your head, and when you believe them, you cause violence. And even if it's just raising your voice to someone you love, inside you it feels like violence. So "I look forward to . . ."

PHILLIPE: I look forward to losing my patience and to feeling a desire to slap her.

KATIE: You can look forward to it because that kind of desire is so crazy that it wakes you up to your own deluded state of mind. The Work is preventive medicine. And I love that you've found it.

PHILLIPE: Thank you so much.

KATIE: You're very welcome.

19

INCONCEIVABLE WEALTH

The Buddha said, "Let me ask you something, Subhuti. If someone filled a billion worlds with inconceivable wealth and then gave it all away in support of charitable causes, would the merit gained by this person be great?"

"Extremely great, Sir."

The Buddha said, "It would indeed. But if this merit were real, the Buddha would not have called it 'great.' It is because this merit doesn't exist that the Buddha calls it 'great.'"

Every time I give something away, what comes back to me is freedom. I allow the whole world to enter the space that had been filled by my possessions. When I gave away possessing, I gained the whole world. I saw that there was nothing to possess in the first place, so everything was mine. And even though I appear to own things today, that can never be. Possessing is a state of mind. You only need to watch a building burn to understand that, or the burial of someone you love. Once you understand it, you notice that everything is yours, and it always has been. When I drive through a neighborhood and see a man watering his lawn, I know that it's my lawn, it's my house, it's my friend, though we've never met. I know him. He's taking care of my world. He's doing what's necessary. There's merit in all things. There's merit in every moment. There's not even a need to wake up to it, since it is what it is, whether we notice it or not.

I identify with the person the Buddha is talking about here, the man or woman of inconceivable wealth, the richest possible person in all possible universes, who gives everything away. Wealth is a state of mind; if anything is held back, it's not true wealth. True wealth, the apparently meritorious state of mind, gives everything because it gives itself. It *can't* hold back. When the mind matches the heart (my name for our natural wisdom), it doesn't discern right from wrong; it's completely right with itself, always. It's the song of the self, the song of our true nature. I never have to go out of my way to think, "Who needs this?" That's a task I would never think of taking on. My abundance is so great that it can never be spent—not even a fraction of it. Every time I spend it, it multiplies again. It's completely self-sustaining. It's a well that never runs dry. It's fun to be the richest person in the universe, because you're completely at leisure, always. Your wealth can never diminish, and you don't have to do anything for it or with it. You're simply a conduit.

It's equally wonderful to be the poorest person in the universe. I own nothing, I have nothing, I am nothing, and that leaves me with everything. What I give away isn't mine. The well never stops flowing. It pours out whether or not a need is expressed.

In 1997 a couple came with their young children to see my little one-bedroom guesthouse, which I was selling. When they looked at the guesthouse, they knew it wasn't what they wanted. But as the conversation continued in my own house, which was a lot bigger, the woman turned to her husband and said, "I'd do anything to own a house like this, wouldn't you?" They laughed and sighed, then she turned to me, looked me straight in the eyes, and said with a smile, "Would you give us your house?"

I said, "Yes."

"Are you kidding?" she said.

"No."

So I gave them the house I was living in. They were amazed, and so grateful. As they were moving in, they said that they loved my dog, so I gave them the dog too.

At no time in this whole transaction did I think that I was doing something generous. The house was theirs, obviously, as soon as they asked; it was no longer mine to give. They loved it so much that I would have been a fool not to give it to them. They belonged there. I was simply recognizing the fact. There was no decision to make. And this was true about my dog as well. They obviously loved him. Roxann, my youngest, had moved out of the house many years before, and I knew that the dog would be happy to have young children to play with.

Abundance isn't a word about yesterday or tomorrow. It's recognized now, lived now, given now. It doesn't ever stop; it just keeps pouring itself out. Once you understand this, all striving falls away. You need only notice and let the giving happen through you, excited to see where it will go next, always knowing that you'll never run out of what's needed.

You've said that you always found it easy to make money. Have you always felt wealthy?

Before 1986, absolutely not. Wealth is freedom of mind. Making money was easy for me even when I was ten or eleven and sold Christmas, birthday, and holiday cards. In my twenties and thirties I made a lot of money, but I felt the opposite of wealthy. Though I owned several businesses, a wonderful house, other real estate, cars, a boat, etc., I never trusted that I was going to have enough money to support it all.

After 1986, there was nothing that needed wealth, because I realized that everything belongs to me, so there is never a reason to own anything. Other people are taking care of it for me and being generous for me or not, and whether they're keeping it or giving it, it's all as it should be, nothing out of order, everything a gift.

When you gave away your house, how did Paul react?

At first he went nuts. He was used to my strange actions by then, but he considered this "a doozy." According to him, our whole world was tied up in that house. But after a while, he calmed down and signed the papers. He must have trusted me in this, in spite of what he was believing.

Every time I give something away, what comes back to me is freedom.

20

THE PERFECT BODY

The Buddha said, "Let me ask you something, Subhuti. Can the Buddha be perceived by his perfect body?"

Subhuti said, "No, Sir. The Buddha cannot be perceived by his perfect body. The Buddha has said that a perfect body is not a perfect body. It is only *called* 'a perfect body.'"

"Can the Buddha be perceived by any special Identifying characteristics?"

"No, Sir. The Buddha cannot be perceived by any special identifying characteristics. The Buddha has said that any special characteristics are not special characteristics. They are only *called* 'special characteristics.'"

Everyone is the Buddha. Everyone has the perfect body. If you weren't able to compare your body to any other, what could possibly be lacking? Without the mind's comparison, no one can be too fat or too thin. That's not possible; it's a myth. Comparison keeps you from the awareness of what is. You could weigh five hundred pounds, you could be dying of cancer, and still you would have the perfect body, the one that you need in order to be exactly who you are in this moment.

People sometimes use The Work with the motive of healing their bodies. They don't understand that sanity is the cure, and that's not up to the body. Ultimately the body's not going to make it. This is very good news. It's over, forget it, let's work with cause. If this body story were true, it would mean that no fat person could ever be self-realized, no one in a wheelchair, no one old or sick, no one who's not beautiful. That would leave out practically the whole human race! Under this theory, none of us would have a chance for freedom. People think they need to get their life perfect first, and *then* they'll have peace. Can we just do it from here, now?

I suggest that you not do The Work with the motive of healing your body. Go in for the love of truth. Heal your mind. Meet your stressful thoughts with understanding. You may spend years eating the right food, exercising every day, and getting your body in optimal shape, and then a truck hits you in the crosswalk. Can you be happy right now?—not tomorrow, not in ten minutes? I use the word *happy* to mean the natural state of peace and clarity. That's what The Work gives us.

Bodies don't crave, don't want, don't know, don't care, don't love, don't hate, don't get hungry or thirsty. The body only reflects what the mind attaches to. There are no physical addictions, only mental ones. Body follows mind; it doesn't have a choice. (Actually it all happens simultaneously, but as long as we seem to be living in a world of duality, let's say that body follows mind.)

When the mind is at peace, it projects the body as perfect, even on its way to the hospital in an ambulance, in the midst of a heart attack. There's no fear of anything that may happen. Fear isn't possible for the sane mind. It loves every moment of what might be its last trip identified as a this or a that, in an ambulance or alone. It's no longer at war with reality.

One day in 1986, a few months after my experience on the attic floor of the halfway house, I was sitting on a couch, and when I tried to get up, I couldn't move. My legs were paralyzed. It was as if they had nothing to do with me. I remember putting my hands on them and talking to them as I would to dear old friends. "Oh sweethearts," I said, "you've carried me for so many years without any demands. You don't ever have to move for me again. Not ever." I felt an inexpressible gratitude that they had brought me that far. And I just sat there with them and waited, without any expectations, to see what they would do. About forty-five minutes later, they came back to life at a level that I had never experienced before. They seemed to have more strength and vitality than they'd had even when I was a child. It was as if they had just been born into a new life as if love was so attractive that they would move beyond themselves to join it.

The clear mind understands that the body is not personal. It can't cause any problem; mind's identification with the body is what causes the confusion and suffering. Identified mind fears bodilessness. It doesn't know how to be homeless, selfless, apparently lost forever. It isn't realized enough to let go, and when it has a rare moment of no identification, it scares itself small again and doesn't know how to regain its freedom.

The Work is one way the mind can lose its grip safely as it awakens to reality. Mind is limited when it thinks that the body it identifies as is less than perfect. It sees the body and realizes that it's dying, and it panics over its thoughts of what it would be without any identification at all. It doesn't realize that the identification was false to begin with. How can mind be body? How can it live or die? As long as it thinks it is capable of living or dying, it's stuck in an illusion.

People are afraid to die. They think they don't know how. But the truth is that everyone knows how to die. We do it perfectly every night of our lives. When you're exhausted, and for all you know you're never going to see daylight again, would you rather go to sleep or stay awake? No contest. We take ourselves to that obliteration every night.

And without sleep, we don't feel right; we may even go crazy from sleep deprivation. What do we wake up to? Mind. Mind wakes up to mind. If we love what we think, we love sleeping (the nothing) as much as we love waking (the something).

To identify as a body, as a "you," is such a delusional state of mind that with it comes arrogance. If mind believes that it is what it's not, then it has to imagine that everything it projects is real. And in that arrogance, it thinks it has to preserve what can never be preserved. If mind had a choice, why would it identify as a body and live under the threat of death? Wouldn't it want to understand how without any identification it is apparently resurrected in the joy of its own bodiless, infinite being?

My heart, for example, is always perfect, because I never believe that it's mine. Whether it's beating strongly or blasting into oblivion, it's as it should be. Even if it were having an attack, it would be perfect for that moment. If you argue with what's happening when you're having a heart attack, you'll have it with a lot of fear. But without a story, you can experience a heart attack in peace. A heart attack can even be exciting.

It's 1999, and I'm driving home to 35th Street in Manhattan Beach from Peet's Coffee. The radio is playing music I love, and as I listen, a pain shoots through my chest and arm. It's excruciating and thrilling at the same time. I am fascinated. The traffic is heavy. I look for a parking place, then pull over. I see everything in slow motion: the sky, the trees, the buildings, my hands on the wheel. It's a beautiful day. Is this how she dies? Is this the end of the story? I don't want to miss any of it—not one moment of what could be the final scene. Sky, buildings, asphalt, hands, wheel, silence. What grace! And as the joy continues to fill me, the pain begins to subside. It goes back to where it came from, and I laugh out loud at the way of it. It's as good that the story continues as that it ends. I love being present enough not to miss one moment, one breath, of this beautiful apparent life.

You almost died in February 2014. What was that experience like?

In my *doctor's* opinion I almost died—not in mine. I had acute pneumonia and jaundice and liver failure and kidney failure. Alison Garb, my doctor and friend, put me in the emergency room and called in three specialists for the organs that were failing, and for seven days they were all unable to stop the shutting down. It was a natural process, like a sunset: so beautiful.

At one point Ali said to Stephen, "This is really serious. I'm alarmed. We might lose her." Then she decided to try one last procedure, on the lungs. With Stephen standing at the bedside, she said to me, "Your heart might stop during the procedure. We need your permission to resuscitate you. Is that what you want?" I didn't answer, since I could find no preference for life or death. Actually, I thought she was kidding. Then I realized that she really believed I could die, and so as not to confuse her, I let Stephen answer. He told her that *he* would supply the preference: she was to resuscitate me, as long as there was no major brain damage. That was fine with me. I went into the procedure with no preference and no drama. For me there was nothing serious in the whole experience. All of it was mind-play.

Ultimately the body's not going to make it. This is very good news.

21

NOTHING TO LOSE

The Buddha said, "Subhuti, don't ever think that the Buddha has something to teach. If someone says that the Buddha has anything to teach, he is slandering the Buddha; he doesn't understand what the Buddha is teaching. In teaching the truth, there is no truth that can be taught. That's why it is called 'teaching the truth.'"

Subhuti said, "Sir, thousands of years from now will there be beings who gain confidence when they hear these words of yours?"

The Buddha said, "The beings who gain confidence aren't beings, nor are they non-beings. The Buddha has taught that all beings aren't really beings. They are only *called* 'beings.'"

One of my favorite expressions is "I have nothing to lose." Nothing belongs to me, and I experience that as freedom. That said, as long as something is in my care I am an excellent caretaker. I want it to be as pristine as possible, because you may be the one it's passed on to, and I project that you'll love it as much as I do.

How can I have anything? It's not possible. What do I have to lose but my illusions? When mind is no longer fearful of itself, that's the end of separation. Eventually it comes to understand that it can possess nothing, not even its own self.

The only thing worth learning is to unlearn. The way to do this is to question everything you think you know. Once you've found the key to yourself, you discover a freedom so vast that no physical body can contain it; not even a universe can contain it. Unlearning is how the vastness reveals itself. As long as we're stuck in what we think we know, the world remains small, and life is lived in apparent suffering.

When you believe that there's a problem and you go to the Buddha, he won't teach you anything. The Buddha is yourself reflected. He'll point you back to your own mind, where all the answers are. Only mind exists, if anything exists, and the Buddha will always point away from the physical world, back to the only place where self-realization can be experienced.

The Buddha lives in the sureness of the don't-know mind, with no past or future to dictate his movements, as though he were a leaf blowing in the wind, always landing in the perfect place. The only way that the unenlightened mind can ever keep up with him is to walk the path of "I can't know." This isn't a doing, even though it appears to be. It's not what the Buddha says or does that is his power. His power is what he lives out of: awareness. As he walks his path, people follow because they're drawn to it. He never says, "Follow me."

It takes an open mind to question your certainties. It takes a mind that is fearless in its journey inward, a mind willing to go to places it has never been to before. It's a journey into what is true. And everything dissolves into the truth. Nothing survives it. It is love itself, and there's nothing that it isn't. It's the mind finally resting in itself, at home with itself. It's the end of contradiction, war, unkindness—the end of identity as a body, the end of a separate self. The enlightened mind understands that nothing exists but its own joyous nature.

When everything dissolves into the truth, you say, the mind discovers that it is love itself. Would you elaborate on this?

The nature of mind is clarity, expansiveness, joyous creation, endlessly at play in itself. There are no limits to its generosity. It's the revelation of what isn't, appearing to be. It's nothing and everything and nothing. It's faster than instantaneous, vast, all-inclusive, always alone, and more beautiful than you can possibly imagine. What was lost is forever found; what was found is forever gone.

The only thing worth
learning is to unlearn.
The way to do this
is to question everything
you think you know.

22

PICKING UP THE GARBAGE

The Buddha said, "Let me ask you something, Subhuti. When I attained enlightenment, was there anything that I attained?"

Subhuti said, "No, Sir. As I understand it, there was nothing that you actually attained."

The Buddha said, "Exactly so, Subhuti. When I attained Absolute Perfect Enlightenment, I attained absolutely nothing. That is why it is called 'Absolute Perfect Enlightenment.'"

No one has ever attained enlightenment. Enlightenment is not a thing. It's a figment of the imagination. It happens in a past that doesn't exist. Are you enlightened to your own stressful thinking right now? That's the only enlightenment that matters.

Having no past, I have no reference points. No one does. When a story appears and we focus on it, that story overrides awareness. It becomes our whole world. It's like sitting in a theater, watching a movie that is so all-consuming we think it's real, and we get chills or are moved to tears. The focus on an unexamined story is like that. We call it a past. But if you look around for the past, you can't find it. You can only find where you are in the present moment.

Whatever job is in front of me is never more difficult than I can handle, since I never have to handle it. Either I pick up the garbage, or if I don't notice it, it's left for others to notice. When you notice the garbage on the ground, what do you project out of it? Is it ugly, a bother, a disgrace? Or is it your perfect job in the moment? To clear your mind so that you can live in a beautiful world, the real world, is the ultimate job. Heaven is created out of this, or hell. The job of the Buddha is simply to pick up the garbage, to do the dishes, to sweep the floor. In this, he changes the world a little bit, for the better. But the ultimate job is not to change the world; it's to understand the world within you.

No one can change the world forever. You can pick up the garbage, and there will always be more garbage somewhere else. The only world we can truly change is the world of our own perception. That's what matters, until the perception rings your heart as though it were a bell. The world penetrates you, and seeing the garbage becomes a moment of grace. There's nothing that can't enlighten you, because everything is perception. So question anything that would cost you the awareness of your true nature. There's nothing kinder than *nothing*.

You say that you have no past. But you remember things like taking care of your mother when she died. Doesn't that mean that you have a past?

Not at all. I'm simply reporting the movie of an apparent past that is appearing now. And not now. And not now. These are pointers and symbols of what isn't. If you're suffering, I'll say anything, I'll go anywhere, I'll speak your language, I'll pretend that I exist, and only by your invitation.

Are you enlightened
to your own stressful
thinking right now?
That's the only
enlightenment
that matters.

23

GRATITUDE HAS NO WHY

The Buddha said, "Furthermore, Subhuti, in the enlightened mind everything is equal; there is neither higher nor lower in it, neither better nor worse. That's why it is called 'enlightened.' When someone who doesn't believe the concepts 'self' and 'other' acts in a selfless way, that person is able to embody and live the state of enlightenment."

We're not doing anything; ultimately, we're being done. When I say, "I love you," there's no personality talking. It's self-love: I'm only talking to myself. More accurately, *it* is only talking to itself. If I say, "Let me pour you some tea," *it* is pouring its own tea for itself, and the tea is itself. It's so self-absorbed that it leaves no room for any other. Not a molecule is separate from it. That's true love.

It's the ultimate self: the non-self. It's self-consuming always, and always loving it. In the apparent world of duality, people are going to see a "you" and a "me," but in reality there is only one. Everything is equal. There's no "this" or "that." And even to say "one" is delusional. It doesn't matter how you attempt to be disconnected, that's not a possibility. Any thought you believe is an attempt to break the connection. But it's only an attempt. It can't be done. That's why it feels so uncomfortable.

When I woke up to reality, I had never heard of meditation; there was no one to tell me that thoughts were enemies. It was only natural that I could meet each thought arising and welcome it as a friend. I can't meet you as an enemy and not feel it as stress. So how can I meet a thought as an enemy and not feel it as stress? When I learned to meet my thinking as a friend, I noticed that I could meet every human being as a friend. What could you say about me that hasn't appeared within me as a thought? It's so simple.

I can't *not* love the person or people I'm with—that would be insane. I just expect nothing of them, absolutely nothing. They give what they give for their own sake, their own happiness, and I receive it with open arms, loving the generosity of whatever arises from the human heart. People come and go; I love it when they come and when they go. I know I can't pick and choose who stays. I can't cheat myself with my little choices. Why would I do that? Why would I go for the small when the universe is so vast? I don't dictate who should be in my life, or when people should enter or leave. How would I know that?

When people are generous, I'm grateful—not to them, but grateful, period. When a reason shows up later, it's always valid. Gratitude has no why. The story of "because" can be wonderful, as stories go, but in the end we're simply grateful. There is nothing believable enough to challenge the goodness of this moment. And the only thing better than this moment is *this* one . . . Oops, where did it go? And each now . . . now . . . now . . . is only now, and now it's then. I can't stand all this gratitude! Is that true? I think not. Test it for yourself.

The Buddha says that generosity isn't generosity. That's because it doesn't feel like generosity when we're being generous. We're just doing what we know to do. It comes naturally. We give because that's who we are. It's not a choice.

The greatest example of generosity I ever experienced was an old woman who first appeared to me in August 1986. I called her "my Lady." It was early in the morning, and I was lying in bed asleep, next to Paul. As I woke up and looked, there she was, sitting on a chair next to our bed, against the wall. She was the sweetest, most harmless-looking old woman, in her sixties, which today we would call her eighties. She was fat but not obese, about five feet two and weighed maybe 175 pounds. She was wearing black lace-up leather shoes with buckles and small wide heels, a black and off-white paisley print dress with buttons down the front of it, a thin belt made of the same material, with a small black cloth buckle, and sleeves more than halfway down her upper arms. The hem came further than mid-calf, but I knew that under the dress she was wearing stockings that were rolled up below her knees. Her hair was pulled loosely back in a bun. She sat with her legs apart and held her hands in her lap in front of her, making interlocking rings of her thumbs and forefingers. She was absolutely benign, absolutely without malice, and I felt a trust I had never felt before. If I had trusted Jesus or known about the Buddha, I might have projected either of them. But I projected what I could love and trust.

Then, suddenly, I was stunned to find myself *in* the Lady, *as* the Lady, without knowing that I had ever been a Katie. And I went to what I later called "the school." It was as if I had shot straight up out of my (the Lady's) head and into another dimension. I felt I was being shown all physical creation, from the beginning of time to the end of time. It was all numbers. Everything in the universe was a number, and the numbers all had their own colors and sounds and began to travel all the way out and all the way back and returned to zero. I saw everything in the universe, and it all added up to nothing. I don't know how long this experience lasted. It felt like an eternity.

Then I found myself back as the Lady on the chair. I looked toward the Katie woman and the man lying on the bed, and I felt a vast, indescribable love. I saw how primitive they were, as if they came from an ancient world of darkness. I could see the animal in their eyes, the density, the ignorance. I saw the two of them as equally dense. The woman on the bed was not enlightened; the only enlightened part of her was sitting on the chair as the observer. But as the Lady, I wasn't sitting on a chair; I was without form. I was everywhere. I had never seen these people, I had never seen *any* humans, I had never seen anything. Through all the density of their suffering, I could see their innocence. I understood all that they couldn't understand. They were unaware that they didn't have to suffer. In their confusion they really believed that they were victims and that there was no way out.

I watched them as a being of total compassion, from the place where all suffering has been transcended, where the physical realm isn't remembered even as a possibility. I watched from the other end of time. The two people on the bed were all humanity, every man and woman. They weren't guilty of anything, but they suffered as though they were. They thought they were separate, but they weren't. They thought there was something wrong, but there never had been. I felt such compassion for them. At the sight of their innocence, I dissolved into that vast love. Looking out from the Lady's position, I was seeing from a place of understanding, which to Katie would have felt like more than she could have endured. The love was so vast, so fierce, that she would have felt burned to ashes in the intensity of it.

When I found myself back in the body of the Katie person, I looked over to the chair. The Lady wasn't there. I felt devastated. I asked Paul, "Where did she go?" He said, "Who the hell are you talking about?"

After that, I saw my Lady whenever I lied or exaggerated or tried to control or change a person or situation, or when I said or did something with a self-directed motive. She was my teacher, as real to me as an actual human being, as concrete as my own children. Any time I tried to manipulate anyone to see me as important or wise or kind, or as anything that would gain their love or approval, I would feel the Lady's absence inside me, and I would see her standing across the room with her head bowed, looking at the floor, and I knew there was something unbalanced or unfinished in me. I knew that I had to identify whatever motive had been running in me, take back what I had said, and tell the truth straight from my heart. I would go to the person I had lied to or tried to manipulate or impress, and I would say, "I lied to you" or "I wanted you to see me as important." I would clean up the interaction immediately, because I felt I would rather die than lose my Lady. I didn't know then that she was me. I only knew that I couldn't live without her. I would have done anything to keep her. She was separate from me until I cleaned up my act. And I got to be very fast at that. After I had cleaned up my act, I wouldn't see her anymore; I would just feel her presence. It was immediate: an immediate flow, from itself back to itself.

Whenever my Lady left me, I would feel a panicked emptiness and longing for her return. There was a silent plea that would have sounded like "Come back! Please come back!" She couldn't be bribed, she couldn't be persuaded, she couldn't be faked out. Her integrity was absolute. And so I would clean up my mess and apologize to someone, and I would truly mean it. That's the only way she would come back: it had to be genuine. She was attracted only to humility. When I was insincere even in the slightest way, or involved in even the slightest kind of lie or manipulation, she had no interest in a home in this apparent Katie body. I had become so dense that my body couldn't contain her. She was too light to be experienced in such density; the density would send her out of me. But it was simple to get her back. All I had to do was admit the lie or unkindness or lack of integrity, and truly mean it. I didn't care who overheard me or what they might think of me; I didn't care if there were a hundred people in the room. Whatever the consequences might be, I found my error and made it right, and I left nothing out when I told people. When I made it right, I became spacious enough to contain her. She wouldn't come back into me unless I had spoken from the heart.

With this honesty came peace. That was the way I found my integrity. I learned humility from her. I learned absolute honesty. I came to live more and more within her awareness, as the apparent Katie continued to fall away and be seen as not real, as nothing but a bunch of stories and concepts.

Later, I came to see that I had projected the Lady. I didn't have a teacher, so I projected this harmless old woman in a paisley dress with funny shoes and her hair in a bun. She was nothing more than a symbol for the truth within me. But I projected her, because people from my culture didn't have spiritual teachers. I had no religion and didn't even know there was such a thing as a spiritual teacher. I thought they were all dead and buried in a Bible somewhere.

After seven or eight months, it was over. As soon as there was a balance, as soon as I could see that she was my projection, she was gone, and I knew that she would never appear again. We had merged completely. She had always been me.

At that time, people began telling me that I should go to college (I had dropped out when I was eighteen), so in 1989 I took some courses at the city college in Barstow. It was radical. I had never seen humans trying to learn like this. "You are learning so many things," I thought. "Don't you know how important it is to *unlearn*?" One day, as I was speaking with the head of the psychology department, he casually mentioned that apparitions were a myth. I told him about my Lady, and he said that what I was describing was impossible, that it couldn't have happened. I nodded my head. And yet there she had been nonetheless—projected, just like my classmates, my children, and everyone else. The professor, too, was projected. But I didn't tell him that.

As I think of my Lady now, I realize that she was showing me the pure generosity of the Buddha. I saw the compassion on her face from my position on the bed as the former, confused Katie, and I experienced her compassion from within her as I witnessed the woman on the bed. Freedom has to penetrate completely, at every level, until all the echoes, all the shadows, disappear.

When Paul didn't see the Lady, I was alarmed. If he couldn't see her, how would I ever find her again? She had left without a trace. And what I realized, months later, is how generous the mind is, that it would split off its most loving, compassionate self as a separate form, that it would come into this dense world of suffering to show me what compassion is, and speak not a single word. There was no introduction, no acknowledgment, no hello or goodbye. She came into this world for my sake, with the utmost generosity, and she said nothing. So I say nothing, though I appear to speak. She came back to the ancient world of suffering; that's why I keep coming back to that ancient world, when people ask me to. She understood my suffering; I understand people's suffering. She had compassion; I have compassion. It was all as if seen in a mirror. She was a mirror image of myself. Everything she taught, I learned, and she spoke to me without speaking. Love is entirely recognizable. There's no one who doesn't recognize genuine love.

You say that thoughts aren't enemies, so you don't try to get rid of thoughts. What kind of thoughts do you think?

Once I understood my thinking, life became pure joy. I love what is, so that's where my mind is. If I have the thought *I love to walk*, it's because I'm walking. If I have the thought *I love to be still*, it's because I'm being still. If I have the thought *I love to do the dishes*, it's because I'm doing the dishes. My mind is in harmony with reality. I'm always aware of the match.

Do you enjoy thinking?

Very much. More accurately, I love being thought. I love never finding one thought that can be captured.

Why did you need the visions of the Lady in 1986? The Work was already alive inside you. Why was anything else necessary?

Because that's the way of it. I had no idea I needed the extra help, and yet there she was. We all get what we need, exactly when we need it. Today "I" am the lady who stays as long as she is needed, and not one moment more.

Strange things can happen when the mind understands and rests silently in itself, but these are no more miraculous than the simple act of breathing or walking or biting into an apple. When the past is over (and it always is), I forget it until someone asks me about it, because there's nothing to remember. It's done, it's gone without a trace, as if it had never existed. What is happening right now? That's where my focus is.

Would you say more about your experience of seeing everything in the universe as a number?

The universe started with nothing, went out to everything, to infinity, and at the point of infinity, it arced and came back to itself. It was like a circle of numbers, and each number was not just a number but also an energy or vibration of light and sound and color, all perfectly coordinated without separation. Every being, every material object, every atom was also a vibration and a number. All the numbers were there, from zero to infinity. All mathematics was there, all the fractions, all the fractals, all the equations. Everything that could ever exist found its way through mathematics and back, and each number was a different color; all the words, all the sounds that belonged to it, everything, was within it and contained. Everything was a number: fire was a number, and ice and water and stars and galaxies. Everything was vibrating as a different number or frequency. Pencil, sky, dog, rug, red, yellow, blue.

The numbers went all the way out and all the way back and returned to zero. I saw the beginning, the middle, and the end. I saw everything, all of it, from the beginning to the end of time and everything in between, happening all at once, in fire, water, ice, air, rock, clay, human, animal, silence. And it all added up to nothing. It was prior to zero. I saw everything anyone has ever wanted to see, and it meant nothing. I saw that I was nothing, that everything in the universe was nothing, that I had never left and I hadn't come back, that none of it was real. I experienced all the levels and dimensions within one thought, all the veils and loops of it, and how not even the deepest knowledge has any meaning.

At some point, I found myself in a place I couldn't return from. It was so far away that the distance is unimaginable. There was total darkness, with no one and nothing there. It felt as if I were alienated from all beings, forever. I didn't know how I got there or how to get back. There was no way to die, because being has no opposite there. In that place there's no death and you live alone forever. There's no light, no up or down, no possibility of movement, no anything. There's nothing, forever, with no way out. I felt such terror.

And then the questions arose to meet the thought: *Can I really know that this is true? How do I react when I believe that there is something better than this? Who would I be without my story of forever?* And because of this inquiry, the darkness became friendly. I was totally present and comfortable in it.

When that reality became as comfortable as this reality, I found myself again as "woman sitting on chair in house on Fredricks Street in paradise." I was at home in that darkness, forever, just as much at home as I am here. But now it looked like a Katie, a window, trees, mountains, sky. And people wonder why I can look at my hand or your hand and become ecstatic. It's no different from being out there in that place of apparent terror, as a motionless speck, alone for all time. Inquiry can hold any condition. After that trip, everything was play, the freedom of having no body, the dance and the bodilessness of it all.

*We all get what
we need, exactly
when we need it.*

24

THE CAUSE OF ALL SUFFERING

The Buddha said, "Subhuti, if someone filled a billion worlds with inconceivable wealth piled up as high as Mount Sumeru and then gave it all away in support of charitable causes, the merit gained by this person would be incomparably less than the merit of someone who, upon realizing what is taught in this sutra, wholeheartedly embodied it and lived it and explained it to others. The merit of someone who is able to embody and live this truth would be hundreds of thousands of millions of billions of times greater. In fact, no number could express how much greater it would be."

Here the Buddha repeats what he has said in previous chapters, about the relative merits of philanthropy and a clear mind. He uses very big numbers to make his point, numbers intended to make your head spin. But the point is simple. Even the greatest philanthropist confers less benefit than someone who understands and lives the central truth of this sutra: that there is no self and no other.

It's not hard to understand why this is so. Imagine someone who owns a billion mountains of gold, each one as high as Mount Everest, and who gives away all this wealth to feed and house the poor, cure diseases, protect the environment, save animals from extinction, and so on. This philanthropist would be able to give security and comfort to everyone on earth. But could he or she give one person peace of mind? Of course not. Security and comfort, and even great abundance, can't ever satisfy us. You can have a beautiful, healthy body, live in a mansion, drive an expensive car, eat the finest food, and still your life may be filled with suffering. It's like dying of thirst in the middle of a clear lake. With all the security and comfort in the world you can be miserable; with nothing but a robe and a begging bowl, like the Buddha, you can be supremely happy.

This is not to undervalue philanthropy. I do whatever I can to help people, in many ways, and this includes giving money to the poor and to organizations that care for people's welfare. But that kind of help goes only so far. The greatest gift you can give others is your realization that there is no self and no other.

When I woke up to reality, I woke up to The Work; actually, I woke up *as* The Work. There was nothing left of me. In an instant I saw the cause of my suffering, and The Work shows this to everyone else as well. I saw that I suffered because I was believing my thoughts, and I saw that thoughts and the images that appear with them as proof weren't true and that they had nothing to do with reality. In that first moment of new life, born out of the death I had been living, I saw that nothing that appeared in my mind was true—absolutely nothing, no thoughts, no names, not even my own. The real world is the world before names, and in that nameless, unseparated, beautiful life I witnessed names, identification, and stories entering and separating everything. As mind identified objects, it created its own suffering with each unquestioned thought.

As I noticed this, I noticed the world that instantly sprang out of the first story, "I," and I realized that the illusion of life had just happened and that it was nothing more than imagination. I also noticed that in this world of names and meaning I had imagined I was really a Byron Katie. Apparent people believed—appeared to believe—that my name was Byron Katie, but I could no longer make that happen. They appeared to believe all the things I had believed, and they were suffering as I had suffered. So, with the ones who wanted to know what had happened, who were honest, open, and courageous enough, I began asking the questions that allowed them to travel into their own identified selves, through the depths of what lies below the belief systems they were operating out of.

In the moment on the attic floor when my eyes opened, I saw that nothing was true. The first two questions ("Is it true?" and "Can you absolutely know that it's true?") were answered automatically for me, and they're answered this way for other willing travelers too. The world of suffering begins when the first thought is believed, and this world is described by the answer to the third question ("How do you react, what happens, when you believe that thought?"). Here's how you react: the entire world of suffering is created in that moment, with that thought, and as long as you believe it, you have the illusion of past and future. That's how it is. You can't see what you don't believe. Belief creates the world of illusion—all of it.

Before thought began in that first moment, there was the pure unknown: love. That's one of the many revelations that people discover when they sit deeply in the fourth question ("Who or what would you be without the thought?"). They begin to recognize the real world, the world of *being* love, the fearless, the nameless, the beautiful, the world where nothing is separate and creativity is allowed to flow without interruption, and the new is witnessed and appreciated at every moment, and you're always alone with yourself, and you're everyone and everything, free to take full responsibility as the creator of the entire world—your world, the world of your imagination.

I look around and I see people attempting to frighten themselves by believing what they think, innocently creating their own fear, anger, and misery, with all their arguments against reality used as proof. And I wait. Every mind ultimately finds its way back. It's wonderful to watch the mind that was so convinced dissolve into nothing and rest in that simple reality.

When someone loves what is, she makes use of anything life happens to bring her way, because she doesn't con herself anymore. What comes her way is always good. She sees that clearly, even though people may say otherwise. There's no adversity in her life. And from her experience, others learn the way of it. If someone says, "I'm leaving you," she feels the excitement rising inside her, since she can see only the advantages that come from that. What could be a more fulfilling experience than to witness the gift of reality? If someone says, "I'm joining you," she can see only the advantages in *that*. What could be a dearer experience than having you join me? She's going to die: good. She's not going to die: good. She's going to lose her eyesight: good. She's not going to lose her eyesight: good. She's crippled; she can walk again: good, good, good. She, like everyone and everything else, is the beautiful, simple flow of reality, which is always kinder and more exciting than our thoughts about it.

———————————

Why does the Buddha keep comparing the merit of a philanthropist to the merit of someone who understands the mind? Is it helpful to think that one is better than the other?

One isn't better than the other. The Buddha is using this untruth to call people's attention to the truth that the best thing you can do for yourself and for others is to understand the nature of the mind.

You've said that you'd be excited if your husband left you, that you'd be happy as you helped him pack. Isn't it glib of you to say that? After all, you haven't had that experience. How do you know how you'd react?

I love Stephen, and I want him to be happy always. I want what he wants. Anything less than that awareness would be *me* leaving *him*, not the other way around. So to celebrate what he wants is to stay connected. It doesn't require *him* to stay connected to *me*. That would be conditional love on my part. My true nature, this clear mind, my gift and my delight, is to stay connected to him. When you love someone, it's an uninterrupted joy. It's your true nature in harmony with all of life. The moment you go to war with the person you love, the connection is broken, and you're always, necessarily, the one who has broken it. Why would you wage war with yourself, since war is a hopeless, loveless state of being? Self-realization is the end of war. Whether or not Stephen leaves me—for any reason, including death—I love him with all my heart. And in my world, he can never leave me.

The greatest gift
you can give others
is your realization
that there is no
self and no other.

The Work in Action

"Daniel Doesn't Keep His Promises"

KRISTEN [*reading from her Worksheet*]: *I'm angry at Daniel because he doesn't keep his promises.*

KATIE: What's the situation?

KRISTEN: We have two little girls, ages four and six. I was going to put the little one to bed, and Daniel was going to take care of the older one. That was what we planned to do so that at eight o'clock we could do something together. I tucked the little one in bed on time, but Daniel wasn't finished, because he read a good-night story to our older daughter, and it was a very long story.

KATIE: Did you walk in and see him reading to your daughter?

KRISTEN: Yes.

KATIE: So that's the situation. "He doesn't keep his promises"—is it true? You don't have to guess. The images of what happened will show you. Just be there now. And remember, the answer to the first two questions is either yes or no. It's not "Yes, because . . ." or "No, but . . ." We're going to meditate on a moment in time. Some of the things that happened in our pasts are pretty spooky. But we're always safe from them here. So let's get still and meditate on that moment, to see if there's something we missed when we were so angry. So if yes is the answer, good. If no is the answer, good. Just allow the situation to show you the truth. "Daniel doesn't keep his promises"—is it true?

KRISTEN: No.

KATIE: Interesting. Now close your eyes and look at yourself. There's your husband. There's your daughter. How do you react when you believe the thought "He doesn't keep his promises"?

KRISTEN: Right away, the anger rises.

KATIE: What else?

KRISTEN: I go into that peaceful situation with my anger.

KATIE: And look at yourself.

KRISTEN: It's as if I'm imprisoned. I don't know what else to do. I can't get out of it.

KATIE: Now, who would you be without the thought "He doesn't keep his promises"?

KRISTEN: I would be lighter. More peaceful. Kinder. Fair.

KATIE: And the three of you would be enjoying the moment. You would feel appreciation for your husband, for your daughter, for yourself. All that, without the thought. Now look at the situation again *with* the thought, and notice the difference. Do you see how helpless you are? And how helpless they are?

KRISTEN: Yes.

KATIE: "Daniel doesn't keep his promises." Turn the thought around.

KRISTEN: Daniel does keep his promises.

KATIE: What does that mean to you?

KRISTEN: He puts my daughter to bed.

KATIE: It could be that he promised her he'd read to her.

KRISTEN: Yes.

KATIE: It could be that he's doing what he promised to do. Can you find another example of how "Daniel does do what he promised to do" might be true?

KRISTEN: Yes. Many examples.

KATIE: That would be Daniel. Good, sweetheart. "Daniel doesn't keep his promises." Can you find another turnaround?

KRISTEN: *I* don't keep my promises.

KATIE: In that situation, what promises did you break to yourself, to Daniel, to your daughter?

KRISTEN: I didn't participate any longer in putting my girls to bed. I was just sitting on the couch and waiting for him to come, but I didn't participate in it anymore.

KATIE: Any other thing in that situation where you broke your promise to yourself, to them, or to Daniel?

KRISTEN: Yes, because this date that Daniel and I had was about working on the quality of our relationship. [*The audience laughs.*] And after I got angry, of course we weren't able to work on it anymore.

KATIE: So we're noticing here what happens when we believe our thoughts. Believing that Daniel doesn't do what he promised to do caused the separation. It created the very thing you had a date to work on. It lowered the quality of your relationship. It separated you from your family. Let's look at statement 2 now. What did you want from Daniel?

KRISTEN: *I want Daniel to do what he says.*

KATIE: Is that true? Look at him reading to your daughter. "You want him to do what he says"—is that true?

KRISTEN: No.

KATIE: So what I'm hearing from you is that you'd rather have him read to her than keep his promise to you.

KRISTEN: Yes, basically. Yes.

KATIE: And notice how you treat him when you believe the thought "I want him to do what he says." Notice what happens to your life together. [*To the audience*] How many of you have had that thought about someone? How many of you believed it in the moment? [*Many people raise their hands.*] [*To Kristen*] How do you react when you believe the thought "I want him to do what he says."

KRISTEN: I get really pushy. I bring stress into that situation.

KATIE: Yes. That beautiful husband who is reading a story to his daughter, keeping his promise to put her to bed. Now witness. Who would you be without the thought?

KRISTEN: Relaxed. I could enjoy our being together.

KATIE: It's beautiful. It's what people imagine happy families look like, and there it is just waiting for you to see—this amazing, beautiful moment, where you can just be there in that beauty, that intimacy. And thoughts like "I want him to do what he says" are the cause of war when we believe them. So are you guilty? Or are you simply hypnotized? Are you simply believing your thoughts? [*To the audience*] Is there anyone in this room who can stop believing what you're believing in the moment you're believing it? [*To Kristen*] It's against our true nature to be anything less than connected with people, the way you are in your daughter's bedroom with your husband when you don't believe your thoughts about him. You're awake to what is. Nothing terrible has ever happened. It's not happening now, and it never will. I've come to understand that this is a friendly universe, and I invite all of you here to test it for yourselves. You can see the world as it really is when you stop believing your stressful thoughts. Then mind matches its true nature. Husbands are here to wake us up, and so is everyone and everything else in your life. Let's turn it around. "I don't want Daniel . . ."

KRISTEN: I don't want Daniel to do what he says.

KATIE: No. He had a better idea, one that would give your daughter and you what you wanted. Once you understand this, you're living with the master, always wise, without exception. Our husbands are here to wake us up. Do you see another turnaround? "I want me . . ."

KRISTEN: I want me to do what I say.

KATIE: Which was to keep that agreement to work on peace in your family. You're doing that now. It's never too late. Okay. Now read statement 3.

KRISTEN: *Daniel should talk less and act more.*

KATIE: Turn it around. "In that situation with Daniel and my daughter, I should . . ."

KRISTEN: I should talk less and act more.

KATIE: So that advice to Daniel was really advice to yourself.

KRISTEN: Yes. I should talk less and act more to question my thoughts.

KATIE: That was good advice. Notice how you react when you believe the thought. You try to force your husband. And he doesn't understand. But when you turn it around and follow your own advice, it always makes sense. It's kinder. It allows awareness. Let's look at statement 4.

KRISTEN: *I need Daniel's deeds to follow his words, to walk his talk, and to do what he promises.*

KATIE: Close your eyes. Look at him reading to your daughter. "You need his deeds to follow his words"—is that true? Is that what you need to be happy in that moment?

KRISTEN: No.

KATIE: How do you react, what happens, when you believe that thought?

KRISTEN: I get very upset. I see him as doing something wrong. I become a victim.

KATIE: And notice who you would be without that thought.

KRISTEN: It would be beautiful.

KATIE: Turn it around.

KRISTEN: I need my deeds to follow my words.

KATIE: Yes. Not so easy, is it? Believers have a lot of suffering in their lives. And if The Work becomes your daily practice, you'll find that there's no longer any war in your life. When the war ends in you, it ends in your family. You're the one who can end it. You're the only one. Our husbands or wives can't do it for us. Can you find another turnaround?

KRISTEN: I don't need Daniel's deeds to follow his words.

KATIE: Yes. When he's reading to your daughter, he's actually doing what you prefer. When you question what you're believing, it wakes you up to reality. And when you turn around those wants, needs, and shoulds on your Worksheet, they'll give you clear guidance. The guidance is always there. Okay, now turn statement 4 around to yourself all the way.

KRISTEN: I need my deeds to follow my words, and I need to walk my talk and to do what I promise. Yes. It happens very often that I wait for him to do something in our relationship.

KATIE: Wonderful, sweetheart. When you realize this, it means you never have to wait again. He's always doing what you want, believe it or not. That's very liberating. You don't have to agree with it. But I am here to invite you to question what you believe about it and to wake yourself up to this friendly universe. What did you write for statement 5?

KRISTEN: *Daniel is unreliable, has no respect for me, and isn't interested in working on our relationship.*

KATIE: Okay. "Daniel is unreliable." In that situation, is it true?

KRISTEN: No. For my daughter, he was very reliable.

KATIE: And is he doing what you prefer?

KRISTEN: He's being a loving father, yes.

KATIE: So, he's reliably a loving father, which is what you want.

KRISTEN: Yes. If it weren't what I want, I wouldn't be able to sit here.

KATIE: Good. Now get very clear. Close your eyes. Would you rather that he be there reading to your daughter or with you on the couch? Look at him with your daughter. Get clear about what you really want.

KRISTEN: Yes. [*Smiling*] To tell the truth, I didn't feel that much like working on our relationship. [*The audience laughs.*]

KATIE: "He has no respect for you, and isn't interested in working on your relationship"—is it true?

KRISTEN: No.

KATIE: We just can't know about him and his motives. So let's see what we *can* know. "In that situation with myself and with my family, I am . . ."

KRISTEN: I am unreliable, have no respect for him, and am not interested in working on our relationship. Yes, completely.

KATIE: You're just not interested in what he wants or what he's doing. And blind to what you really want, even though it's right there before your eyes. Confusion is the only suffering in this world. And when we hear what you were believing and how it affected you in that situation, it's easy to see the price of confusion. Let's turn this around again. "He is reliable . . ."

KRISTEN: He is reliable, full of respect for me, and very interested in working on our relationship.

KATIE: That's Daniel, when you're awake to yourself. When you believe your thoughts, you're angry at the Daniel of your imagination. It's not the Daniel of reality. When you walked into the bedroom, you saw the Daniel of your imagination. You attacked an innocent man. And you are just as innocent. So any time you experience anger, I invite you to identify your thoughts and write them down on a Judge-Your-Neighbor Worksheet. And then question what you are believing. That way you and your husband never have to work on your marriage again. It takes only one person to have a happy marriage, and that one is always you. You don't have to wait for him. Let's look at statement 6.

KRISTEN: *I never want to hear Daniel promise something and later do something else.*

KATIE: "I'm willing to . . ."

KRISTEN: I'm willing to hear Daniel promise something and later do something else.

KATIE: "I look forward to . . ."

KRISTEN: I look forward to hearing Daniel promise something and later do something else.

KATIE: Because he's here to wake you up. And so are your children.

KRISTEN: Thank you, Katie.

KATIE: You're so welcome.

25

EQUAL WISDOM

The Buddha said, "Subhuti, the Buddha doesn't entertain the thought 'I will liberate all sentient beings.' Why? Because not even one being exists for the Buddha to liberate. If there were beings for the Buddha to liberate, it would mean that the Buddha believes the concepts 'self' and 'other.' Though the Buddha says 'I,' in reality there is no 'I.' Yet immature beings take this to be an 'I.' And for the Buddha, there are no immature beings; they are only *called* 'immature beings.'"

The Buddha says here that there are no mature or immature people. We all have equal wisdom. It's equally distributed. No one is wiser than anyone else. The only difference is that some of us believe what we think, and some of us have learned to question the thoughts that separate us from our inborn wisdom.

The Buddha also says, as he has said in previous chapters, that there are no suffering beings to liberate. This is an amazing statement. Can you feel how shocking it is? Some people might see it as cold and heartless. "What do you mean, there are no beings to liberate? Are you crazy? What about all the ignorance and brutality in the world?

What about all the innocent victims of greed and violence?" His statement might even be seen as dangerous, because people might think that it could sap people of their motivation to do good. "If there were no one out there to liberate, I would just sit back and do nothing."

But "no beings to liberate" is the simple truth, and the truth is what sets us free. Far from making us passive and self-absorbed, it leads to generosity. If we truly understand that the self isn't real, how can we act selfishly? And if there is no self, how can there be others that you can oppose? All beings are simply me, and it would be as crazy to hurt another human being as to purposely break my own leg. The Golden Rule isn't a *should*. It's not a matter of ethics; it's a matter of *fact*. I do unto others as I do unto myself, because I realize that others *are* myself.

As you begin to question your mind, mind loses the ability to believe that it's a this or a that. It ceases to identify itself. It becomes free. It understands that identification is just a state of mind. Some people lose identification accidentally, or in meditation, and it frightens them, and in reaction they become very controlled. The ego attempts to make sure that that freedom never happens again; it attempts it through fear; it tightens in on itself. But it's okay to let go of identity. It's also okay to believe you're a "you." There's nothing serious going on here. It's just that you're not a "you." Believing that you are doesn't make it so.

One day, in the late '80s, as I was sitting on the edge of a cliff in Big Sur, pausing from a long day's drive, I looked down toward the ocean—way, way down, where there were waves and sharp rocks. At that moment, a seagull appeared, at eye-level, just in front of me. And as it flew by, mind was so free that it took on that identity. One moment I was the woman on the ledge, and the next moment I was the seagull, inside the seagull's body, looking out from its eyes. I was elated, and yet peaceful too, feeling myself as the spaciousness of all flight.

Then something shifted. The "I" was born within the seagull. It glanced down. It had the thought "I don't know how to fly." And then it thought, "Oh my God, I'm going to fall!" I felt so heavy, as if I weighed a hundred pounds. And I noticed more thoughts: "I don't want to be a bird that can't fly. I want to be the woman sitting there, safe and solid." These thoughts were the only cause of my fear. I knew that as a bird I wasn't actually falling—that was the reality of it. And immediately each thought that argued with reality was met with inquiry: "Is that true? Can I really know that it's true?" Each thought had a question as its mate. This brought things back to their natural balance. Within that balance I was free.

In slow motion it felt like this: *"I can't fly"—can I really know that that's true?* No. *How do I react when I believe that thought?* I get scared. *What would I be without it?* Totally confident. And immediately the thought dissolved, and I flew. I had the time of my life as a seagull. I just kept soaring, thrilled with the joy of flight. And as soon as I made peace with that identity, I once more became the woman sitting on the edge of the cliff, ecstatic and ordinary.

You say that there are no mature or immature people. Yet didn't you yourself mature after your early ecstasies?

Yes, you could say that, though the understanding always remained the same. In the early days I was in love with it all, as I still am. I loved everything I laid eyes on. It was all beautiful to me—all of it was ultimate reality. I was in passionate love with everyone and everything. Every time I saw people, I fell in love. I would walk up to someone and look into his or her eyes with all the love I was feeling. "You are God" would have been my words. "You are my dearest, most intimate self." I was so wild with love that I couldn't help it. But I soon learned not to do that. People seemed to pull back. They seemed to be frightened.

I learned that if I didn't speak, what came through was what I called "the cleanse," the cleansing of itself. It purified itself from any teaching. The cleansing looked like tears and humility and death, the death of the personality, the death of any self that might remain. I could see that any time I spoke when someone hadn't asked, I was met with confusion. People would look at me, and their eyes would reflect back a crazy woman. That was okay with me, but there was no value in speaking that way, except in learning to experience a truth from within and not speak it to myself outside.

I had such a hunger to burn up whatever thoughts arose in my mind that whenever a physical reaction came through me, I let it come. I would shake or burst into tears or laughter or express whatever needed to be expressed. They were the tears and laughter of someone who was intoxicated with love. I was like a very young child, totally uninhibited. It didn't matter if the reaction occurred in a mall or a supermarket or when I was walking down the street. I would just stand or drop onto the sidewalk and let the emotion have its way. People were always kind. They would stop and say things like, "Do you need help?" "Would you like a tissue?" "Is there someone I can call?" "Can I take you somewhere?" That's how I met the world. It was tender. It was sensitive. These people were all pieces of me.

When I was in public I experienced the whole of it, the unraveling of it, the knots being untied, through the four questions of The Work, which were always alive in me. In them I was always met. I would sometimes ask people to hold me. I would be in tears of joy and would walk up to a stranger and say, "Would you hold me now?" No one refused. Not one person ever refused. Sometimes a woman would rock me and sing me lullabies, and the only thing I had done was ask. I love telling that I was never turned down. The truth about who we are is obvious when there's no motive. Anyone will hold innocence. It doesn't matter if you're a forty-three-year-old woman—people will hold you like a baby.

One morning, on the streets of Barstow, a Latino man walked up to me and said, "I watch you walking every day, and so often I see you crying. Why do you do that to yourself?" This was the first time I realized that I was crying when I walked. I remember being shocked that he didn't know I was undoing everything in the universe, for everyone, for all time. I was amazed that he would have to ask about something so obvious. "I'm undoing all of creation," I said, "and this is what it looks like." He just shook his head and walked away.

I loved to sit down on a curb or the sidewalk in Los Angeles and watch as people approached me. I knew that everyone is God (that was my word for *Buddha*), including the street people, so I was never afraid or separate from anyone. They would say things like "I need help." "Will you give me money?" "What are you doing?" "Who are you?" "Can I sit with you?" Sometimes people were volatile, and sometimes sad or angry. I saw every emotion and understood it. This is what happens when you sit on the sidewalk without an agenda, just loving what is. I would sit when I knew to sit. I was in what I called "earth school," and everyone was showing me who I was through my thoughts about who they were. Life kept giving itself up to me—to itself.

Sometimes I would meet some of the homeless people in Barstow as I was walking with one of my children or with Paul. They might come up to me silently and put their arms around me and then walk on. Our relationship was often one of silence, especially if I was talking to one person and two or three others came and listened. Sometimes tears would flow from the most bitter of them. I watched and heard and understood. Often people I hadn't met approached me. One day, for example, as I was walking the streets with Paul, I noticed an obese, very dirty woman, in her fifties, wheeling a shopping cart with many bags on it and carrying other bags with her. She dropped her bags when she saw me and moved into my arms. I held her, kissed her face, held her head, and melted into her beautiful eyes. Paul stood by, aghast. Later I helped her gather her bags and put them onto her cart. Then I took Paul's hand and continued on my way.

Another time two very tough-looking young men approached us. As they came toward us, I opened my arms and began to move toward one of them. Paul said, in his usual gruff way, "God damn it, Kate, those guys would cut you up and kill you in a heartbeat." The young man walked into my arms the way a child would come to his mother. There were tears and thank-yous, and the other man was just as grateful for whatever he thought was happening. These were people who might have met me before or heard about me. The homeless people called me "the woman who made friends with the wind"—the wind in Barstow can be relentless—and there were other names for me that had evidently stuck. It was clear to many people that they could be with me and not have to pretend or change in order to be loved. My arms were open to anyone. They still are.

When you apparently became a seagull, wasn't this just a hallucination? What value do you find in telling this story?

It *was* a hallucination, just as everything is. For me, the story is a vivid illustration of the power of inquiry. There's no experience, however strange it might be, that I fear—as far as I know. I love the adventure, wherever it may take me. I would rather fall to the rocks below than miss that. I understand that the universe is friendly. In other words, mind is everything, and its nature is good. So whatever mind projects has to be good. This means that nothing terrible can happen. Those unquestioned thoughts—"I can't fly," "I'm going to fall"—seemed matters of life and death, they were so elemental. Each one arose in my chest; each one had an excitement about it. So I allowed *it* to show *me* what was true and what wasn't. That's inquiry lived. Love showed me that I *could* fly. And if I fell, it would be the same. Both ways were equal. What a trip! And it was all a projection of mind.

In each experience, I know I am nothing, even as the woman on the cliff seeing the seagull. I'm aware that I am prior to thought, that I'm not the woman or the bird or anything but awareness. I am nothing, looking out at itself—a completely silent mind. Awareness knows nothing, and therefore it's hidden to itself. In this infinite loving state, it shoots out to know, to see, to revel in itself, to realize what it hasn't yet revealed to itself. Everything in the universe is a reflection of mind. It is whatever identity you believe it is. It stays as a throbbing gratitude, whether it is woman, seagull, or rock.

*I do unto others as
I do unto myself,
because I realize that
others are myself.*

26

A BUDDHA IN THE HOUSE

The Buddha said, "Let me ask you something, Subhuti. Can the Buddha be recognized by his thirty-two distinguishing physical characteristics?"*

Subhuti said, "No, Sir."

The Buddha said, "If the Buddha could be recognized by his thirty-two distinguishing physical characteristics, then righteous kings† who possess these distinguishing physical characteristics would also be buddhas."

Subhuti said, "Sir, I understand that the Buddha cannot be recognized by his physical characteristics."

Then the Buddha recited this verse:

Those who see the Buddha with their eyes,
or hear him with their ears, can never know.
How with your body's senses can you find me
and realize that I neither come nor go?

---

* See footnote, chapter 5.
† The Sanskrit term is *chakravartin*, an ideal king who rules benevolently over the whole world.

We can't recognize the Buddha. We can't ever know who is a buddha and who isn't. So the reasonable thing is to assume that everyone is a buddha, no matter how mistaken he or she may seem to be. Think of that person you just can't stand (you know the one). What lesson has he or she incarnated as, in order to teach you?

When Roxann was pregnant with Marley and feeling sick and cranky, her husband, Scott, would say to her, "I'm sorry I did this to you. It's all my fault. What can I do to make it right?" He didn't have to mean it. Roxann would usually react by thinking, "'It's all his fault'—really?" She felt checkmated in her annoyance at him. When Stephen heard this, he suggested that Scott write a handbook for men. It would be titled *The Secret of a Happy Marriage,* and it would be one page long—one sentence long, actually. In the center of the first and only page there would be this advice:

> **Whenever there is a problem between you and your wife, no matter who is at fault, go to her and say the following: "I'm sorry I did this to you. It's all my fault. What can I do to make it right?"**

The truth is that your partner is your mirror. He or she always reflects you back to yourself. If you think there's a flaw in him, that flaw is in you. It *has* to be in you, because he's nothing more than your story. You are always what you judge him to be in the moment. There's no exception to this. You are your own suffering. You are your own happiness.

People think that relationships will make them happy, but you can't get happiness from another person; you can't get it from anywhere outside you. What we usually think of as a relationship is two belief systems that come together to validate that there is something outside you that can bring you happiness. And when you believe that that's true, growing beyond your common belief system means losing the other person, because that's what you had together. So if you move forward, you leave this old belief system behind in what you call the other person, and then you feel it as separation and pain.

The only relationship that is ever going to be meaningful is the relationship you have with yourself. When you love yourself, you love the person you're always with. But unless you love yourself, you won't be comfortable with someone else, because he or she is going to challenge your belief system, and until you question your beliefs, you've got to make war to defend them. So much for the relationship! People make these unspoken contracts with each other and promise that they won't ever mess with the other person's belief system, and that's not possible.

I don't want other people's approval. I want them to think the way they think. That's love. You can't control someone else's thinking. You can't even control your own. There's no one thinking anyway. It's a house of mirrors. Seeking approval means being stuck in the thought "I'm a this," this speck, this tiny limited thing.

You can't disappoint another human being, and another human being can't disappoint you. You believe the story of how your partner isn't giving you what you want, and you disappoint yourself. If you want something from your partner and he says no, that's reality. It leaves you as the provider. This is good news, because it allows you to get what you want. If you don't have him to help you, you have yourself. Obviously, if he says no, you're the one who is supposed to help you.

Wanting Stephen to love me would assume that he doesn't. It would be the opposite of love. I want him to love whomever he loves. People see how much I love him, and they call that love, but I'm just a lover of what is. I know the joy of loving, so I know it's not my business how he directs his love. My business is simply to love him.

No one you love can leave you. Only you can do that. Whatever his commitment is, your commitment is what you can count on, until it changes (if it changes). The one marriage vow that Stephen and I took was "I promise to love you until I don't." A long-term commit-ment is for this moment only. Even if someone says he is committed to you forever, you can never know that, because as long as you believe that there is a "you" and a "him," it's only a personality committing to a personality, and, as I often say, personalities don't love, they want something.

There's a lot to be said for monogamy. It's the ultimate symbol for One, because it keeps your mind focused on one primary person. You just have to question everything you believe about him, every story of him that arises in your mind. Monogamy is a sacred thing, because the mind can be very still in that position. One person will give you the experience that a million people could give you. There's only one mind. Your partner will bring up every concept ever known to humanity, in every combination, so that you can come to know yourself and realize that you are the creator of all suffering. If you can just learn to love the one you're with, you have met self-love.

We *are* love, and there's nothing we can do to change that. Love is our very nature. It's what we are when we no longer believe our own stories.

"The only relationship that is ever going to be meaningful is the relationship you have with yourself." Are you saying that your marriage isn't meaningful?

I'm living a love affair with the self, which doesn't exist. It excludes no one. It excludes nothing. It's whole unto itself and responsible for no other, since there *is* no other. As love would have it, I'm always connected with Stephen, because I'm always connected with myself.

Is there any conflict between your commitment to your marriage and your commitment to yourself?

The commitment to myself is my connection with Stephen. No judgment of him as less than perfect would be worthy of him, or of me. And if there were ever any discord between us, I would look to my own unquestioned thoughts about him for the solution.

Love is our very nature. It's what we are when we no longer believe our own stories.

27

THE SPACE
BETWEEN THOUGHTS

The Buddha said, "Subhuti, don't think that the Buddha attains enlightenment because of any distinguishing physical characteristics. The Buddha doesn't attain enlightenment because of any distinguishing physical characteristics. And don't think that someone who attains enlightenment sees all things as nonexistent. Someone who attains enlightenment doesn't see all things as nonexistent."

Think of your feet. Did you have feet before I asked you to think about them? Did they exist in your awareness? Did you put them in the position they're in right now? *Some*thing did. But until a few moments ago, you didn't have feet. No story: no feet. It's like that with everything.

In the months after my experience of waking up to reality, I cried many tears that came from losing everything in the world. There was no sorrow in these tears, just gratitude and the awareness that nothing in the world belongs to me. It wasn't my body I was losing; I had already lost it from the first experience on the attic floor. It was like this. You see a chair, for example, and you realize that it's not; you've lost even that. It leaves you with nowhere to walk, no one walking, no floor—nothing. Then someone comes in and says, "Hello, Katie," and you're talking, and you *know* you're not talking to anyone but your own mind. There's no one else talking. You know it. You can't backtrack—there's no going back, because you can't create something to go back to. And it falls away to a deeper level. But there's always something stable. And you can't even cling to that, because you know that that's not real either.

You can't have anything. You can't have any truth. Inquiry takes all that away. The only thing that exists for me is the thought that just arose. Prior to that there was no existence at all. There's nothing to create. There's no one, creating nothing. So again and again we return to the space between thoughts.

There are teachers of non-duality who say that nothing exists. This isn't untrue, but it's not true either, as the Buddha says here. The truth can't be expressed in words. It's not on one side of an either/or. It has a billion sides, and it has no side. If an apparent truth has an opposite, it can't be valid.

People don't really care whether things exist or not. They just want to be happy. Our natural state is happiness, but when we believe our thoughts, we feel the effect as stress. If people are suffering, what good does it do in the long run to tell them that they're perfect or that their natural state is happiness? You might give them a glimpse of who they really are, but there's a whole underworld of unquestioned thoughts that will override that perception and bring them right back into their bad dream. If someone comes to you and says, "I'm lost," it's a kindness to give him directions, if you know the direction. "Take a right here, and a left there, and you'll be on Main Street. Then just keep walking straight ahead."

Everything created can be uncreated. All of it is pure imagination. To say, "There's nothing" leaves out the one who believes it. You can never say that there's nothing, because the first thought is the beginning of the universe. There was never anything before the beginning.

This is not to say there was nothing. There's only one. You can't have a zero. A zero is actually a one imagining a zero. Only a something could think of nothing.

We can notice that everything we perceive or think is already in the past, and this awareness is a beautiful thing if the claim is authentically realized, since there's no truth in it to prove or teach. But to teach that there's nothing—no matter how well-intentioned the teaching is—is to point to something. That's why silence is a more accurate expression of what is. It's a reflection of the Buddha's mind, knowing that all words are untrue, spilling out as continual creation, with its deep, silent laughter.

The only thing that you have to work with is your thinking. People tell me they want a quiet mind; they think that freedom is the mind stopped. That's not my experience. What I knew to do, since my mind wouldn't shut up, was to meet my thoughts with understanding, through inquiry. And then I noticed that people were saying the same thoughts I had been thinking. So because I had met my thoughts with understanding, there was no one to meet; there were only concepts understood, which I called "people."

The Work wakes us up to reality. When we take it on as a practice, it leaves us as flawless, innocent, a figment of pure imagination. Practicing inquiry takes us to the Buddha-mind, where everything, without exception, is realized as good. It leads to total freedom. Why would you want to experience a problem and pretend it isn't there—to skip over it and find just some tiny place inside you that's free? Don't you want to find freedom with every breath? Nothing exists but the concept in the moment. Let's meet that now with understanding.

You've said that The Work leads to self-responsibility. Do you think that people are responsible for everything that's happening to them?

In one sense, yes, of course. People who do The Work find that when they question their stressful thoughts, the whole world changes for the better. They discover that everything happens *for* them, not *to* them. They begin to realize that they are 100 percent responsible for their own happiness. This is very good news, because we can't change the world right now, but we can certainly change how we experience the world.

"I am responsible for everything that's happening to me" is not a mere concept; it's an experience. I often tell people, "Don't pretend yourself beyond your evolution"—in other words, don't believe anything that you haven't actually realized out of deep personal experience. Many people read books that teach positive thinking, or the so-called "law of attraction," and they do affirmations, and then they feel guilty when they get sick or when they don't become rich. "Oh dear, I have cancer. I'm responsible for it. I must be doing something wrong." Or "I'm not a millionaire by now. I must not be sending out enough positive energy." That's like saying, "May my will be done, not God's will," rather than realizing, deeply, that God's will *is* your will at every moment. It's trying to get what you want, rather than wanting what you have, which is the only way you can ever be happy.

You say that after you woke up to reality, the major stressful thought for you was "My mother doesn't love me." Is that the thought that was making you miserable for ten years?

No. I used one symbol to unravel the shadows of identity. You can use any stressful thought to unravel identity; it doesn't matter which one. In my own experience, the shadows were consistently delicious, since I understood the power of bringing each one to inquiry, respectfully and openheartedly, kissing it hello and goodbye. It was an incredible privilege. There was nothing out of order. Every illusion was the gift. There was no mother to work with, only a hallucination identified through language and seen for what it really was: nothing.

You say that The Work leads to total freedom. How many other people have you met who live in total freedom through The Work?

I have no way of knowing another person's mind. But I have heard from a few people who practice inquiry that they haven't had a problem in years.

Practicing inquiry takes us to the Buddha-mind, where everything, without exception, is realized as good.

28

"BRUSH YOUR TEETH!"

The Buddha said, "Subhuti, if someone filled worlds as many as the grains of sand in the Ganges with treasure and then gave it all away to support charitable causes, and someone else were to understand the truth that there is no such thing as 'self' and 'other' and wholeheartedly embody and live it, the merit gained by this second person would be far greater than the merit of the first. Why? Because bodhisattvas don't see merit as something to be gained."

Subhuti said, "Sir, how is it that bodhisattvas don't see merit as something to be gained?"

The Buddha said, "Bodhisattvas don't see merit as something belonging to them or as separate from them. That is why the Buddha says that bodhisattvas don't see merit as something to be gained."

Merit is always a judgment that comes from the outside. In reality there is no merit. No one is counting. No one is keeping score.

We can also turn the statement around. "There is no merit" turns around to "There is merit," and that's true as well. There's value to everything we do, and nothing is more valuable than anything else.

That billionaire philanthropist, the one who has built so many hospitals and funded so much scientific research? When you stop comparing, the value of what he has done exactly equals the value of what you have done. You're benefiting humanity every time you do the dishes, sweep the floor, or drive your kids to school. Benefiting one person equals benefiting a million. When you do your job completely—that is, when you do it with a clear mind—you're absorbed in the action, you disappear into it. The only things that exist are the dish, the soapy water, the sponge, the hand moving in its own rhythms. There's no self in it, no other. You are not the doer; you're being done.

When you follow the voice inside, you lose your sense of self. In my world, I can't do anything wrong. There's no plan. I am just an internal yes. That voice is clear to you, it's clear to all of us, but it's overlaid by the thoughts we believe. I used to call it the voice of the heart. I didn't have a teacher to tell me, "This is spiritual and this isn't," so I just kept following the voice and losing everything. People would say, "You're crazy," and I would just say, "Oh," and keep on following the voice. It's a wonderful experiment, and what happens is that you expand into that awareness and lose yourself in a deeper and deeper way. And then other people, who are just you again, say things like "You're so loving," and there's no one to thank, and you receive it fully. It's the space that opened as you.

Just say yes. Just do the dishes. To say yes to that voice, to enter that great experiment, is true co-creation, and you lose yourself in it, you become it. And when you don't want to do the dishes, that's okay too; just notice. This isn't about guilt or shame. Just notice that you don't, and if you can find the thought that's keeping you from following the voice—"I'll do them later," "It's not my turn," "It's not fair"—then write it down and question it. And maybe the next time, you find that the dishes are done and you wonder who did them, and someone says it was you.

One day in 1986, soon after I returned from the halfway house, I heard a voice, the same voice I'd heard thousands of times before. It said, "Brush your teeth!" I had thought revelation would be a great burning bush, and all it turned out to be was "Brush your teeth!" I had heard that before, and sometimes, in my depressed state, I wouldn't brush them for weeks. I *couldn't* brush them; dozens of reasons arose why not. And then on this day I heard "Brush your teeth!" without any interference, and I fell out of bed and crawled on my belly to the bathroom sink. It wasn't about cavities; it was about doing the right thing, honoring the truth inside me.

This life doesn't belong to me. If the voice says, "Brush your teeth," I say yes. I just move right on through, and I don't know what it's for. If it says, "Walk," I walk. If someone sincerely asks me for something, I do it if I can, since even the apparent outer voice is an inner voice. I have no life of my own; my life is not my business. I'm following orders. So each moment is new. "Brush your teeth" doesn't sound very spiritual, but it was the real deal. I just opened to it and became more of a listener. That voice is what I'm married to today. All marriage is a metaphor for the marriage to the inner voice. It's wonderful to follow such a wild thing, to say yes to it.

But to be more exact, there's no voice. It's an inner direction, a resonance within me, within us all, and when we don't follow it, we hurt. I am movement, as we all are when we don't believe our thoughts. You just watch it do itself. You create nothing. What it does, and when and how, aren't your business. You just move with it, and every judgment you have about it falls away.

———————

Why do you say that the voice that said "Brush your teeth" wasn't even a voice?

It appeared as a voice. It was wisdom translated into this specific direction. I had to project a voice apparently outside myself. But from this time on, it was me just following right mind, without question, whatever it said or did. It was always able to discern. It never said, "Jump off this cliff," though I would have been willing to do that too, since I had nothing to lose.

That particular morning I crawled to the bathroom. It had to be in slow motion. I didn't know how to get there, I only knew that I had to do it. The voice was the gift of wisdom, showing me the most mundane, simple directions. It didn't tell me I had to get out of bed and walk to the bathroom; it didn't give me a way to do it, and I didn't know that crawling wasn't the right way. I was just following the simple directions. And because my mind was so clear at that point, no reason arose internally to stop following it.

You are not the doer;
you're being done.

29

BEING TRANSPARENT

The Buddha said, "Subhuti, people call the Buddha the Tathagata.* But anyone who says that the Tathagata comes, goes, sits, or lies down doesn't understand the point of my teaching. In reality the Tathagata doesn't come from anywhere and doesn't go anywhere. That is why he is called 'the Tathagata.'"

Before Stephen read me the Diamond Sutra, I had never heard the word *Tathagata*. It's a Sanskrit word, he explained, and it means "the one who has thus come (or gone)" or "the one who has arrived at the truth, just as it is" or, according to one interpretation, "the one who appears just as he is." This last meaning describes us all, in a sense, since to a clear mind we all can't help appearing just as we are. But in another sense it describes a buddha in particular. There's no difference between the way she appears in public and the way she appears in private. She's transparent. She doesn't wear any masks; what you see is what you get. She says her truth honestly, without trying to please you or gain your approval. When she speaks in front of an audience of a thousand people, she is speaking as intimately as if she were speaking to one friend.

---

* Pronounced tuh-tah'-guh-tuh.

In reality, the Buddha hasn't "thus come" or "thus gone." Any concept of coming and going evaporates when you examine it closely. There *is* no coming or going. If you're coming from somewhere, you need a past; if you're going somewhere, you need a future. As this chapter says, the Buddha doesn't come from anywhere or go anywhere; he or she is beyond coming and going.

Everything comes and goes in its own time. You have no control. You never had any control, and you never will. You only tell the story of what you think is happening. Do you think you cause movement? You don't. It just happens, but you tell the story of how you had something to do with it: "I moved my legs. I decided to walk." I don't think so. If you inquire, you'll see that that's just a story. You know that you're going to move because everything is happening simultaneously. You tell the story before the movement, because you already are that. *It* moves, and you think that you did it. Then you tell the story of how you're going somewhere or how you're doing something. The only thing you can play with is the story. That's the only game in town.

In the months after I woke up to reality, Paul or one of my children would ask me, "Where are you going?" Going, going . . . what does that mean? How is it possible to go, when I haven't come? And how could I answer such questions, since I was committed to speaking the truth? My honest answer would have been, "I don't go, I don't come, I'm not what appears to your dreamed senses." But that kind of answer, I knew, would have freaked them out.

So when someone asked, "Where are you going?" I learned to say, in the name of love, "Oh, I'm going out for a walk" or "I'm going to the market." I learned how to join people without frightening or alienating them. Love joins, because it's not ever separate. The first few weeks, I was telling the truth without much concern for joining people. If someone asked, "What's your name?" I would say, "I don't have a name" or "My name is your name." But once I learned the scam we run on ourselves here, once I understood that people were pretending not to know who they are, it became simpler to talk. These people were parts of me pretending to be asleep, cells still dense, not yet ignited. So if someone said, "Hello," I'd say, "Hi." If someone asked me what my name was, I'd say, "Katie." But if he or she was sincerely interested and asked, "Is your name really Katie?" then I'd say, "No." In this way I could join people and answer their questions without alienating anyone.

It can be different for people on their deathbeds. Some of them have stopped pretending. I have already died—that's one way of saying it. What I know about death is that when there's no escape, when you know that no one is coming to save you, beliefs drop away. You just don't bother. So if you're lying on your deathbed and the doctor says it's all over for you and you believe him, all the confusion stops. There's no longer anything to lose. In that sweet peace, there's only you. You're it.

I know what death is: nothing. When I speak with dying people, I can sometimes tell them the truth without frightening them. I was once called to the deathbed of a friend who was in the final stages of cancer. He had been evicted from his house a month before, because the owners had sold it, and his Volkswagen van had caught fire and burned. So he had a big garage sale and sold everything he owned, and he moved into a hospice center, with his toiletries and a dozen books and CDs that he loved. (I noticed *Loving What Is* on his night table, and the pocket edition of Stephen's *Tao Te Ching*.) He was very thin and frail; he obviously had just a few weeks left. After we had talked for a while, he turned on a voice recorder, and asked me to say something about death, something he could listen to again. I said, "There's one thing I can promise you, sweetheart, and that is that death will never happen. You can depend on that." Since he had lost just about everything, there were no concepts standing between my words and his hearing. His face lit up, and tears poured down his cheeks.

One reason I love the School for The Work is that during those nine days I don't need to lie so blatantly. People can join me there. They can begin to track my world, the world of inquiry, where everything is grace and there are no problems, ever. As they question their minds, our worlds begin to merge. And I get to witness the one mind waking up to reality, the mind that has always been yours: astonished, delighted, grateful, and head over heels in love.

Do you ever find yourself trying to please people or gain their approval?

I please myself, and I approve of myself, and I project that onto everyone. So in my world, I already please everyone, and I already have everyone's approval, though I don't expect them to realize it yet.

You mentioned your School for The Work. Would you say more about it?

Anyone who's interested can read more at www.thework.com/en /school-work.

Why did you create the School?

People would tell me that they could never live their lives with the freedom they saw in me, and I knew that as long as they believed their stories about this, they were right. Since my experience on the attic floor, I had been living without a story and hadn't left myself anything to be afraid of. There was nothing to stop this free flow of happiness. People asked if they could come live with me, and I said yes. It got to the point where at night their sleeping bags covered the floors of my five houses on Fredricks Street. People would come and go; some would stay for a short time, and some would stay for months, learning and teaching how to do The Work. I would travel all over the country and in Europe, giving Work events, and when I returned to Barstow some of the people would still be there, and there would be a lot of new faces.

Then someone told me that a habit is established in twenty-eight days. So I created a twenty-eight-day immersion in inquiry. That made sense to me. I called it the School for The Work, and the first one took place in August 1998 in Barstow. The School exercises had, in a sense, already been written, because I had lived them all. They were all based on my experiences of the first two years, 1986 and '87, and were designed to bring people directly into a new awareness. I revised the exercises and wrote new ones as I listened closely to people's responses. I still do this today. By now, I have compressed the curriculum into nine days.

In the School, I take people through every waking nightmare I ever experienced. I show them how to walk themselves through their own fears, until they're confident that they understand how the mind creates suffering and how the mind can end it. If they have a problem, real or imagined (and all problems are imagined), we question it. I go with them into the depths of hell and we come out again into the sunlight. These brave people are tired of suffering; they long for freedom, they really want to know the truth, and they're ready for peace on earth. Once the four questions are alive inside them, their minds become clearer and kinder, and therefore the world they project becomes clearer and kinder. This is more radical than anyone can possibly express.

I already please everyone, and I already have everyone's approval, though I don't expect them to realize it yet.

30

A WORLD THAT'S COMPLETELY KIND

The Buddha said, "Let me ask you something, Subhuti. If a good man or woman took a billion worlds and crushed them into particles of dust, would there be many particles?"

Subhuti said, "Very many, Sir. But if all these particles had a separate existence, the Buddha wouldn't have called them 'particles.' Particles of dust aren't in fact particles of dust. They are only *called* 'particles of dust.' A billion worlds aren't in fact a billion worlds. They are only *called* 'a billion worlds.' To the extent that these worlds really exist, they do so as a collection of particles. Nor is a collection really a collection. It is only *called* 'a collection.'"

The Buddha said, "Subhuti, to call something a material object is just a conventional way of speaking. Only immature beings attach to such terms."

———————————

Again and again in this sutra, the Buddha points us to the world beyond names. When you were a child, before you had language, before words had any meaning for you, where was the world? There *was* none. You didn't have a body, because you hadn't yet believed yourself in one. You had no separate identity; you couldn't separate reality into an "I" and a world. When your mother pointed to a tree and said, "That's a tree," you looked up at her and said, "Goo goo, ga ga." Then, one day, she said, "That's a tree," and you believed her. Suddenly there was a tree and a mother and a "you." You had a world. You had a body. And before long, your body was too short, too tall, too skinny, too fat, not good enough for this, not good enough for that. A whole world of suffering arose when you began to name things in a world separate from you.

You think that you're the image you see in the mirror, and you compare that image, which is now an image in your head, with your image of the people you consider beautiful. The unquestioned thoughts that attack your imagined body only support the imaginary self you believe you are. But you've never seen your own face. And you can believe that your body is too anything only if you believe the world of names that your own thinking has created.

When mind realizes that it isn't this body, it ceases to experience threats, because threats don't make sense to what has no substance. Unquestioned mind is still conflicted, argues with itself, and worries about its safety, and there is no peace until it understands that there's nothing to deal with other than its own unquestioned thinking. Its life is mirrored out, since that's the only way to see itself, its bodiless journey projected as form. But when mind wakes up, it can see itself only as brilliant imagination perfected, with nothing to get stuck on or to slow its infinite journey.

As it does The Work, mind can lose its grip on identity safely, gently. When you question your stressful thoughts and surrender everything that "you" thought you were, you come to the place where you wonder, "Without that thought, what am I?" Just because an identity appears doesn't make it true. No one knows what he or she is. The minute it's said, it isn't.

Once it thoroughly questions its thoughts, the mind projects a world that's completely kind. A kind mind projects a kind world. If someone else sees something that's not perfect, the questioned mind can't comprehend that at first, because it can't project it. But it remembers its ancient dream-world, when it believed that too, so in the stillness there's a kind of reference point, an echo. It's always grateful for how it sees things, and it understands how others see them. That leaves a lot of energy for it to make amazing changes in the moment, because its clarity keeps none of the options hidden. This is a fearless state of being. There's no limit to it.

———————————

"Fear is not possible for the sane mind," you say. But isn't fear a biological reaction that happens before thinking?

Not at all. You can't feel fear unless you believe a thought about a future. The thought you're believing happens so fast that you have no way to track it; you're aware only of the physical or emotional effects. For example, if you woke up experiencing fear, even though you may be unable to identify why you're afraid, you're simply reacting to the idea that something terrible has happened or is going to happen. Believing one or the other or both thoughts is the cause of your fear, not anything happening in reality. You just woke up with your head on your pillow and with all your needs met in the moment. This is also true of situations where you're actually in what people call danger. When you see a bear, you can run in terror or you can just run. Except for the unquestioned thoughts you're believing, life is always good.

As it does The Work, mind can lose its grip on identity safely, gently.

The Work in Action

"Glenn Is Drinking Again"

EMMA [*reading from her Worksheet*]: *I'm angry at, disappointed in, confused by Glenn*—that's my son's name—*because he's drinking non-alcoholic beer and smoking again.* He's been in an alcohol rehab clinic since January.

KATIE: What's the situation? Where are you?

EMMA: He came home to Zurich this weekend to take care of our dog so that I could come here to your event.

KATIE: And you saw him drinking?

EMMA: Yes.

KATIE: Okay. So "He's drinking non-alcoholic beer"—is it true?

EMMA: Yes.

KATIE: And how do you react? What happens? Close your eyes. You look at him. You see the non-alcoholic beer. You see him drinking it. You see images of past and future. How do you react when you think the thought "He's drinking non-alcoholic beer"?

EMMA: I feel terrified.

KATIE: You *have* to feel terrified, because you see him in some kind of terrible condition.

EMMA: He's such a beautiful person. It's almost impossible for me to watch this beautiful young man not be happy.

KATIE: As he happily sits on the couch, happily drinking his non-alcoholic beer. [*The audience laughs.*]

EMMA: I'm not at all convinced that he's happy.

KATIE: So you're psychic too.

EMMA: Yes. He's my son.

KATIE: And as you see those images in your head, your real son is sitting on the sofa, drinking his non-alcoholic beer. Who's upsetting you: you or your son?

EMMA: Pardon?

KATIE: Is it the images in your head that are upsetting you, or your son?

EMMA: It was a tie. I was upset about him and about myself. When I heard the beer can go "click," my whole body reacted.

KATIE: That's the moment the dream began in your head—the nightmare. You saw those images of the past, and then you saw images of the future. Is it your son you're seeing, or is it your imagination? I don't know why this is such a difficult question, sweetheart. Imagine a juicy, ripe lemon. Now imagine taking a big bite out of it. Did you notice what happened?

EMMA: Yes. My mouth puckered. I felt the saliva.

KATIE: That's what you're up against. You didn't really bite into a lemon. You imagined it. You imagined it, and your body reacted. What color was the lemon?

EMMA: Yellow.

KATIE: I didn't say "yellow"; you imagined it. So, your son pops the can. You go straight into this movie in your head. And your son's just taking a harmless drink. The beer has no alcohol in it. He's there on the couch, perfectly safe and sober. He lights a cigarette. He has come to do a service for his mother so she can be here. One of you has your act together. [*The audience laughs.*] So, you're angry and disappointed in your son. Turn it around. "I'm not . . ."

EMMA: I'm not angry and disappointed in my son.

KATIE: He's sitting on your couch, sober. That's your real son. The other one, the one you're angry at, is imagined. Is your real son the cause of your suffering, or is it caused by what you're imagining?

EMMA: What I'm imagining.

KATIE: Now, notice how you treat your son when you believe the thought. And all he's done is to pop a can.

EMMA: I cut him off, and then I pretend to love him.

KATIE: That's what fear looks like. "I'm disappointed in my son"— turn it around. What's the opposite of *disappointed*?

EMMA: I'm happy about.

KATIE: Okay, close your eyes. Look at your son on the couch, popping the top of the non-alcoholic beer. Who would you be without the thought that you're angry at him for doing what he isn't doing?

EMMA: I'd be so grateful that he came from Lucerne just to watch the dog. And after years of drinking alcohol, he's trying what it's like to drink non-alcoholic beer.

KATIE: He's not trying. He's *doing* it.

EMMA: Right. He's drinking a non-alcoholic beer.

KATIE: He's sober.

EMMA: Sober.

KATIE: In service to his mother. Let's look at statement 2.

EMMA: Am I allowed to say bad words?

KATIE: Of course. The ego isn't polite when it's afraid. Just read what you wrote.

EMMA: *I want him to stop that shit and to stop bullshitting himself and take his life by the horns.*

KATIE: I love that one. Is it true? Do you want him to stop drinking non-alcoholic beer?

EMMA [*looking sheepish*]: No.

KATIE: And how do you react, what happens, when you believe that thought?

EMMA: I'm terrified. I get furious at him.

KATIE: Who would you be if you didn't believe the thought?

EMMA: I'd be perfectly calm. I'd be grateful. I'd just see a young man opening a can of non-alcoholic beer.

KATIE: Now turn it around. "I want me . . ."

EMMA: No!

KATIE: "In that situation, I want me . . ."

EMMA [*grimacing*]: I want me to stop that shit and to stop bullshitting myself and take my life by the horns.

KATIE: *He's* got his stuff together. He's sober. That's reality. You're stuck in the future and the past.

EMMA: Oh my God, Katie! You're right.

KATIE: Let's look at the next statement.

EMMA: *Glenn should do therapy. He should finish his bachelor's degree. He should do what I suggest, because I know what's best for him.*

KATIE: Ah, we're just so lost in those moments when we believe we know. "He should do therapy and finish his bachelor's degree and do what you suggest"—is it true?

EMMA [*shaking her head*]: No.

KATIE: And how do you treat him when you believe that thought?

EMMA: I make him small.

KATIE: Who would you be in that situation without the thought?

EMMA: I would be open to whatever he's doing.

KATIE: Maybe having a sip of it yourself.

EMMA: Maybe what?

KATIE: Having a sip of the non-alcoholic beer.

EMMA: Oh! [*Smiling*]

KATIE: The next statement?

EMMA: *I need Glenn to choose a path of healing. I need him to be happy so I can be happy. I need him to wake up.*

KATIE: "You need him to choose a path of healing"—is that true?

EMMA: No.

KATIE: No. He's already chosen one. He's sober. So he has already chosen a path of healing. You don't need him to choose one. Let's turn it around. "In that situation, I need myself . . ."

EMMA: I need myself to choose a path of healing.

KATIE: In that moment. Your path is all over the place. It takes you to the past; it takes you to the future. The path for healing is always right here, right now, realizing that the universe is friendly. You can see the amazing gift of sobriety in your son. And it's so simple to choose a path of healing when you don't enter the hell of past and future. There's nothing to break the connection with your son, because you're staying in reality. Continue to turn the thought around. "I need myself . . ."

EMMA: I need myself to be happy so I can be happy.

KATIE: Yes. Now notice how you react when you believe the thought that you need him to be happy. Notice how you treat him. You pretend to be okay when you're not. You live a lie, to him and to yourself. Let's look at statement 5.

EMMA: *Glenn is lazy, terrified, fat, unhealthy, self-deceptive, and avoidant.* I'm not going to turn that around. [*Loud laughter in the audience.*]

KATIE: "In my head, I am . . ." And read it. "In my head, I am lazy."

EMMA: In my head, I am lazy.

KATIE: You're looking at past and future. You're too lazy to look at now. And now is so clear. But when we believe these thoughts of past and future, we think that the image of our son in our head is our real son. And it's not. The next word: "In that moment, I am . . ."

EMMA: In that moment, I am terrified.

KATIE: You're terrified by your projections about your son. And the next: "In that moment, I am . . ."

EMMA: I am unhealthy.

KATIE: I'm unhealthy because I avoid what is.

EMMA: Yes.

KATIE: Let's look at statement 6.

EMMA: *I never want to experience that fear again.*

KATIE: "I'm willing to . . ."

EMMA: I'm willing to experience that fear again.

KATIE: "I look forward to . . ."

EMMA: I look forward to experiencing that fear again.

KATIE: So, now let's say he is sitting on the couch and it's real beer he's drinking, and he's completely drunk. You see him on the couch? Which is kinder: reality, or what you're believing about him in the past and future?

EMMA: Reality. I see that.

KATIE: Whether he's drunk or sober, you are the cause of all of your terror and separation. And I love that that's always true. I love that we had these moments together. And if you take on The Work as a daily practice, you'll eventually realize that you have the perfect son and that he has the perfect mother.

31

THE TRUE NATURE
OF EVERYTHING

The Buddha said, "Subhuti, if someone claims that I teach the concept of 'self and other,' would you say that that person has understood my teaching?"

Subhuti said, "No, Sir. That person has certainly not understood the Buddha's teaching. What the Buddha has explained as the concept of 'self and other' isn't in fact a concept of 'self and other.' It is only *called* 'the concept of self and other.'"

The Buddha said, "Subhuti, all those who aspire to attain enlightenment should be firm in their understanding that all things are without a trace of self or other. There is no such thing as a 'self' or an 'other,' and there is no such thing as a concept. A concept is only *called* 'a concept.'"

I often say, "No story: no world." If you have no story, not only can't you have a world, you can't even have the "you" you identify yourself as. Isn't your life based totally on what you believe to be you? Isn't your world all about the self that sees it? The idea of "tree" is just another way of holding a "you" in place. If the tree is real and separate, then "you" must be a valid entity. Who would you be if you could just *be* the seeing, without the imagined "you" that sees? Without a "you," how can the tree exist separately, or at all? If you don't believe in a "you," there's no identity that can believe in a tree, a sky, a world, and therefore nothing can exist. This is where life gets really exciting!

The questioned mind just watches. There is never any danger to avoid; it's always safe within its own marvelous creation. There is never anyone to be, or anything to know or do, as you watch it singing, dancing, creating, serving, loving. Whenever you get angry or frustrated, you can be sure that you're identifying yourself as someone separate, and that's okay too. It's just the signal that allows you to know that your true nature is being overridden, while "you" live this out as justification, defense, or attack.

I love the world as myself, my imagination lived. But the imagined world is more than one. Even one is more than one, since it implies something after it. It implies two, and then three, and then everything else is born out of it: sight, sound, taste, touch, earth, sky, trees, humans, dogs, cats. I love this world even when it appears to die. How could I not? Look what it leaves room for. Look what fills that vacuum.

Destruction of the environment is, for the time being, like it or not, the way of it. If you came to love death, you would love life with all your heart. You'd love how everything must die, must step back in order for other things to live and grow. There's nothing unkind about the falling away of a species, or even of the earth, except for the way you understand it. Do you see the deterioration of your own body as terrible? *Do* something about it! Then, ten years later, do something about *that!* And later, as you notice that you're even older, that your body has deteriorated beyond anything you could prevent, do you see it as terrible? Your body is like the earth. Take another look.

Maybe the right word isn't *destruction*. It certainly isn't for me. I see everything in apparent time as the natural evolution that makes way for something even sweeter than what you think reality is at its most beautiful. I have never seen, touched, smelled, kissed, or loved anything more dearly than my ninety-year-old mother's flesh in the last moment she lived and the first moment she died. And still that beauty remains, and it penetrates my heart.

I love the way of it. Because I understand death, I love it as life, and in the clarity of that, great change takes place in the world around me, and the change that takes place is peace, in the kindest manner. It's the place of balance, and out of it solutions are born. It's the place where clarity allows solutions to live and thrive. I follow that. It feels right. Where change is possible, I help make it happen. That willingness is built into me. It's built into you. It's called love.

With the planet looking down the barrel of an environmental catastrophe, how do we live our lives?

I have looked down the barrel of a real gun pointed at me, and on several occasions I have heard fearful, innocent people threaten to kill me, and never for an instant was I afraid. Fear is the story of a future. How could I know that the man would pull the trigger? How can I know that an environmental catastrophe will happen or, if it does happen, that it will be a bad thing for the planet? Once you understand this, and begin to live in reality, not in your thoughts about reality, life becomes fearless, loving, and filled with gratitude, whatever the nonexistent future may bring.

The war with reality always sees catastrophes looming, whether these are planetary or personal. It's a very painful way to live. Maybe an environmental catastrophe will happen; maybe it won't. In the meantime, I go about my business as if there were no life or death (and there isn't). My house is powered by the sun, the car I drive is electric, I'm careful about recycling, I vote for people who say they are concerned about global warming, I'm happy to be taxed for the public good, I support environmental causes. I'm fearless, worry-free, and I do whatever I can. "Get solar panels," the mind says, and there is no valid reason not to, since all thoughts have been tested by inquiry. The panels are installed, my electric bill is a few dollars a month, and at some point I will have put back all that I've used, and more. This will match my existence: all traces gone, a grateful life given back to what it came from.

I once gave a talk to a group of environmental activists, at a Bioneers conference in San Francisco, and hundreds of people came to listen. Many of these people had dedicated their lives to saving the planet. I talked for a while about my commitment to environmental action, which seems to me the sane and kind thing to do. Then I asked for their thoughts about the environment. They were living with a great deal of anxiety, even terror, they said—an enormous burden on their shoulders. But many of them had open minds and were willing to question the thoughts that were causing them so much stress. I helped them do The Work on thoughts such as "Something terrible is going to happen," "I need to save the planet," and "People should be more conscious." They discovered how these thoughts were driving them crazy, and how the thoughts have opposites that could be just as true.

After a few hours of intensive inquiry, I asked them to imagine the worst things that can happen if we continue to poison our beautiful planet, and I invited them to make a list. "The planet will become uninhabitable for humans. Thousands of species will become extinct." And so on. Once they had made their list, we questioned some of their statements, and I asked them to turn the list around: instead of "The Worst Things That Can Happen to Our Planet," I asked them to retitle their list "The Best Things That Can Happen to Our Planet," then to find specific, genuine reasons why each item on the list was appropriate. How could it be the best thing for our planet to become uninhabitable by humans, for example? Many of them didn't want to go there at first; there was a lot of resistance, and many upset questions. But these were courageous people, and eventually they found valid reasons why every item on their lists was the best thing that could happen. "It would be the best thing for endangered species not to have humans around." "It would be the best thing for insects." "It would be the best thing for the rain forests." "We wouldn't be pumping and mining the life blood out of the planet." "Who knows what intelligent species would evolve if we were gone?" They had been dealing with discouragement and burnout for years, and some of them later thanked me and told me how empowering this exercise had been for them.

One of the things you discover when you begin to practice inquiry is that the world doesn't need saving. It has already been saved. What a relief! The most attractive thing about the Buddha was that he saved one person: himself. That's all he needed to save, and when he saved himself, the whole world was saved. All his years of teaching—forty years of apparent compassion—were just the forward momentum of that one moment of insight.

The world doesn't need saving. It has already been saved.

32

LOVING THE DREAM

The Buddha said, "Subhuti, if on the one hand there were someone who filled worlds as infinite as space with inconceivable wealth and then gave it all away in support of charitable causes, and on the other hand there were a good man or woman who upon realizing what is taught in this sutra, wholeheartedly embodied it and lived it and explained it to others, this second person's merit would far exceed the merit of the first. And what is the essential truth that that person has realized? Simply this: that the world is not what we name it or think it, and that there is no such thing as a self or an other. Listen now to this verse:

> Each object in this fleeting world is like
> a lightning flash, a bubble in a stream,
> a wisp of smoke, a cloud, a drop of dew,
> a fading star at dawn, a breath, a dream."

After the Buddha had finished speaking, the monk Subhuti and all the other monks, nuns, laymen, and laywomen who had been listening were filled with confidence and joy, and they vowed to take these teachings to heart and put them into practice.

The name creates the thing. It's how eternity separates itself out into illusion, as though it could ever exist in parts and not as the whole. Naming is like eternity, until the name is believed. The moment a name is believed—table, chair, tree, sky—a sadness, however subtle, arises in the namer. But when you understand that even the present is in the past, it's easy not to get attached to names and the apparent things they name. They're all a dream, as the Buddha says here.

I love my dream. How could I not, since I love everything I think? But if you're having a nightmare, even a small one, a moment of anxiety or upset, you can wake yourself up through inquiry. These things that are so fleeting that they don't even exist in the first place, these things that are pure innocent imagination, no longer have the power to make us suffer when the mind understands how they are created. The more it understands, the less it knows.

The don't-know mind is a container that's always full. Everything flows into it, and there's never a need to hold on to a drop for itself. It's the innocent that watches the whole world come to it. Things enter with their best and worst behavior, their most shameful, their most glorious, their richest, their poorest. Everything is allowed. It is always vast enough to contain what flows into it. And in it everyone gets what they came for: a look, a glimpse, the gift of love.

The don't-know mind is constant. It's the floor, it's the voice of someone across the room, it's the tapping of a fingernail, a patch of sunlight on the white wall, the fireplace tools, the smell of cooking, the touch of a hand. All of it is precious. None of it is real.

When you love the dream, is there any need to wake up from it?

None, absolutely none. Realizing that it's a dream, you can just lean back and enjoy it—every moment of it.

The more the
mind understands,
the less it knows.

APPENDIX

How to Do The Work

The one criticism of The Work I consistently hear is that it's just too simple. People say, "Freedom can't be this simple!" I answer, "Can you really know that that's true?"

Judge your neighbor, write it down, ask four questions, turn it around. Who says that freedom has to be complicated?*

Putting the Mind on Paper

The first step in The Work is to identify the thoughts that are causing your stress and to write them down. These thoughts can be about any situation in your life, past, present, or future—about a person you dislike or worry about, someone who angers or frightens or saddens you, or someone you're ambivalent or confused about. Write your judgments down, just the way you think them. Use short, simple sentences. (Use a blank sheet of paper, or go to thework.com, to the section called "Tools to Do The Work," under "Resources," where you'll find a Judge-Your-Neighbor Worksheet to download and print.)

Don't be surprised if you find it difficult at first to fill out the Worksheet. For thousands of years we have been taught not to

---

* This appendix is adapted from *Loving What Is* and thework.com.

judge—but let's face it, we still do it all the time. The truth is that we all have judgments running in our heads. Through The Work we finally have permission to let those judgments speak out, or even scream out, on paper. We may find that even the most unpleasant thoughts can be met with unconditional love.

I encourage you to write about someone whom you haven't yet totally forgiven, someone you still resent. This is the most powerful place to begin. Even if you've forgiven that person 99 percent, you aren't free until your forgiveness is complete. The 1 percent you haven't forgiven that person is the very place where you're stuck in all your other relationships (including your relationship with yourself).

If you are new to inquiry, I strongly suggest that you not write about yourself at first. When you start by judging yourself, your answers come with a motive and with solutions that haven't worked. Judging someone else, then inquiring and turning it around, is the direct path to understanding. You can judge yourself later, when you have been doing inquiry long enough to trust the power of truth.

If you begin by pointing the finger of blame outward, then the focus isn't on you. You can just let loose and be uncensored. We're often quite sure about what other people need to do, how they should live, whom they should be with. We have twenty-twenty vision about other people, but not about ourselves.

When you do The Work, you see who you are by seeing who you think other people are. Eventually you come to see that everything outside you is a reflection of your own thinking. You are the storyteller, the projector of all stories, and the world is the projected image of your thoughts.

Since the beginning of time, people have been trying to change the world so that they can be happy. This hasn't ever worked, because it approaches the problem backward. What The Work gives us is a way to change the projector—mind—rather than the projected. It's like when there's a piece of lint on a projector's lens. We think there's a flaw on people on the screen, and we try to change this person and that person, whomever the flaw appears to be on next. But it's futile to try to change the projected images. Once we realize where the lint is, we can clear the lens itself. This is the end of suffering, and the beginning of a little joy in paradise.

How to Fill in a Worksheet

Please avoid the temptation to continue without writing down your judgments. If you try to do The Work in your head, without putting your thoughts on paper, the mind will outsmart you. Before you're even aware of it, it will be off and running into another story to prove that it's right. But though the mind can justify itself faster than the speed of light, it can be stopped through the act of writing. Once the mind is stopped on paper, thoughts remain stable, and inquiry can easily be applied.

I invite you to contemplate for a moment a situation where you were angry, hurt, sad, or disappointed with someone. Be as judgmental, childish, and petty as you were in that situation. Don't try to be wiser or kinder than you were. This is a time to be totally honest and uncensored about why you were hurt and how you felt in that situation. Allow your feelings to express themselves as they arise, without any fear of consequences or any threat of punishment.

Write down the thoughts and stories that are running through your head, the ones that really cause you pain—the anger, the resentment, the sadness. Point the finger of blame first at people who have hurt you, the ones who have been closest to you, people you're jealous of, people you can't stand, people who have disappointed you. "My husband left me." "My partner infected me with AIDS." "My mother didn't love me." "My children don't respect me." "My friend betrayed me." "I hate my boss." "I hate my neighbors; they're ruining my life." Write about what you read this morning in the newspaper, about people being murdered or losing their homes through famine or war. Write about the checker at the grocery store who was too slow or about the driver who cut you off on the freeway. Every story is a variation on a single theme: *This shouldn't be happening. I shouldn't have to experience this. God is unjust. Life isn't fair.*

People new to The Work sometimes think, "I don't know what to write. Why should I do The Work anyway? I'm not angry at anyone. Nothing's really bothering me." If you don't know what to write about, wait. Life will give you a topic. Maybe a friend didn't call you back when she said she would, and you're disappointed. Maybe when you were five years old, your mother punished you for something you didn't do. Maybe you're upset or frightened when you read the newspaper or think about the suffering in the world.

Put on paper the part of your mind that is saying these things. You can't stop the story inside your head, however hard you try. It's not possible. But when you put the story on paper, writing it just the way the mind is telling it, with all your suffering and frustration and rage and sadness, then you can take a look at what's swirling around inside you. You can see it brought into the material world, in physical form. And, finally, through The Work, you can begin to understand it.

When a child gets lost, he or she may feel sheer terror. It can be just as frightening when you're lost inside the mind's chaos. But when you enter The Work, it is possible to find order and to learn the way back home. It doesn't matter what street you walk down, there's something familiar; you know where you are. Someone could kidnap you and hide you away for a month and then throw you blindfolded out of a car, but when you take off the blindfold and look at the buildings and streets, you begin to recognize a restaurant or a grocery store, and everything becomes familiar. You know what to do to find your way home. That is how The Work functions. Once the mind is met with understanding, it can always find its way back home. There is no place where you can remain lost or confused.

The Judge-Your-Neighbor Worksheet

After my life changed in 1986, I spent a lot of time in the desert near my home, just listening to myself. Stories arose inside me that had been troubling mankind forever. Sooner or later I witnessed every concept, it seemed, and I discovered that even though I was alone in the desert, the whole world was with me. And it sounded like this: "I want," "I need," "They should," "They shouldn't," "I'm angry because," "I'm sad," "I'll never," "I don't want to." These phrases, which repeated themselves over and over in my mind, became the basis for the Judge-Your-Neighbor Worksheet. The purpose of the Worksheet is to help you put your painful stories and judgments into written form; it's designed to draw out judgments that might otherwise be difficult to uncover.

The judgments you write on the Worksheet will become the material that you'll use to do The Work. You'll put each written statement—one by one—up against the four questions and let each of them lead you to the truth.

Here is an example of a completed Judge-Your-Neighbor Worksheet. I have written about my second husband, Paul, in this example (included here with his permission); these are the kinds of thoughts that I used to believe about him before inquiry found me. As you read, you're invited to replace Paul's name with the name of the appropriate person in your life.

1. **In this situation, who angers, confuses, saddens, or disappoints you, and why?**

    I am angry with Paul because he doesn't listen to me.

2. **In this situation, how do you want them to change? What do you want them to do?**

    I want Paul to see that he is wrong. I want him to stop lying to me. I want him to see that he is killing himself.

3. **In this situation, what advice would you offer them?**

   Paul should take a deep breath. He should calm down. He should see that his behavior frightens me. He should know that being right is not worth another heart attack.

4. **In order for *you* to be happy in this situation, what do you need them to think, say, feel, or do?**

   I need Paul to hear me when I talk to him. I need him to take care of himself. I need him to admit that I am right.

5. **What do you think of them in this situation? Make a list. (Remember, be petty and judgmental.)**

   Paul is unfair, arrogant, loud, dishonest, way out of line, and unconscious.

6. **What is it about this situation that you don't ever want to experience again?**

   I don't ever want Paul to lie to me again. I don't ever want to see him ruining his health again.

Worksheet Tips

Statement 1: Be sure to identify what most upsets you in that situation about the person you are writing about. As you fill in statements 2 through 6, imagine yourself in the situation that you have described in statement 1.

Statement 2: List what you wanted him or her to do in this situation, no matter how ridiculous or childish your wants were.

Statement 3: Be sure that your advice is specific, practical, and detailed. Clearly articulate, step by step, how he or she should carry out your advice; tell him or her exactly what you think he or she should do. If he or she followed your advice, would it really solve your problem in statement 1? Be sure that your advice is relevant and doable for this person (as you describe him or her in statement 5).

Statement 4: Did you stay in the situation described in statement 1? If your needs were met, would that take you all the way to "happy," or would it just stop the pain? Be sure that the needs you have expressed are specific, practical, and detailed.

Inquiry: The Four Questions and the Turnarounds

1. **Is it true? (Yes or no. If your answer is no, move to question 3.)**

2. **Can you absolutely know that it's true? (Yes or no.)**

3. **How do you react, what happens, when you believe that thought?**

4. **Who would you be without the thought?**

    And **Turn the thought around.** Then find at least three specific, genuine examples of how each turnaround is true for you in this situation.

Now, using the four questions, let's investigate the portion of the statement from number 1 on the Worksheet that is the cause of your reaction: *Paul doesn't listen to me.* As you read along, think of someone you haven't totally forgiven yet, someone who just wouldn't listen to you.

Question 1: Is it true?

As you consider the situation again, ask yourself, "Is it true that Paul doesn't listen to me?" Be still. If you really want to know the truth, the honest yes or no from within will rise to meet the question as you recall that situation in your mind's eye. Let the mind ask the question, and wait for the answer that surfaces. (The answer to the first two questions is just one syllable long; it's either yes or no. Notice if you experience any defense as you answer. If your answer includes "because . . ." or "but . . . ," this is not the one-syllable answer you are looking for, and you're no longer doing The Work. You're looking for freedom outside yourself. I'm inviting you into a new paradigm.)

Reality, for me, is what is true. The truth is whatever is in front of you, whatever is really happening. Whether you like it or not, it's raining now. "It shouldn't be raining" is just a thought. In reality, there is no such thing as a "should" or a "shouldn't." These are only thoughts that we superimpose onto reality. Without the "should" and "shouldn't," we can see reality as it is, and this leaves us free to act efficiently, clearly, and sanely.

When asking the first question, take your time. The answer is either yes or no. (If it's no, move to question 3.) The Work is about discovering what is true from the deepest part of yourself. You are listening for *your* answers now, not other people's, and not anything you have been taught. This can be very unsettling at first, because you're entering the unknown. As you continue to dive deeper, allow the truth within you to rise and meet the question. Be gentle as you give yourself to inquiry. Let this experience have you completely.

Question 2: Can you absolutely know that it's true?

Consider these questions: "In this situation, can I absolutely know that it's true that Paul isn't listening to me? Can I ever really know when someone is listening or not? Am I sometimes listening even when I appear not to be?"

If your answer to question 1 is yes, ask yourself, "Can I absolutely know that it's true?" In many cases, the statement *appears* to be true. Of course it does. Your concepts are based on a lifetime of uninvestigated beliefs.

After I woke up to reality in 1986, I noticed many times how people, in conversations, the media, and books, made statements such as "There isn't enough understanding in the world," "There's too much violence," "We should love one another more." These were stories I used to believe too. They seemed sensitive, kind, and caring, but as I heard them, I noticed that believing them caused stress and that they didn't feel peaceful inside me.

For instance, when I heard someone say, "People should be more loving," the question would arise in me, "Can I absolutely know that that's true? Can I really know for myself, within myself, that people should be more loving? Even if the whole world tells me so, is it really true?" And, to my amazement, when I listened within myself, I saw that the world is what it is in this moment and that in this moment people couldn't possibly be more loving than they are. Where reality is concerned, there *is* no "what should be." There is only what is, just the way it is, right now. The truth is prior to every story. And every story, prior to investigation, prevents us from seeing what's true.

Now I could finally inquire of every potentially uncomfortable story, "Can I absolutely know that it's true?" And the answer, like the question, was an experience: no. I would stand rooted in that answer—solitary, peaceful, free.

How could no be the right answer? Everyone I knew, and all the books, said that the answer should be yes. But I came to see that the truth is itself and will not be dictated to by anyone. In the presence of that inner no, I came to see that the world is always as it should be, whether I oppose it or not. And I came to embrace reality with all my heart. I love the world, without any conditions.

If your answer is still yes, good. If you think that you can absolutely know that that's true, that's as it should be, and it's fine to move on to question 3.

Question 3: How do you react, what happens, when you believe that thought?

With this question, we begin to notice internal cause and effect. You can see that when you believe the thought, there is an uneasy feeling, a disturbance that can range from mild discomfort to fear or panic.

How do you react when you believe that Paul doesn't listen to you? How do you treat him? Be still; notice. For example: "I feel frustrated and sick to my stomach; I give him 'the look'; I interrupt him; I punish him; I ignore him; I lose my temper. I start talking faster and louder, and I try to force him to listen." Continue your list as you witness the situation and allow the images in your mind's eye to show you how you react when you believe that thought.

Does that thought bring peace or stress into your life? What images do you see, past and future, and what physical sensations arise as you witness those images? Allow yourself to experience them now. Do any obsessions or addictions begin to appear when you believe that thought? (Do you act out on any of the following: alcohol, drugs, credit cards, food, sex, television, or computers?) Also, witness how you treat yourself in this situation and how that feels. "I shut down. I isolate myself, I feel sick, I feel angry, I eat compulsively, and for days I watch television without really watching. I feel depressed, separate, resentful, and lonely." Notice all the effects of thinking the thought "Paul doesn't listen to me."

After the four questions found me, I would notice thoughts like "People should be more loving," and I would see that thoughts like these caused a feeling of uneasiness in me. I noticed that prior to the thought, there was peace. My mind was quiet and serene. This is who I am without my story. Then, in the stillness of awareness, I began to notice the feelings that came from believing or attaching to the thought. And in the stillness I could see that if I were to believe the thought, the result would be a feeling of unease and sadness. When I asked, "How do I react when I believe the thought that people should be more loving?" I saw that not only did I have an uncomfortable feeling (this was obvious), but I also reacted with mental pictures to prove that the thought was true. I flew off into a world that didn't exist. I reacted by living in a stressed body, seeing everything through fearful eyes, a sleepwalker, someone in a seemingly endless nightmare. The remedy was simply to investigate.

I love question 3. Once you answer it for yourself, once you see the cause and effect of believing a thought, all your suffering begins to unravel.

Question 4: Who would you be without the thought?

This is a very powerful question. Picture yourself standing in the presence of the person you have written about when he (or she) is doing what you think he shouldn't be doing. Consider, for example, who you would be without the thought "Paul doesn't listen to me." Who would you be in the same situation if you didn't believe that thought? Close your eyes and imagine Paul not listening to you. Imagine yourself without the thought that Paul doesn't listen to you (or that he even *should* listen). Take your time. Notice what is revealed to you. What do you see now? How does that feel?

For many people, life without their story is literally unimaginable. They have no reference for it. So "I don't know" is a common answer to this question. Other people answer by saying, "I'd be free," "I'd be peaceful," "I'd be a more loving person." You could also say, "I'd be clear enough to understand the situation and act in an appropriate, intelligent way." Without our stories, we are not only able to act clearly and fearlessly; we are also a friend, a listener. We are people living happy lives. We are appreciation and gratitude that have become as natural as breath itself. Happiness is the natural state for someone who knows that there's nothing to know and that we already have everything we need, right here now.

Turn the thought around.

To do the turnarounds, find opposites of the original statement on your Worksheet. Often a statement can be turned around to the self, to the other, and to the opposite. First, the turnaround to the self. Write it as if it were about you. Where you have written someone's name, put yourself. Instead of "he" or "she," put "I." For example, "Paul doesn't listen to me" turns around to "I don't listen to myself." Find at least three specific, genuine examples of how this turnaround is as true as or truer than your original statement.

Next is the turnaround to the other. "Paul doesn't listen to me" becomes "I don't listen to Paul."

A third type is a 180-degree turnaround to the extreme opposite. "Paul doesn't listen to me" becomes "Paul does listen to me."

Don't forget, for each turnaround find at least three specific, genuine examples of how the turnaround is true for you in this situation. This is not about blaming yourself or feeling guilty. It's about discovering alternatives that can bring you peace.

Not every statement has as many as three turnarounds, and some have more than three. Some turnarounds may not make any sense to you. Don't force these.

For each turnaround, go back and start with the original statement. For example, "He shouldn't waste his time" may be turned around to "I shouldn't waste my time," "I shouldn't waste his time," and "He *should* waste his time." Note that "I should waste my time" and "I should waste his time" are not valid turnarounds; they are turnarounds of turnarounds, rather than turnarounds of the original statement.

The turnarounds are a very powerful part of The Work. As long as you think that the cause of your problem is "out there"—as long as you think that anyone or anything else is responsible for your suffering—the situation is hopeless. It means that you are forever in the role of the victim, that you're suffering in paradise. So bring the truth home to yourself and begin to set yourself free. Inquiry combined with the turnarounds is the fast track to self-realization.

The Turnaround for Statement 6

The turnaround for statement 6 on the Judge-Your-Neighbor Worksheet is a little different from the other turnarounds. "I don't ever want to . . ." turns around to "I am willing to . . ." and "I look forward to . . ." For example, "I don't ever want Paul to lie to me again" turns around to "I am willing to have Paul lie to me again" and "I look forward to having Paul lie to me again." Why would you look forward to it? These turnarounds are about embracing all of life, just as it is. Saying—and meaning—"I am willing to . . ." creates open-mindedness, creativity, and flexibility. Any resistance you may have is softened, and that allows you to open up to the situation in your life rather than keep hopelessly applying willpower to eradicate it or push it away. Saying and meaning "I look forward to . . ." actively opens you to life as it unfolds. Some of us have learned to accept what is, and I invite you to go further, to actually *love* what is. This is our natural state. Freedom is our birthright.

If you feel any resistance to a thought, your Work is not done. When you can honestly look forward to experiences that have been uncomfortable, there is no longer anything to fear in life; you see everything as a gift that can bring you self-realization.

It's good to acknowledge that the same feelings or situation may happen again, if only in your thoughts. When you realize that suffering and discomfort are the call to inquiry and to the freedom that follows, you may actually begin to look forward to uncomfortable feelings. You may even experience them as friends coming to show you what you have not yet investigated thoroughly enough. It's no longer necessary to wait for people or situations to change in order to experience peace and harmony. The Work is the direct way to orchestrate your own happiness.

After sitting with the turnarounds, you would continue a typical inquiry with the next statement written on the Worksheet—in this case, *I want Paul to see that he is wrong*—and then with every other statement on the Worksheet. For further instructions, read *Loving What Is* or visit thework.com.

Your Turn: The Worksheet

Now you know enough to try The Work. First relax, get very still, close your eyes, and wait for a stressful situation to come to mind. Fill in the Judge-Your-Neighbor Worksheet as you identify the thoughts and feelings that you were experiencing in the situation you have chosen to write about. Use short, simple sentences. Remember to *point the finger of blame or judgment outward*. You may write from your point of view as a five-year-old or at any time in your life. Please do *not* write about yourself yet.

1. In this situation, who angers, confuses, saddens, or disappoints you, and why?

_____

_____

_____

2. In this situation, how do you want them to change? What do you want them to do?

_____

_____

_____

3. In this situation, what advice would you offer them?

_____

_____

_____

4. **In order for you to be happy in this situation, what do you need them to think, say, feel, or do?**

_____

_____

_____

5. **What do you think of them in this situation? Make a list. (Remember, be petty and judgmental.)**

_____

_____

_____

6. **What is it about this situation that you don't ever want to experience again?**

_____

_____

_____

Your Turn: The Inquiry

One by one, put each statement on the Judge-Your-Neighbor Worksheet up against the four questions. Then turn around the statement you're working on and find at least three specific, genuine examples of how each turnaround is as true as or truer than the original statement. (Refer to the examples in the previous section, "Inquiry: The Four Questions and the Turnarounds." You can also find help at thework .com or with The Work App, which includes a tutorial with Byron Katie.) Throughout this process, explore being open to possibilities beyond what you think you know. There's nothing more exciting than discovering the don't-know mind.

This Work is meditation. It's like diving into yourself. Contemplate the questions, drop down into the depths of yourself, listen, and wait. The answer will find your question. No matter how closed down or hopeless you think you are, the gentler polarity of mind (which I call the heart) will meet the polarity that is confused because it hasn't yet been enlightened to itself. You may begin to experience revelations about yourself and your world, revelations that will transform your whole life, forever.

Questions and Answers

I have a hard time writing about others. Can I write about myself?

If you want to know yourself, I suggest you write about someone else. Point The Work outward in the beginning, and you may come to see that everything outside you is a direct reflection of your own thinking. It's all about you. Most of us have been pointing criticism and judgments at ourselves for years, and it hasn't solved anything yet. Judging someone else, questioning those judgments, and turning them around is the fast path to understanding and self-realization.

Do I have to write? Can't I just ask the questions and turn it around in my head when I have a problem?

Mind's job is to be right, and it can justify itself faster than the speed of light. Stop the portion of your thinking that is the source of your fear, anger, sadness, or resentment by transferring it to paper. Once the mind is stopped on paper, it's much easier to investigate. Eventually The Work begins to undo you automatically, even without writing.

What if I don't have a problem with people? Can I write about things, like my body?

Yes. Do The Work on any subject that is stressful. As you become familiar with the four questions and the turnarounds, you may choose objects such as the body, disease, career, or even God. Then experiment with using the term "my thinking" in place of the object when you do the turnarounds. Example: "My body should be strong, flexible, and healthy" becomes "My thinking should be strong, flexible, and healthy." Isn't that what you really want—a balanced, healthy mind? Has a sick body ever been a problem, or is it your thinking about the body that causes the problem? Investigate. Let your doctor take care of your body as you take care of your thinking. I have a friend who can't move his body, and he loves his life, because he loves what he thinks. Freedom doesn't require a healthy body. Free your mind, and the body will follow.

I've heard you say that you're a lover of reality. What about war, rape, poverty, violence, and child abuse? Are you condoning them?

How could I condone them? I'm not crazy. I simply notice that if I believe they shouldn't exist when they do exist, I suffer. Can I just end the war in me? Can I stop raping myself and others with my abusive thoughts? If not, I'm continuing in myself the very thing I want to end in the world. Sanity doesn't suffer, ever. Can you eliminate war everywhere on earth? Through inquiry, you can begin to eliminate it for one human being: you. This is the beginning of the end of war in the world. If life upsets you, good! Judge the war makers on paper, inquire, and turn it around. Do you really want to know the truth? All suffering begins and ends with you.

So what you're saying is that I should just accept reality as it is and not argue with it. Is that right?

It's not up to me to say what anyone should or shouldn't do. I simply ask, "What is the effect of arguing with reality? How does it feel?" The Work explores the cause and effect of attaching to painful thoughts, and in that investigation we find our freedom. To simply say that we shouldn't argue with reality just adds another story, another spiritual concept. It hasn't ever worked.

Loving what is sounds like never wanting anything. Isn't it more interesting to want things?

My experience is that I do want something all the time. What I want is what is. It's not only interesting, it's ecstatic! When I want what I have, thought and action aren't separate; they move as one, without conflict. If you find anything lacking, ever, write down your thoughts and inquire. I find that life never falls short and doesn't require a future. Everything I need is always supplied, and I don't have to do anything for it. There is nothing more exciting than loving what is.

Is inquiry a process of thinking? If not, what is it?

Inquiry appears to be a process of thinking, but actually it's a way to *undo* thinking. Thoughts lose their power over us when we realize that they simply appear in the mind. They're not personal. Through The Work, instead of escaping or suppressing our thoughts, we learn to meet them with unconditional love and understanding.

I don't believe in God. Can I still benefit from The Work?

Yes. Atheist, agnostic, Christian, Jew, Muslim, Buddhist, Hindu, pagan—we all have one thing in common: we want happiness and peace. If you are tired of suffering, I invite you to The Work.

I understand the process of inquiry intellectually, but I don't really feel anything shifting when I do it. What am I missing?

If you answer the questions superficially with the thinking mind, the process will leave you feeling disconnected. Try asking the question and going deeper. You may have to ask the question a few times to stay focused, but as you practice this, an answer will slowly arise. When the answer comes from inside you, the realizations and shifts follow naturally.

I've been using the turnarounds whenever I make judgments, and somehow it doesn't do anything but make me depressed and confused. What's going on?

To simply turn thoughts around keeps the process intellectual and is of little value. The invitation is to go beyond the intellect. The questions are like probes that dive into the mind, bringing deeper knowledge to the surface. Ask the questions first, and then wait. Once the answers have arisen, the superficial mind and the deeper mind meet, and the turnarounds feel like true discoveries.

CONTACT INFORMATION

To find out more about The Work of Byron Katie, visit thework.com.

Byron Katie International, Inc.
P.O. Box 1206
Ojai, CA 93024
1–805-444-5799
International (001) 805-444-5799
E-mail info@thework.com

When you visit the website, you'll be able to read detailed instructions about The Work; watch video clips of Katie facilitating inquiry with people on a wide variety of issues; view Katie's calendar of events; download free materials; register for an upcoming School for The Work, a No-Body Intensive, a weekend program, or Turnaround House; find a facilitator; learn how to call the free *Do The Work* helpline; learn about the Institute for The Work and its Certified Facilitators; download Judge-Your-Neighbor Worksheets; listen to archived interviews; download apps for your iPhone, iPad, or Android; subscribe to the free newsletter; and shop at the online store. We also invite you to Katie's Facebook, Twitter, Google+, and Pinterest pages. For videos, visit TheWorkofBK YouTube channel, and for live-streaming events, visit livewithbyronkatie.com.

We invite you to help us move The Work in the world by supporting scholarships for the School and other projects of The Work Foundation, a 501(c)(3) charitable organization. We deeply appreciate your donation, which you can make on our foundation website, theworkfoundationinc.org; by calling Byron Katie International at 1-805-444-5799; or by mailing a check to The Work Foundation, P.O. Box 638, Ojai, CA 93024.

ACKNOWLEDGMENTS

We would like to express our gratitude to Martha Beck, whose discerning enthusiasm provided the necessary momentum at a critical moment; to Josh Baran and John Tarrant, who read an early draft and offered helpful suggestions; to Michele Penner, who collected a few passages that are spliced in here and there; to our agent, Linda Loewenthal, who knew and kept knowing exactly what to do; and to Gideon Weil, our editor, thanks to whose astute questioning this book reached its final form.

ABOUT THE AUTHORS

BYRON KATIE discovered inquiry in 1986. She has been traveling around the world since 1992, teaching The Work directly to hundreds of thousands of people at free public events; in prisons, hospitals, churches, corporations, battered women's facilities, and universities and schools; and at weekend intensives, the nine-day School for The Work, and her twenty-eight-day Turnaround House. She is the author of three bestselling books: *Loving What Is, I Need Your Love—Is That True?*, and *A Thousand Names for Joy*. Her other books are *Question Your Thinking, Change the World; Who Would You Be Without Your Story?; A Friendly Universe*; and, for children, *Tiger-Tiger, Is It True?* and *The Four Questions*. Her website is thework.com, where you'll find many free materials to download, as well as audio and video clips, a schedule of events, and a free helpline.

STEPHEN MITCHELL's many books include the bestselling *Tao Te Ching, The Selected Poetry of Rainer Maria Rilke, Gilgamesh, The Gospel According to Jesus, The Book of Job, The Second Book of the Tao, The Iliad, The Odyssey*, and *Beowulf*. You can read extensive excerpts from all his books on his website, stephenmitchellbooks.com.